A Word About the Author of

LATIN AMERICA: MYTH AND REALITY

PETER NEHEMKIS

practices law in Washington, D. C., specializing in Latin American and international affairs, and is a member of the National Council of the Federal Bar Association. He took his B.A. at Swarthmore and his LL.B. at Yale Law School. He has lived and traveled in Brazil and has visited most of the other Latin American countries. He was a member of a Harvard University study group of businessmen and academicians who in December 1960 prepared for President-elect John F. Kennedy a report entitled "Alliance for Progress." In 1962 he was appointed by the Organization of American States to the Inter-American Commission to monitor the first free elections in the Dominican Republic, and was subsequently invited by the Dominican Government to prepare a comprehensive plan for holding elections, from the village to the national level. He has served on the Committee for the Alliance for Progress of the U. S. Department of Commerce, is a member of the International Committee of the Chamber of Commerce of the United States, and serves as a trustee of the Pan American Development Foundation. He has also served a number of important American corporations as a consultant on Latin American problems.

MENTOR Books on
Early Latin American History

AZTEC: MAN AND TRIBE *by Victor W. von Hagen*

A noted authority on ancient Latin America writes of the history, daily life, religion, and art of the nation that ruled Mexico before Columbus' time. Illustrated.
(MT618—75¢)

THE CONQUEST OF PERU (abridged)
by William H. Prescott

The authoritative history of the Inca empire and its subjugation by Pizarro; abridged and revised with a new Introduction by Victor W. Von Hagen, archaeologist and historian.
(MT675—75¢)

REALM OF THE INCAS *by Victor W. von Hagen*

The history, culture, religion, art, and social and economic life of a fascinating Indian race that achieved a fabulous empire before Columbus discovered America. Copiously illustrated.
(MT636—75¢)

WORLD OF THE MAYA *by Victor W. von Hagen*

A history of the Mayas and their resplendent civilization that grew out of the jungles of Central America. Illustrated.
(MT603—75¢)

LATIN AMERICA:

Myth and Reality

Revised Edition

by PETER R. NEHEMKIS

MENTOR >

A MENTOR BOOK

Published by THE NEW AMERICAN LIBRARY,
New York and Toronto

Published as a MENTOR BOOK
by arrangement with Alfred A. Knopf, Inc.,
who have authorized this softcover edition.

FIRST PRINTING, AUGUST, 1966

Library of Congress Catalog Card Number: 66-24516

MENTOR BOOKS are published *in the United States* by
The New American Library, Inc.
1301 Avenue of the Americas, New York, New York 10019
in Canada by The New American Library of Canada Limited,
295 King Street East, Toronto 2, Ontario

The author gratefully acknowledges permission to reprint here portions of material which appeared in a somewhat different form in *Export Trade* and in *The Caribbean: Venezuelan Development, a Case History,* School of Inter-American Studies, University of Florida; published by the University of Florida Press. To Houghton Mifflin Company, grateful acknowledgment is due for permission to quote from Sir Winston Churchill's *Triumph and Tragedy.*

FOREWORD

IT IS PRESUMPTUOUS for a foreigner to think he knows Latin America. It is an enormous area with many different cultural patterns. Nearly twice as large as the United States, Latin America contains 223 million people in twenty countries. They speak Portuguese, Spanish, French; Quechua and Aymará—the ancient Inca languages; Maya, Guaraní, and numerous other Indian tongues. Cultural influences stem from Spain, Portugal, France, Africa, Asia, and the Indian civilizations. In Mexico and parts of Central America and on the western coast of South America, the influence of the Indian is pervasive. The influence of the Negro has been felt deeply in the Caribbean and in Brazil.

Viewed from an airplane, South America looks like a forbidding lunar wasteland. The works of nature are outsized. The Andean mountains stretch from Venezuela to the tip of Chile. Three to four miles high, they form a wall that separates the western coast from the rest of the continent. There are snow-capped mountains in the latitudes of the tropics. Mount Aconcagua in Argentina near the border of Chile rises to a height of 23,000 feet; it is the highest peak in the Americas. Lake Titicaca on the Peruvian-Bolivian border is 12,507 feet above sea level; it is the highest lake in the world and the largest (3,500 square miles) inland lake in South America. There is a desert that extends from northern Peru to central Chile in which no life or vegetation exists. On the eastern side of the Andes lies the Amazon basin—the largest river system in the world. It covers an area of 2.7 million square miles and drains over one third of the continent. The Amazon River itself is 3,500 miles long. In places it is over 50 miles wide. The Amazon River has an average flow of 3.6 million gallons a minute. This flow is so enormous that, according to Under

Secretary James K. Carr of the U.S. Department of the Interior, in a single day it could flood the state of New York to a depth of six inches. Two hundred miles beyond the mouth of the river, the Atlantic Ocean is muddy with the topsoil of the continent. Much of Latin America is tropical. The southern part of the continent is closer to Africa than to the United States or Europe. The fastest-growing population of any major region in the world today is found not in China or India but in tropical South America.

The attitudes of the people are as varied as the geography. Indeed, geography has conditioned the attitudes of the people. The sophisticated *porteño* of Buenos Aires is apt to be of Italian extraction; he regards Argentina as an extension of Europe. His outlook is different from that of his counterpart in Chile, the *santiaguino* of Santiago, whose ancestry may be Spanish, German, English, Yugoslavian, French, Swiss, or Araucanian Indian. The Spanish conquerors of Chile, principally Basques and Andalusians, intermarried with Araucanian women. The *mestizo* is the predominant racial type. The Chilean upper class represents a merger of the bourgeois and the feudal, of Basque immigrants (who became successful, wealthy businessmen) and traditional landowning families (descendants of the *conquistadores*). The Chilean reminds one of the Swiss. He is frugal, practical, and industrious. But in his outpouring of first-rate books and in his intellectual liveliness, he is like the French. Indeed, there is a striking similarity between the political parties of France and those of Chile.

Both the Argentine and the Chilean are quite different from the aristocratic *limeño* of Lima. His paternal forebears were lieutenants of Francisco Pizarro; his maternal ancestors, Inca royalty. The Peruvian aristocrat retains a medieval social outlook. The economic and social structure of Peru is highly stratified. All three—Argentine, Chilean, Peruvian—are entirely different from the Brazilian, who inhabits a veritable continent comprising 3 million square miles, about half the land mass of South America, and containing half the population of the southern continent. Who and what is the Brazilian? He is Portuguese, Indian, Negro, Dutchman, Italian, Spaniard, German, Japanese, Syrian, and Jew. He has an identity and a national consciousness unlike that of the Spanish-American. He is *brasileiro*—a new type of man in the Western Hemisphere.

Within the same country there are pronounced regional differences among the people. The *nordestino* from the Northeast of Brazil is a migrant. When he comes to Rio de Janeiro or São Paulo in search of a job, he saves his money and invariably returns to his home in the arid *sertão*. The *carioca* of Rio has an infectious humor: his irreverent jokes about prominent public figures are celebrated. The *bahiano* from Bahia is brilliant and a gifted conversationalist. The Brazilians have a saying, *"Bahiano burro nasce morto"* ("The stupid Bahian is a still birth"). The *paulista* from São Paulo, like the North American, believes that man was born to work. São Paulo is a combination of Pittsburgh, Chicago, and New York—its energy is literally explosive. *Paulistas* say their region is the locomotive that pulls the rest of the Brazilian train, mainly sleeping cars.

In Colombia—to take an example from a Spanish-speaking country—the hard-working, entrepreneurial *antioqueño* from Medellín (whose origin is Basque) is different from the somber, dignified *bogotano* in the capital city (whose passionate interest in politics can be lethal). In Ecuador, the *costeño* from Guayaquil, on the hot, humid coast, has different tastes in food and dress than the *quiteño* of Quito, the capital, 9,350 feet above sea level. *Costeños* and *quiteños* are also fierce commercial and political rivals.

There are an indeterminate number of Indians on the high *sierra* of the western coast of South America from Ecuador to Chile. Their habits and customs have scarcely changed since the days of the conquest. At least half of the people in Guatemala, Ecuador, Bolivia, and Peru do not understand Spanish. And in Paraguay, the entire population is bilingual, speaking Guaraní and Spanish. In Haiti, the mulatto elite speak Parisian French and take pride in their French way of life. The Haitian peasant, on the other hand, speaks Creole, a blend of French, Spanish, English, and Dutch, to which have been added words and phrases of African origin. Catholicism is the official religion, but Vodun—imported from Africa during the days of slavery—is the religion of the people. On the other side of the Haitian frontier is the Dominican Republic. Spanish is spoken by all Dominicans. There, before the hate and violence left by the April 1965 Revolution, one could still see the grace, charm, and dignity of colonial Spain. In the Caribbean, attitudes, customs, and political and economic interests are entirely different from those of the rest of Latin America. Castilian Spanish is spoken differently in different countries. There are variations in pronunciation, tempo, gestures that accompany speech, tone of voice, and meaning of words. In

Spanish, "turkey" is *pavo*. But in Mexico it is *guajolote*, and
in Central America, *chompipe*. Brazilian Portuguese has been
enriched by the Indian vocabulary. Argentine Spanish has been
influenced by Italian, Cuban Spanish by the Negro idiom. The
most illustrious name in Spanish-American letters is that of
Rubén Darío, the Nicaraguan poet. His use of New World
Spanish revolutionized the literary language of Spain.

The Latin American political systems are bewildering in
their diversity. There are, for instance, popular, enlightened
democracies; psychopathic dictators; military juntas; a Communist dictatorship; governments run by committees; a coalition government in which the two major parties alternate the
presidency and divide all elective and appointive posts, from
ministries to *municipios* to deans of universities; an associated
commonwealth of the United States.

Latin America is an area of dramatic contrasts: the
twentieth century and the fifteenth exist side by side. Factories
as modern as any in the United States or Europe can be found
in countries whose populations are largely outside the cash
economy. Nuclear physicists pursue their studies in countries
where a majority of the people live under medieval conditions.
Renowned writers are native to countries in which illiteracy
is widespread. Spectacular cities are surrounded by appalling
shanty towns. Class distinctions are as great as in the caste
system of India. The gap between the few wealthy and the
many poor is so enormous as to shock the conscience. This is
Latin America, where an industrial revolution, an agrarian
revolution, and a social revolution are on a collision course.

How can so diversified an area be called "Latin America,"
as if it were a geographical and cultural entity like Japan,
France, or the United States? It was not known by that name
until the nineteenth century, when the French, seeking to re-
establish themselves in the Western Hemisphere, popularized
the term. It is an inadequate expression.

In the search for threads of meaning in the tangled skein of
Latin America's history, politics, and cultural heritage, myth
must be distinguished from reality. Latin Americans and North
Americans have perpetuated a rich lore of mythology about
themselves and each other. These myths are barriers to mutual
understanding. Indeed, they have poisoned our relations. It
is time to discard them. This book is an attempt to unmask the
mythology that blocks understanding of Latin Americans by
North Americans, and of North Americans by Latin Americans. Many more books will have to be written by Latin

Americans, North Americans, and Europeans before this task can be completed.

Over the past twenty years, my Latin American education has been helped by many Latin American friends. I owe them a great debt. It would have pleased me immensely to record the names of my teachers, but the list would be too long. And there would be missing from the acknowledgment those whose names I never knew—patient, suffering, neglected, hungry people. They helped me to understand their Latin America. The teacher is not responsible for the sins of omission or commission of his pupil: my teachers should be absolved.

This book could not have been completed without the grace, tolerance, and understanding of my wife, Bea, and of my daughter, Alexis.

PETER NEHEMKIS

Washington, D.C.
March 1966

Americans, Latin Americans, and Europeans the are prejudices that can be conquered.

During the past twenty years, my Latin American inclinations have been period of many Latin American attitudes over these a great deal. It would I have pleasure and temptation to record diverse names of my teachers, but the day would be too long. And here would be it honor to acknowledge those whose counsel I gratefully quote ... They belong me to understand their Latin America. The author is not responsible for the sins of omission or commission on his part, any reader is should be annoyed.

This book could not have been completed without the co-operation and understanding of my wife, best, and of my daughter, Anne.

—WALTER MILLIARD

Washington, D.C.
March 1964

CONTENTS

CHAPTER ONE

The Setting for Salvation

PRESIDENT KENNEDY was wont to describe Latin America as "the most critical area in the world." President Lyndon Johnson has said that, next to maintaining the peace and freedom of the world, "no work is more important for our generation of Americans than our work in this hemisphere." Latin America is critical and important but not because of the probability of another Cuba, although that contingency cannot be ignored. The real trouble lies much deeper. It is the despair and hopelessness of the ordinary people; the cynicism and social irresponsibility of most of the rich; the pervasive corruption in high places; the sense of inferiority and insecurity of the people; the emotional identification of the middle class with the institutional *status quo;* the flamboyant nationalism; the envy and resentment directed at the United States; the predilection for violence as a substitute for political suffrage; the contempt for and indifference toward the Indian population; the paralysis of the will which prevents action for social reform. These are manifestations of a clinical disorder buried deep in the subsoil of Latin America's historic consciousness. For the truth of the matter is that Latin America is a sick society. It is sick politically. It is sick economically. It is sick spiritually. Each sickness feeds upon the others and the malaise is total.

One of the Western Hemisphere's most distinguished scholars, the Colombian writer, diplomat, and editor Germán

Arciniegas, once described Latin America as consisting of two Americas—the visible and the invisible. The visible Latin America comprises the gleaming, spectacular cities with their breathtaking architecture, and the remnants of a picturesque, postcard Spanish colonialism; the burgeoning new industries that turn out automobiles, automatic washing machines, radios, and TV sets for the emergent middle-income groups; the streets choked with American and European cars; the well-dressed men and the fashionably garbed women.

The visible Latin America looks and acts prosperous. It is.

The invisible Latin America consists of some 140 million people, the two thirds of the population of whom Arciniegas has written: "The day they can make themselves heard there may be a consuming fire or a flood of light."

Because the invisible Latin America can no longer be kept submerged—unseen and unheard—the continent may be likened to a volcano on the verge of violent eruption. This invisible Latin America seethes with the accumulated frustrations, bitterness, and social unrest of more than three centuries of neglect and indifference on the part of its ruling and governing classes.

Latin America's angry millions know that the twentieth century exists: they have a passionate determination to partake of its benefits. They want an end to the tragic hopelessness of their lives, to their grinding poverty, to the hunger that is their pitiless lot from cradle to grave, to the wretched diseases that rack their bodies and deform their children.

The slum dwellers want an end to sleeping on earthen floors under straw thatched roofs; to the absence of drinking water and the most elementary sanitation; to the subhuman conditions in which they live in the miserable hovels of their shanty towns.

The *campesinos* in the backlands want an end to the single-crop sugar-cane, coffee, and banana cultures, which make for economic feasts, and famines; to the hangover of a colonial agricultural system that subjects more than two thirds of the continent's population to the "hidden hunger" of malnutrition.

The progressive leaders want an end to a feudal land tenure that denies landownership to the vast majority of farm families and removes from cultivation many millions

of acres of arable soil—acreage that could, if properly cultivated, feed the continent with diversified crops and with
meat and dairy products and thus reduce the chronic nutri-
tional starvation of 140 million people.

The church wants an end to the unbridgeable class dis-
tinctions, a social inequality that a distinguished Chilean
Catholic, Don Manuel Larraín Errázuriz, the Bishop of
Talca, has characterized as the most severe in the world.

In a word, the invisible ones of Latin America are de-
manding that they be accorded the dignity of human beings
and the rights of citizenship in the twentieth century.

The Western Hemisphere stands at the crossroads of one
of history's great decisions: Is Latin America capable of effecting an orderly transition into the twentieth century? Can
Latin America's social revolution be accomplished peacefully? Or must the continent, for the remainder of this century, run red with blood and Communism?

The problems of social reform are enormously complex.
If Latin America is to solve them peacefully through the
legislative processes, it needs time. But if the progressive
and orderly governments move too slowly, they invite attack by the extremist Left. If they take reform seriously and
undertake to carry it out, they invite denunciation from the
extremist Right. Or they may be toppled by a military
coup d'état aimed at preventing reform. This is the mel-
ancholy dilemma that confronts the area.

To resolve this dilemma, the few progressive Latin American regimes face as difficult and delicate a problem in the
art of government as exists anywhere in the world: how to
preserve a balance between the accelerating demands for
swift change from the people and the resistance to change on
the part of the conservative centers of power. In short, how
to provide enough reform without causing the roof to fall in
by attempting too much.

The risks of failure are great; success is freighted with
heavy odds.

Whether it will be the destiny of Latin America to take
the road of peaceful evolution or that of violent revolution
will depend upon whether the governing and ruling classes of
Latin America will have the wisdom to accept Lord Ma-
caulay's injunction that to preserve you must reform. It will
depend upon the willingness of Latin America's ruling elite
to bend with the winds of change by sharing their economic
and political power with the people.

It will depend upon the diplomatic sensitivity and the organizing skill of the United States Government, upon its vision, and boldness, its dynamic sense of mission, its capacity to embrace new ideas and to discard old myths, to exercise unobtrusive leadership over countries determined to fulfill their own national aspirations. In short, it will depend upon whether the United States can fashion a Latin American policy that will give credibility to its role as defender of democracy and exponent of social revolution.

It will depend upon how soon the United States can purge itself of amateurism in the conduct of its Latin American policy. It is almost three decades since Sumner Welles and Adolf Berle brought their profound knowledge, detailed experience, perceptive insight, and political realism to the management of inter-American affairs. It is not a coincidence that the professionalism of Welles and Berle was distinguished by deep understanding of the Caribbean—the powder keg of the Western Hemisphere. Welles's *Naboth's Vineyard* is the classic study of the Dominican Republic. His diplomatic career was largely preoccupied with the Caribbean. Berle's penetrating insight into the peculiar mentality of the Caribbean was derived initially from his practical business experience with sugar—the lifeblood and the curse of the Caribbean. Indeed, from the days of the early Republic through the first part of this century, Latin American diplomacy was synonymous with Caribbean diplomacy. The Monroe Doctrine was primarily a Caribbean doctrine. When invoked, it was to protect the security of the United States in the Caribbean. Any lingering doubt that the Caribbean is the "Middle East" of the Western Hemisphere was put to rest by the events in Panama during the fateful week of January 9, 1964, and the bloody civil war which erupted in the Dominican Republic on April 24, 1965.

A polar map (rather than Mercator's flat projection) of the Western Hemisphere will show the strategic importance of the Caribbean basin. It looks like an elongated saucer. One edge extends along southern Mexico, Nicaragua, Costa Rica, and the Isthmus of Panama to the northern rim of South America.

On this northern coast are Colombia, Venezuela, the Guianas, and the Brazilian bulge pointing toward Africa. The blighted Northeast of Brazil is potentially an inflammable area. British Guiana obtained independence in May 1966. She has a built-in potential for disaster in the racial conflict

of her East Indian and Negro populations. Under the
American-educated former Prime Minister, Dr. Cheddi
Jagan, Guiana was rapidly becoming the Cyprus of the
Caribbean. The political rivalry of her two outstanding leaders—Negro Prime Minister Forbes Burnham (a brilliant self-
styled Scandinavian Socialist) and East Indian Marxist Cheddi Jagan—has led many Guianese to conclude that their
choice lies between a Caribbean Kwame Nkrumah and another Western Hemisphere Fidel Castro. In Venezuela, Castro-Communist youths wage deadly war against organized
society. The Castroite Armed Forces of National Liberation
(FALN) no longer depends on Cuban shipments of weapons
—it manufactures its weapons locally. Late in October 1965
units of the army and Digepol—the efficient Venezuelan
FBI—raided an underground factory on the outskirts of
Caracas. In an innocent-looking farmhouse, they found a
formidable arsenal of locally produced mortars, machine
guns, ingenious booby traps and small arms: a supply of
armament for a small army. Galleries containing the munitions plant were 9 feet underground and had metal roofs
and walls. Electrically operated steel doors protected the
arsenal. Modern Swedish and Venezuelan machinery was
used in the production of the weapons. The underground
complex contained classrooms for instruction in guerrilla
warfare. A Venezuelan army officer, surveying this impressive munitions supply center, asked the key question: "I
wonder how many more of these factories they have?" After
intensive study, *Diario Las Américas*—the best-informed
journal on Latin American affairs published in the United
States—reported on February 11, 1964 (p. 1), that five of
the long-entrenched bandit zones in Colombia are for all
practical purposes "independent republics." They are organized on Communist lines. *Campesinos* are indoctrinated
with Marxist-Leninist ideology. Proclamations issued by the
jefes of the republics, resemble in style and content similar
emanations from Havana. The "republics" have their own
disciplined "armies" under the command of experienced officers. Like the Communist Viet Cong in Vietnam, the Marxist Colombian bandits also obtain American military equipment through sporadic clashes with the Colombian army.
During 1965, the Colombian army conducted an intensive
campaign against the Red guerrillas. Armored columns fought
their way into the "independent republics." The Minister of
Defense now claims that there are only nine active *cuadril-*

las (bandit gangs), numbering 200 men. Informed Colombians, however, believe that the bulk of the Marxist bandits has moved out of the area, and regrouped elsewhere. They may have joined with the Castro-supported "Army of National Liberation," which operates in three zones along the Venezuelan border.

The other edge of the saucer consists of Cuba, Hispaniola (containing Haiti and the Dominican Republic), Puerto Rico, the Leeward and Windward Islands, and finally Trinidad, which is separated from Venezuela by a narrow channel known as the Serpent's Mouth. In the geopolitics of the Caribbean three islands are pivotal: Cuba, Hispaniola, and Puerto Rico. Captain Alfred Thayer Mahan—the first geopolitical writer of the United States Navy—understood the strategic importance of these three islands for the security of a nineteenth-century United States Navy. American occupation of Haiti, the Dominican Republic, and Nicaragua was motivated by strategic considerations rather than, as popularly believed, by "dollar imperialism." These countries secured the approaches to the Panama Canal at a time when the United States was concerned with the rise of German sea power.[1] Although our two-ocean Navy functions independently of the Canal, and the Navy's largest ships are unable to use it, senior officers of the armed forces nevertheless believe that the Panama Canal and control over the Caribbean basin are of major strategic importance to the security of the United States. American intervention in the Dominican Republic in April 1965 was to ensure the protection of American citizens, and the safety of foreign nationals, to halt the bloodshed and restore order. But the landing of more than 20,000 troops was also motivated by strategic considerations: the Caribbean is a theater of the cold war in the Western Hemisphere.

There is a historic connection between Toussaint L'Ouverture's Haitian slave revolution of the eighteenth century and Fidel Castro's social revolution of the twentieth. Both revolutions were peculiarly Caribbean. Each sent shock waves out into the world. Toussaint L'Ouverture's black revolution un-

[1] Dexter Perkins: *The United States and Latin America* (Baton Rouge: Louisiana State University Press; 1961), p. 24. Dana G. Munro's scholarship supports the contention that American security rather than protection of American business motivated United States intervention in the Caribbean during the early part of this century. Dana G. Munro: *Intervention and Dollar Diplomacy in the Caribbean* (Princeton, N.J.: Princeton University Press; 1964), *passim*.

settled Europe, Africa, and the Western Hemisphere. Fidel Castro's Red revolution almost brought the world to a nuclear holocaust. President Johnson's first State of the Union Message to Congress (January 8, 1964) laid heavy stress on domestic problems. The international scene was subordinated. Ironically, the following day the President was confronted with the first major crisis of his administration—an explosion in Panama. The reverberations were heard throughout the world. If the shock effects of the Panama explosion may be likened to a conventional bomb, the Dominican crisis in the spring of 1965, which led to armed intervention, produced a concussion of megaton proportions.

The Caribbean region is unique in Latin America. Its history, people, problems, politics, and political leaders are *sui generis*.

It is not without significance that American diplomacy sustained three of its most disastrous setbacks on two islands of the Caribbean—Cuba and the Dominican Republic. That the third island of the Caribbean trinity—Puerto Rico—is the showpiece of the area is due to the island's special economic and political relationship with the United States and to the peculiar genius of a Caribbean statesman—Don Luis Muñoz Marín.

In large measure, Latin American policy is a problem of management. It requires responses derived as much from intuition as from knowledge. It involves sensing a mood and employing the appropriate tactical maneuver. It requires what the French call *le sens de l'état*—a feeling for the subtly interrelated strands of political power in the individual countries of the area; in possessing a sense of when diplomatic power can be used and when it must be restrained. Successful management also depends upon having the right ambassador in the right country at the right time.

Latin American policy really entails twenty different policies, with subtle nuances in each country. The management of this policy is difficult because the area is undergoing a vast readjustment. Latin America is responding to General de Gaulle's explosive act of ringing down the curtain on the *pax americana* in Europe. Ever since she achieved independence from Spain, Latin America has been quick to react to European initiatives. In this hemisphere, too, the *fin de siècle* of American hegemony is drawing to a close. Latin America is no longer willing to accept the United States even as the first among equals. Indeed, Hispanic Latin America would follow the "third force" that General de Gaulle aspires to lead but for an obvious fact of life: *la gloire* of Paris is not a substitute for *el dinero* of Washington.

As Professor Federico Gil, one of the most perceptive observers of the Latin American scene, puts it: "The challenge of the Cuban revolution to the influence, might, and prestige of the preponderant power of the Western Hemisphere changed the foreign policies of the Latin American countries." The Hispanic countries from Mexico to Argentina are groping for a new orientation toward one another and toward the United States. Under the regime of the deposed President Goulart, Brazil's diplomatic relations with the United States grew frigid. Brazil was retreating into the isolation of her own continental vastness, and at the same time evolving new relationships with Africa, the West, and the Communist world. Mexico and Argentina are also exploring opportunities for trade with the Soviet bloc and mainland China. Paradoxically, the emergence of a common trade interest in the Communist world may serve to bring Brazil, Mexico, and Argentina into closer relations with one another on Western Hemisphere policies.

The Dominican Republic—before it became a quasi-protectorate of the United States in the spring of 1965—had learned from its own adversities and American diplomatic inanities the great lesson of the 1960's: small countries can help each other. The Treaty of Jerusalem, between Israel and the Dominican Republic, signed in Jerusalem on December 25, 1963, is a historic milestone for Latin America. As Mrs. Golda Meir, that remarkable lady who formerly served her country as Foreign Minister, said to the Dominican delegation upon its arrival in Israel: "Small nations have common enemies—poverty, disease, illiteracy. We understand each other." Israel has much to offer to Latin America: the example of her idealistic youth; highly successful co-operative marketing arrangements; proven experience in soil reclamation and afforestation; an army that has shown its mettle as a first-class fighting machine but also serves as a center for educational and vocational training of immigrants from seventy countries; and a people dedicated to democracy. The Israeli deep-water drilling crews in Brazil, Peru, and Ecuador; the mission in Venezuela to assist that country in establishing procedures for economic planning; the Treaty of Jerusalem, by which Israel will assist the Dominican Republic in establishing rural co-operatives, vocational training, and other types of technical aid—these developments may be the beginning of a new era in technical co-operation for Latin America.

Chile, embarked on major social reforms under President Eduardo Frei's Christian Democratic party, has assumed the role of Argentina in the thirties and is challenging the political and economic hegemony of the United States from the Alliance for Progress to intervention in the Dominican Republic to restructuring of the OAS.

To be sure, President Johnson is confronted with complex domestic issues and problems around the world. Nevertheless, he cannot afford to postpone a serious reappraisal of the management of Latin American policy. Such a reappraisal should not be left to the Department of State alone. What is needed is an American version of the British Royal Commission, by which knowledgeable and distinguished Americans could dispassionately and objectively assist the President in finding new policies and in re-evaluating old ones. The reappraisal would have to begin with the Caribbean—with Panama, Cuba, and the Dominican Republic. The United States is embroiled in an ugly, unfortunate, and permanent controversy with Panama. The Canal—its presence and its future—dominates the economic, political, and emotional life of Panama and Panamanians. For Panama, the Canal *is* the United States—a symbol of Panama's dependency and frustrations. The lessons to be learned from the Panamanian tragedy are of supreme importance. Simplified, they may be stated as: (1) a classic example of what can happen when a running sore is allowed to fester through neglect by the United States; (2) a somber warning of what can happen when a government—in this instance, that of Panama—becomes the captive of uncontrolled nationalistic passions; and (3) the dilemma of a great power that in the age of nationalism endeavors to better relationships with the government of Panama but is unable to overcome the hatreds and passions fanned by nationalist aspirations.

The Communists understand thoroughly that the United States will never permit a Havana-controlled puppet regime astride the Canal. Nonetheless, by identifying themselves with popular grievances, real or fancied, by exploiting psychological and political frustrations, by catering to the need for a scapegoat—for Panamanians, if the United States did not exist it would have to be invented—the Communists will keep Panama in a permanently inflammable state. Consequently, violence will erupt again in Panama sooner or later. Treaties are not sacrosanct. The Hay–Bunau-Varilla Treaty of 1903[2] with Panama has been amended twice before. The treaty was revised in 1936, when the annual rental was increased from $250,000 to $430,000, along with other modifications; and in 1955, when further changes were made, including an increase in the annual rental to $1.9 million, where it now stands. There is, however, a profound difference between revising this treaty—which the

[2] Colonel Philippe Jean Bunau-Varilla was chief engineer in the French company that went bankrupt in an attempt to build a canal through Panama. He organized and promoted a new company that assumed the rights of the defunct company. Bunau-Varilla retained William Nelson Cromwell, senior partner of the famous New York law firm of Sullivan and Cromwell, to promote his interest. Cromwell succeeded in turning Senator Mark Hanna and other prominent American politicians from a canal route through Nicaragua—the original objective of the United States—to Bunau-Varilla's Panamanian scheme. President Theodore Roosevelt became a supporter of the Panamanian route. Bunau-Varilla's plan also called for the United States to pay the stockholders of the Panamanian company $40,000,000. Cromwell's Napoleonic strategy was, in the phrase of Professor Tyler Dennett, "one of the most remarkable propaganda campaigns ever undertaken in the United States to influence legislation." It made history. See Tyler Dennett: *John Hay: From Poetry to Politics* (New York: Dodd, Mead & Company; 1933), p. 365. Under the direction of and with the financial support of Bunau-Varilla, on November 3 and 4, 1903, a handful of Panamanian patriots and American employees of the Panama Railroad Company revolted against Colombia. See Philippe Bunau-Varilla: *The Great Adventure of Panama* (New York: Doubleday, Page & Co.; 1920), pp. 196–247. By a strange coincidence, the U.S.S. *Nashville* appeared on the Atlantic side of Panama, preventing the landing of Colombian troops sent to quell the revolt. On November 6, Washington recognized the new government of Panama. Bunau-Varilla had himself appointed minister of the infant republic for the purpose of negotiating a treaty which was signed on November 18; it gave the United States control over the canal in perpetuity. Theodore Roosevelt's celebrated boast at the University of California on March 23, 1911—"I took the Canal Zone and let Congress debate"—prompted the Rainey resolution for an investigation into the circumstances behind the Panamanian revolt. The documentation of this melancholy episode of United States imperialism is contained in *The Story of Panama, Hearings on the Rainey Resolution, before the Committee on Foreign Affairs of the House of Representatives* (Washington, D.C.: U.S. Government Printing Office; 1913). Many of the documents are reprinted in Earl Harding: *The Untold Story of Panama* (New York: Athene Press, Inc.; 1959), and in Philippe Bunau-Varilla: *Panama; the Creation; the Destruction; the Resurrection* (New York: McBride, Nast & Company; 1914). As Professor Tyler Dennett says: "The saddest aspect of the episode was that it had all been so unnecessary. There had been an alternative, practical and civilized—Nicaragua. Working together, Roosevelt and Hay, with Hanna, Spooner, Cullom, and Aldrich could have chosen it or could have secured the Panama route honorably." (Op. cit., p. 382).

United States originally said it was willing to consider—and scrapping it, as the Panamanian extremists insist, and as the Johnson administration now says it will. A historic guilt complex has led the United States to make atonement to Panama beyond what is necessary or desirable. Abrogating the treaty will not solve our problems with Panama. Indeed, the proposal for three new treaties to supersede the 1903 treaty is likely to founder in Panamanian politics. Former President Arnulfo Arias, who was defeated in the last presidential election by a close vote, charges that the government of President Marco A. Robles is a "spurious and usurping government." Arias heads a United Front coalition that includes virtually all the parties that opposed Robles in the presidential election, the Communists, and even those parties that in the past opposed Arias. The arithmetic of Arias' voting strength in the 42-member National Assembly indicates that Robles will be unable to muster a required two-thirds majority, or 28 votes, for ratification of the treaties. President Johnson may well have placed his personal prestige—unnecessarily—on the quicksand of Panamanian politics.

In the balancing of its international interests and in safeguarding its own security, the United States cannot afford to risk the consequences of an entirely new treaty with Panama, even though the 1903 treaty is, as its signer, John Hay, said, "vastly advantageous to the United States, and we must confess, with what face we can muster, not so advantageous to Panama." [3] To negotiate a new treaty would open a veritable Pandora's box. It would have an immediate impact on the Guantánamo Bay treaty with Cuba, as well as on other United States treaty arrangements for other overseas bases. It could unhinge delicate treaty relations between several Latin American countries—between Chile and Bolivia (involving a Pacific port for Bolivia, who lost her access to the Pacific in a war with Chile); between Peru and Ecuador (whose major foreign policy objective is to obtain revision of existing boundary treaties, universally regarded by Ecuadoreans as unjust and unfair). Indeed, these border controversies flared up, including a shooting incident between Argentina and Chile, on the eve of the Inter-American Conference of Foreign Ministers at Rio de Janeiro.

[3] Letter from Secretary of State John Hay to Senator John Coit Spooner, January 20, 1904. John Hay Papers, John Hay Letterbook No. 3, Manuscript Division, Library of Congress, Washington, D.C.

There are a number of things the United States can do in the interest of maintaining Panama's friendship and co-operation and the goodwill of the rest of the hemisphere without scrapping the treaty or jeopardizing any fundamental security interest. (1) Dr. Víctor F. Goytía, former Justice of the Supreme Court of Panama and a prominent liberal political leader, has proposed several eminently practical changes in the language of the 1903 treaty. He suggests that the phrases "Panama cedes," "Panama grants," and "Panama renounces" be changed to read: "Panama maintains with the co-operation of the United States." This simple change in language, Dr. Goytía believes, will remove the jurisdictional issues between the two countries, restore a sense of dignity to Panama, and take the wind out of the sails of the rabid local nationalists. Incidentally, language similar to that suggested by Dr. Goytía has been used in the treaty for the use of Spanish bases by the United States. (2) The Panama Canal Company (a corporation owned by the United States Government) can be reconstituted as the United States Canal Authority. The board of directors of the Authority could consist of outstanding Americans and Panamanians. The chairman of the Authority should be an individual of the stature of David Lilienthal. The Authority would have direction over the operation of the Canal and the civil administration of the Canal Zone, and would be responsible directly to the President of the United States. (Under the existing organization, the governor of the Canal Zone is also president of the Canal Company. He reports directly to the Secretary of the Army.) The Authority would speak with one voice on all matters pertaining to Canal administration and government instead of three voices—the governor of the Zone, the American ambassador, and the military commander. Divided authority has played into the hands of Panamanian demagogues to the great disadvantage of the United States. (3) We can afford to pay a larger annual rent for the Canal than the $1.9 million that Panama now receives. If this necessitates charging higher toll rates for ships using the Canal, they should be increased. Actually the United States is still charging shippers the rates that were in effect in 1914. (4) A distinction has to be made between those Americans—mainly businessmen—who for years have lived harmoniously with Panamanians and many of whom are married to Panamanians, and the 36,000 Americans who live in the Canal Zone. Among these émigrés there are unfortunately some whose attitude toward the Panamanians resembles that of the former French *colons* toward the Algerians. The Balboa high school student who said: "I am sorry for the rioting because three Army guys are dead, but I couldn't care less about the Panamanians—they have no business here anyway," [4] reflects a parental environment of the era of Teddy Roosevelt. It is probably too late to change the colonial mentality of some of the "Zonians." But the United States Government can take steps to prevent the spread of the disease that infected the *colons* of Algeria. Tours of duty in the Zone can be limited to two years. Return to the United States should be mandatory upon completion of the assignment. (5) We can accelerate training programs for Panamanians in all phases of Canal administration. We can set a time limit for the transfer to qualified Panamanians of jobs now held by Americans. Most American private businesses operating overseas train and employ local citizens in preference to using United States nationals for the same jobs. The United States Government should follow this practice. (6) A chronic grievance of Panamanian businessmen is the system of state socialism in the Canal Zone which enables American civilian personnel to make all their purchases from commissaries at lower prices than local merchants can afford to charge. Under Article XIII of the Treaty of 1903, the United States was granted an exemption from import duties on specified items. A system of state socialism was not contemplated by the signers of the treaty—or, for that matter, by the United States Congress, which ratified the treaty. This point of friction can be eliminated (*a*) by closing the commissaries to civilian personnel or (*b*) by making their prices comparable to local Panamanian prices or (*c*) by restricting the merchandise to items not available in Panama. (7) The United States should restore to Panama some portion of Zone lands not directly used in or needed for running the canal. The original Hay-Herrán Treaty with Colombia, signed on January 23, 1903 (but never ratified by the Colombian Congress, a circumstance that led Theodore Roosevelt to encourage a revolt at Panama City), proposed the lease of a strip 10 kilometers wide for the canal. After recognition of the new republic by the United States, the treaty with Panama

---

[4] *The Washington Post,* January 15, 1964, p. A-10.

(November 18, 1903) used the same figure but changed the unit of distance to miles. Panamanians have always regarded this as an act of duplicity. It still rankles. (8) Facing the trim lawns and neat California-style houses of the Zone is Marañón—one of the most squalid shanty towns in the hemisphere. Marañón is the breeding place for the resentment and bitterness engendered by proximity to an unattainable American paradise. President Johnson could call to the White House several well-known American community-builders and ask them to form a joint company with Panamanians (who have ample capital) to bulldoze this slum out of existence and create a model community in its place.[5] (9) Joseph Farland, former American ambassador to Panama, advocated a concentrated effort by the Agency for International Development (AID) to develop Panama's potentially rich agricultural areas and to provide other forms of technical assistance. He urged the establishment of light industries. Ambassador Farland believes that these programs would reduce the economic dependence of Panamanians on the Canal. These recommendations should be carried out promptly.

These measures can be put into effect with no loss to the United States and with every prospect of gain in the betterment of our relations with Panama. President Johnson's "progress report" on September 24, 1965, on negotiations between Panama and the United States, suggests that several of these measures are to be incorporated in the new treaty. In the long run, however, we delude ourselves if we think we can permanently occupy an area that bisects another country—where the presence of Americans is a bitter reminder of a historic injustice, and where the American high standard of living is flaunted in the face of abject poverty—without creating explosions of the kind that caused the world to shudder on January 9, 1964.

The ultimate solution to the Panamanian problem is for the United States to get out of Panama. The high policy decision has been made for the construction of a sea-level canal. On March 3, 1964, the State Department and the Defense Department presented to the Senate Commerce Committee a joint statement containing this paragraph: "A combination of economic, political, and strategic considerations

[5] A proposal for eliminating the shanty towns is discussed in Chapter 7.

makes it highly desirable to proceed with necessary studies [for building a sea-level canal]. Our evaluations to date indicate that the United States should proceed expeditiously in the belief that eventual construction of a sea-level canal is desirable and in our national interest." President Johnson announced on April 16, 1964, that an American survey group was proceeding to Colombia to make the necessary studies in that country, and other surveys in other countries would follow. Nicaragua, Mexico, and Colombia are possible sites other than Panama. The President's "progress report," however, indicates that the United States plans to make studies and site surveys in Panama. In another ten to fifteen years the present canal will be inadequate for world shipping. A new sea-level canal will eliminate the ever-present danger of sabotage to the existing locks as well as the necessity for maintaining large numbers of American technicians in a foreign country. The use of nuclear explosives could accelerate completion of the new canal. The United States, moreover, could propose that the new canal be operated—as Walter Lippmann has suggested—under hemisphere auspices. It would be appropriate under these circumstances for the other American republics to assume a share of the construction costs.

Some common sense must be introduced into the Cuban situation. Are we to continue an economic blockade that our Japanese, European, and Canadian friends ignore, that strengthens Castro with his own people, and that ties Cuba more firmly to the Soviet Union? Are we to encourage hit-and-run raids by Cuban exiles which accomplish little? Is the mass exodus of refugees a propaganda ploy, an attempt by Castro to be rid of the "unproductive" sick and elderly and the politically dangerous? Or—as some experts believe —is it a genuine effort to relax tensions between the United States and Cuba? In the seventh year of the Cuban revolution, are we prepared to recognize that the new Cuba is a fact of life? And that short of nuclear war we cannot eliminate this revolution and its leader?

A recognized student of international affairs, Louis J. Halle of the Graduate Institute of International Affairs in Geneva, reports world opinion regarding our Cuban policy in these words: "Throughout the free world there is little belief in our Cuban policy, which seems to be dictated less by reason than by the passions of an unsophisticated public opinion in our country." Continuing, Mr. Halle states: "The view is general that, while our boycott clearly hurts the Cubans and the Russians, it can neither bring down the Cuban regime nor force Moscow to withdraw its support. It merely provides the world with a spectacle of a David standing up against an ineffectual Goliath." He concludes: "Most intelligent observers in Europe, at least, believe that the grounds of hope are in an inevitable transformation of the Cuban regime, which we should encourage by our actions, rather than in any prospect of a Cuban counterrevolution and a return to the previous situation."

The Dominican Republic is a microcosm that reveals a false assumption of the Alliance for Progress—that sophisticated economic superstructures can be erected on jerry-built democratic political foundations. The Dominican "problem" cannot be solved by heavy infusions of economic aid because it is primarily a political problem. A preoccupation with the conventional economics of development to the exclusion of political development has demonstrated the bankruptcy of our policy.

The Dominican Republic is not a nation; it is a geographical expression. Since 1821, when the Dominicans threw out their Spanish governor, they have had four tyrants who ruled for seventy-two years. (Trujillo's dictatorship lasted thirty-one years.) Over a period of forty-nine years, there were seventy-two "presidents." Between June 1961—after Trujillo's assassination—and April 24, 1965—when the civil war erupted—six different regimes held office. Constitutional government is to the average Dominican but an empty phrase. The Constitution has no sanctity: it has been changed time and again to satisfy predatory despots or the selfish aspirations of the clique in power. Since 1821, there have been twenty-five Constitutions—a record even under the standards of Latin America.

This brief recital of endemic political instability extending over a century should make it crystal clear that Dominicans do not possess the habits, traditions, experience, social cohesiveness, national purpose, and institutions for democratic government. Ready or not, we are nevertheless determined to force democracy down Dominican throats. A bloody, fratricidal civil war has turned this backward sugar country into a Congo of the Caribbean. Yet we persist in expecting the Dominican Republic to behave like a modern democracy when its political development is about on a level with the Italy of Niccolò Machiavelli. The question is not whether the objectives of democratic government are desirable, but whether they are attainable. The real question is whether the evangelical rhetoric of American policy is relevant to Dominican realities. The harsh truth is that the Dominican Republic needs a long period of tutelage in democracy. This very idea is anathema to American liberals and Latin Americans of the democratic Left; it runs counter to the contemporary political fashion of "one man, one vote"; and it is idle to expect the United States or the OAS to father the thought.

The April 1965 uprising, instigated by Professor Bosch's friends from the extremist Left and dissident army officers, has left a bitter legacy of hate and violence.[6] It is probably too late to offset Dominican extremism with countervailing forces. The United States does not know how to make a progressive revolution in other people's countries. In the Dominican Republic, there are too few socially minded *padres*, the free trade-union movement is too small, there is no significant political party of the Center. Indeed, there are no political parties in the accepted meaning of the term; there are only factions held together by the ambitions of their leaders and the promise of membership in a ruling elite. The traditional power groups are incapable of governing, let alone providing honest and efficient government. The restraints of tradition are dissolving. The gun is the law of the land. Political assassination is becoming a way of life. The Provisional Government supported by the OAS Mediation Committee was a house of cards—mainly red hearts. Its writ did not run beyond the grounds of the Palace. Without the Inter-American Peace Force, President Héctor García Godoy would not have remained in office for one day.

The repudiation of Juan Bosch in the June 1966 election was something of an act of poetic justice: the overwhelming majority of Dominicans, after thirteen months of terror, anguish, and economic chaos, had their fill of a demagogic false messiah. Joachim Balaguer's victory was decisive. By all accounts the election was fair and orderly. Whether Balaguer's election as President will be accepted by the more rabid boschistas and whether organized Communist parties with arms in the hands of their members, shielded by an irresponsible Left, will allow orderly government to function remains to be seen.

The Alliance for Progress is in disarray. In both Latin America and North America, the Alliance has engendered

---

[6] The Dominican Revolution is discussed in an Appendix, pp. 258 ff.

recriminations, distrust, and misunderstanding. The validity of many of the underlying assumptions of the Alliance needs to be re-examined. Some are false, and should be abandoned.

On the southern continent, the paramount diplomatic task is to regain the friendship, trust, and confidence of Brazil. Without a partnership with Brazil, the United States is diplomatically isolated in Latin America; it cannot effectively utilize its diplomatic power over the hemisphere. Perhaps the outstanding achievement by Former Under Secretary of State Thomas Mann, the principal architect of Latin American policy in the Johnson administration, has been the *rapprochement* with Brazil. It is not a coincidence that Brazil is the United States' closest partner in the Dominican strife and that a senior Brazilian military officer, Lieutenant General Hugo Panasco Alvim, first commanded the Latin American Peace Force in Santo Domingo, with its largest contingent consisting of American troops. Nor is it a coincidence that Brazil's President Castelo Branco should urge at the November 1965 Conference of Foreign Ministers at Rio de Janeiro that the American republics must adopt a new concept of "counterintervention" to meet "demonstrable attempts" by Communist groups to seize power. Former Ambassador Juracy Magalhães (now Foreign Minister and coordinator of political affairs in the Castelo Branco government) was the most popular and effective Brazilian ambassador to Washington in a generation. The United States has staked its prestige and almost $1 billion in aid and grants on the ability of Brazil's government to solve its enormously complex economic and political problems.

The Itamaraty (Brazil's Foreign Office) practices the most sophisticated diplomacy in the Western Hemisphere; its foreign policy has both continuity and uniformity. Brazil is conscious of her strategic position in the Western Hemisphere and of her potential role as a world power. Her nationalism was not invented by João Goulart, her demagogic former President. On the contrary, it is part of the historic consciousness of Brazil. She has no intention of becoming a carbon copy of the United States—in her economics, politics, or foreign affairs. Brazil has traditionally been a good neighbor and a close ally, and the Brazilian people admire the United States. In her agonizing struggle to attain economic independence and to find the right political formula by which to govern herself as a modern state, Brazil deserves sympathetic understanding by the people of the United States.

A meaningful reappraisal of the management of Latin American policy can result in an awareness that *respect* for Latin America and *dignity* in the conduct of our relations with her are probably more important than financial assistance. This was the essence of the Good Neighbor Policy. It provided very little tangible financial aid.

Whether Latin America goes the way of violent revolution or follows the path of a peaceful social revolution will depend upon the willingness of the industrialized nations to adopt a more effectively helpful attitude toward Latin America's export of primary commodities. Aid to the developing nations is not a matter only of loans and grants; it is much more importantly a matter of trade. It is sheer folly —if not downright hypocrisy—to demand that Latin America help itself, that she undertake long-range development plans, when she is unable to earn her way by the export of primary commodities and when we ourselves impose restrictions and barriers upon her ability to trade on profitable terms.

The most beneficial action that could be taken by the industrialized countries in assisting Latin America would be to grant free entry of Latin American exports of raw materials, semi-processed products, and manufactured goods, while accepting continued protective tariffs against their own exports. A one-way "free trade" would serve as an incentive for increasing agricultural and industrial production. It would enable the Latin American countries to increase their foreign earnings. Through an increase in their foreign earnings, Latin American countries would be able to meet their payments on loans from the international banks and foreign governments. Greater earnings from the export of primary commodities would reduce Latin America's reliance on foreign aid.

Latin America's social and economic progress will depend upon a sharper perception of the difference between an enlightened capitalism, such as prevails in the United States and in Western Europe, and an obsolete capitalism, which is still the rule in much of Latin America. To equate one with the other not only makes for confusion but also acts to inflame anti-Americanism. A doctrinaire insistence that the American form of private enterprise is the only alternative to Communism or that Latin America's development must be modeled in the image of American private enterprise can serve only to blunt Latin America's national purposes and our own. The mixed economies of Latin America and Europe are alternatives to both Soviet Communism and American capitalism. United States capitalism can continue to play a vital role in the modernization and economic integration of Latin America if some of its leaders will cease bemoaning the absence of "political stability" and "a climate of confidence." Latin America is a volatile, diverse, and ineluctably changing society. It is a society powered by three revolutions moving at the same time: an industrial revolution, an agrarian revolution, and a social revolution. In Latin America, the twentieth century is in headlong collision with the fifteenth. In this environment of turbulence, violence, and anarchy, it is futile to indulge in a will-o'-the-wisp pursuit of political stability or to insist upon a climate of confidence as a condition for doing business. There is precious little political stability to be found in most parts of the world, and its absence does not appear to be a deterrent to private investment. To insist upon it south of the Tropic of Cancer will lay us open to the charge of having a double standard of values. We appear to have forgotten *who* is expected to go *where* for foreign investment. To take advantage of Latin America's profitable business opportunities requires steady nerves, the kind of money that can afford to take big chances and to wait for big returns—and doesn't become jittery at the first alarming headline. This is the area for risk capital. The "widow and orphan" money should stay home.

The way that Latin America goes will depend upon the extent to which Fidel Castro's tarnished Cuban revolution still retains its magnetism for the revolutionary impulses that are running throughout Latin America. In the responsible centers of Latin American public opinion, the lesson of the Cuban experience has been driven home: an *abrazo* by the Russian bear can have nearly fatal (nuclear) consequences. By denouncing his former Chinese friends as blackmailers, subversives, hypocrites, and traitors, Dr. Castro has made it clear that, in the bitter Sino-Soviet conflict, he belongs to the side that butters his bread. He believes that Cuba is the spearhead of Latin America's social revolution and that he is destined to be its leader.

Latin America's future will depend upon the skill with which Moscow and Peking play the game of brinkmanship in the Western Hemisphere. Stressing the solidarity of color, the Peking Chinese have issued the call for the mobilization of the dispossessed and the disinherited. In September 1965, Peking enunciated a view of the world—in a document

entitled "Long Live the Victory of the People's War"—
which should be pondered as attentively in the United
States as it is being studied by young men throughout
Latin America. The signer of the document, Lin Piao, Vice
Chairman of the party's Central Committee, Vice Premier,
and Minister of Defense, contends that Communism came
to power by Mao's tactic of surrounding the cities from the
rural countryside. This tactic, however, was more than a
guerrilla operation. It embraced politics, economics, and
psychological warfare. Now, the time has come, Lin Piao
states, to apply this tactic to the whole world. He puts it
this way:

> Taking the entire globe, if North America and West-
> ern Europe can be called "the cities of the world,"
> then Asia, Africa, and Latin America constitute "the
> rural areas of the world."
>   In a sense, the contemporary world revolution also
> presents a picture of the encirclement of cities by the
> rural areas. In the final analysis, the whole cause of
> world revolution hinges on the revolutionary struggles
> of Asian, African, and Latin American peoples who
> make up the overwhelming majority of the world's
> population. The socialist [i.e., Communist] coun-
> tries should regard it as their internationalist duty to
> support the people's revolutionary struggles in Asia,
> Africa, and Latin America.

In Guatemala and along the *cordillera* of the Andes Mountains from Venezuela to Bolivia, "wars of national liberation," employing Mao Tse-tung's classic guerrilla warfare
tactics, are operative. The revolutionary ferment in the
Caribbean should be viewed against the backdrop of Lin
Piao's dictum that the attack on American influence must
employ the tactic of the united front and play upon local
nationalism but with Communists in actual control.

To Latin America's young men in a hurry, Peking's militant
summons to incendiary action against both progressive and
dictatorial regimes has greater appeal than the siren song of
the more cautious Moscow brethren who prefer the route
of co-existence, trade, aid, and subversion.

The course that Latin America takes will depend upon the
ability of this generation of Latin Americans to produce a
responsible democratic leadership. Many of the new genera-

tion share the conviction of the younger political leaders of
Europe that Marxism, conservatism, and liberalism are out of
date. This generation of Latin Americans has yet to recognize
that democratic government in Latin America has failed in
large measure because of the irresponsibility and emotional
instability of some of their political leaders—a Quadros and
a Goulart in Brazil, an Arosemena in Ecuador, a Bosch in
the Dominican Republic.

Cancellation of the contracts of the foreign oil companies
by the Illia regime in Argentina represents obsolete political thinking by a confused minority leadership out of touch
with world affairs. It reflects the provincialism and isola-
tionist thinking of an Argentina of the twenties. (In Peru,
the oil workers' unions have shown more common sense than
the politicians. They have declared that the Peruvian Government lacks the capital and trained personnel to run
a nationalized oil industry, and that "immediate nationalization" of the privately owned oil industry "is against the
national interest.")

Admiration for Betancourt as the first Venezuelan President to complete his term of office should not blind us to
his shortcomings as a democratic leader. The photograph in
American newspapers of the citizens of Caracas being
guarded by soldiers so that they might cast their ballot
against Acción Democrática—the party of the successful presidential candidate—is a stirring tribute to democracy,
but a withering indictment of Rómulo Betancourt and his
party. Despite the hold of Betancourt's party on the trade
unions and the presence of 125,000 civil servants and 65,000
city workers on the government's payroll, an informed public in the capital city repudiated Acción Democrática. Although Betancourt was pro-United States, anti-Castro, and
the idol of American liberals, the fact remains that his
suspension of constitutional guarantees was used as much
to harass his political opposition as to cope with extremists.
After five years in office, Betancourt did not succeed in
integrating the youth of Venezuela into the national community. Instead, the radicalism of the university students
was converted into outright warfare against society. Betancourt's party was long on forging a tightly knit political
machine, but woefully short on creating new ideas and a
new ideology to capture the allegiance of the majority of
Venezuela's youth. The vacuum was filled by the half-baked
revolutionary theories of Ché Guevara. Terrorism and

guerrilla warfare will continue in Venezuela because many of the young people have repudiated democracy as a method for attaining Venezuela's social revolution.

This generation must rediscover its own Latin America by distinguishing between reality and myth. How relevant are the conventional beliefs regarding the *oligarquía*—the landowning aristocracy, the military, and the Church? To what extent is actual power in the hands of an industrial and financial class, millionaire politicians, and opportunistic demagogues? Is it fact or fiction that American business is harmful to Latin America's development? Would Latin America require massive foreign aid if its own capitalists possessed a sense of social responsibility and repatriated their Swiss and United States bank accounts? Except in Argentina, is there a "middle class" with democratic aspirations? Can reform movements be built on middle-income groups who are tied emotionally to the institutional *status quo*?

Still another basic question that this generation of Latin Americans must face is whether it is really committed to representative government. And what kind of representative government? Is it the Mexican variety, in which a dominant party muffles or suspends political controversy? Is it the representative government of Great Britain, Switzerland, and the Scandinavian countries? Or is it the "authoritarian democracy" of General de Gaulle, who believes that representative government is no longer workable? If these questions can be answered satisfactorily, the analysis must proceed to an examination of the Hispanic concept of political power. Is representative government campatible with a concept of power that cannot be shared through political collaboration?

Realistically, can this generation of Latin Americans take political command while the existing political parties are controlled by the aging lions and tired oxen of democracy? What essential difference is there between the old-style dictators who ruthlessly exterminated the young revolutionaries at the universities, and the modern democratic *caudillos* whose stranglehold on their parties prevents new ideas and new personalities from rising to the surface? The leader who considers his own opinions to be holy writ and regards any deviation from his political platform as treasonable conduct is an anachronism. The day is past when political parties can be owned by dictators or democratic *caudillos*. The complex problems of mass urbanization and industrialization cannot be solved by old-fashioned political parties led by charismatic leaders. Today, realistic political platforms are more important than brilliant personalities. Political effectiveness depends upon organizations with deep roots in the rural areas as well as in the cities. Political organization rather than political grandiloquence is the key to electoral success. The most urgent business today is the formulation of the specific programs by which social justice can be attained.

If this generation of Latin Americans intends to serve democracy, it must produce leaders who possess political realism, a deep sense of public responsibility, impeccable honesty, and respect for other people's ideas. This generation of Latin Americans must produce leaders who are not political dilettantes. Dilettantism has been the bane of Latin American politics since the break-up of the Spanish and Portuguese empires. The art of governing is too complex and the stakes are too high to be entrusted to political amateurs. If they cannot supply these indispensable ingredients of organization and leadership and if the aging leaders are unwilling to relinquish control over their parties, there is little hope for democracy in Latin America.

Attainment of social justice in Latin America will depend upon an increasing concern with and a more active support of social reform by the Catholic Church. *"El deber: social y político"* ("The duty: social and political"), the eloquent declaration by the Chilean bishops which depicted the misery of the Chilean peasants and workers; the denunciation by Dom Helder Câmera, Archbishop of Recife, of those in Brazil's moneyed class who are blind to the need for change; the increasing awareness of the desperate need for birth control; the dramatic radio campaign to overcome illiteracy by Monsignor Salcedo of Bogotá; the establishment of credit unions for the Peruvian Indians by the Maryknoll priest Father McLellan—these acts reflect the historic concern with social justice in Latin America, and are indicative of the Church's growing awareness of its own social responsibilities and of its desire to move with the tides of social reform.

Pope Paul VI has revealed that one of the late Pope's preoccupations as he lay on his deathbed was the future of the Church in Latin America. We are told that, after receiving the last sacraments, John spoke of "the great work to be done in Latin America." If only the *padres* of the backlands of Latin America would ponder the meaning of Pope John's compassionate solicitude and begin the fulfillment of his concern. For in their parishes can be heard the premonitory tremors of a violent explosion.

Whether Latin America can develop democratically will depend upon the attitudes of the military, who throughout Latin America are almost universally the ultimate arbiters of power. By its support of progressive and orderly government, an enlightened military can act as a midwife in delivering its country into the modern world. The trained manpower of Latin America's armies is needed to build highways, schools, and sanitation and water systems. The $1.4 billion that Latin America spends on armaments each year is a tragic burden for improverished peoples to bear. In a nuclear age this investment in obsolete armaments has no relation to the defense of the Western Hemisphere. Caste-ridden military establishments concerned solely with their own pelf and power, content to be merely a praetorian guard to make and break presidents, having no other ambition than to sit on the backs of their people—this type of military acts as a brake on peaceable reforms, exacerbates social and political tensions, and hastens Castro-Communist take-overs and its own inevitable liquidation.

Latin Americans live in the shadow of doom. Uncontrolled population growth and unproductive agriculture menace Latin America with misery, starvation, violent revolutions, and perpetuation of an abysmally low standard of living. Man has made it his business to control death. He knows how to control birth. The right to prevent a new life from entering into human degradation can no longer be withheld. It is beyond Latin America's capability to organize agricultural production on a scale adequate to feed her expanding population and to transform peasant tillers of the soil in subsistence economies into modern farmers who can use agricultural technology and are consumers of the goods and products of industry. But the West can help—before it is too late.

Almost fifty years ago, in a memorable passage in *The Economic Consequences of the Peace*, John Maynard Keynes admonished the peacemakers at Paris in words that are a somber warning to today's political leaders in Latin America and the West:

Men will not always die quietly. For starvation, which

brings to some lethargy and a helpless despair, drives other temperaments to the nervous instability of hysteria and to a mad despair. And these in their distress may overturn the remnants of organization, and submerge civilization itself in their attempts to satisfy desperately the overwhelming needs of the individual. This is the danger against which all our resources and courage and idealism must now co-operate.

The Western world cannot be a disinterested spectator of the epic drama of Latin America, which, as in the Greek tragedy, moves inexorably toward its inevitable fate. A massive failure in Latin America would constitute a fatal blow to the world leadership of the United States. Latin America's rejection of progress through a pluralistic society would permanently turn the new sovereignties of Africa and Asia away from the West and to the side of the coercive societies of authoritarianism.

Throughout the Western Hemisphere, as well as in Europe, there are thoughtful men who believe that the disintegration of Latin America would threaten the foundations of the Western world. Were Latin America to be seized in the convulsive grip of disaster, this company of men would experience moral repugnance in emulating Emmanuel Joseph Sieyès, Vicar General to the Bishop of Chartres, who, when asked what he had done during the Reign of Terror, is said to have replied: *"J'ai vécu"* ("I survived").

Dark though the horizon may appear, it is premature to succumb to despair or to subscribe to the belief that Latin America will have to be written off. Although it is late, it may not be too late for men of good purpose to avert what former President Alberto Lleras Camargo of Colombia has called a "historic disaster."

CHAPTER TWO

The Politics of Disorder

NORTH AMERICANS are prone to forget that Latin America is no Johnny-come-lately to independence from colonial rule. Only thirty-four years separated the beginning of the Wars of Independence of Spanish America from the Declaration of Independence of England's colonies. As all the world knows, the results of these two quests for independence were spectacularly different. In the North, as Don Salvador de Madariaga once observed, a *United* States of America developed; in the South, the achievement was a *disunited* states of America. The reasons for the difference have fascinated Hispanic men of letters since the Great Liberator, Simón Bolívar, expressed his bitter disillusionment over the Spanish-American incapacity for representative government. These speculations need not detain us. The point to be made is that more than one hundred and fifty years after the break-up of the Spanish and Portuguese empires, representative, popular government is still largely an elusive aspiration, is still in the main a search for a political Holy Grail. Constitutional trappings borrowed from the United States and parliamentary edifices appropriated from France are largely theatrical stage props and latter-day Potemkin villages.

The first thing to be kept in mind about the colonial liberation from Spain is this: it was a revolution from on top. The men of Caracas, Bogotá, Quito, Buenos Aires, and Santiago who sought their independence in 1810 were stout royalists at heart. As colonials, they had been denied access to the governing establishment, although they were thrown an occasional sop in the form of a commission in the King's regiments. What these proud New World aristocrats resented was the humiliation of being treated as second-class citizens. But even these annoyances could be suffered. On the other hand, when their King, Ferdinand VII, was imprisoned by the upstart Napoleon, the situation was intolerable. The revolt in Spanish America was triggered by Napoleon's occupation of Madrid and the placing of his brother Joseph on the Spanish throne.

The Indian, the Negro, the New World's men of mixed blood—the *mestizo* and the mulatto—were conscripted into the armies of liberation. The legions of Bolívar, Sucre, and San Martín performed heroic feats and suffered appalling hardships in brilliantly led campaigns across the craggy peaks of the Andes. But with victory over Spanish arms, the legionnaires remained as before: hewers of wood and drawers of water. The end of Spanish rule witnessed only a transfer of power at the apex; the native-born *criollo* aristocracy took over from the *peninsulares*, the governing aristocracy of Madrid.

A second point to be kept in mind with respect to Spanish America's independence is the nature of the political organization under the empire. The Spanish Crown was astute enough to sense that the epic conquest by that motley company of noblemen, adventurers, soldiers of fortune, poets, convicts, and peasants had carved out a potentially golden empire and that the power of the *conquistadores* would eventually jeopardize any effective exercise of the Crown's authority. The development of the territories and the conversion of the pagan population required a trained, experienced administration, both civilian and ecclesiastical. The Casa de Contratación, with control over maritime and commercial policy, was established at Seville as early as 1503. By 1524 a permanent Royal and Supreme Council of the Indies at Madrid was entrusted with jurisdiction over military, ecclesiastical, legislative, and judicial affairs. By 1535 Don Antonio de Mendoza (a member of one of the greatest families of Castile) arrived at Mexico City to assume his duties as viceroy, governor-general, and president of the *audiencia* of New Spain. Eight years later, in 1543, a viceroy was appointed for Peru, with his capital at Lima, "The City of the Kings" founded by Francisco Pizarro and his followers. Until the eighteenth century, the viceroyalty of Peru would rule all of South America. The work of immobilizing the aging and quarreling *conquistadores* was begun. Organization of the commercial potential of the colonies for the benefit of the Crown was undertaken. Political control was centralized in the hands of men who, with few exceptions, were of commanding stature and were tied to Madrid by the closest bonds of tradition and loyalty.

Spain's dominion over the New World has been more widely condemned than praised, but judging the administration of that empire by twentieth-century standards is little more than an exercise in sentimentality. The fact remains that Spain's empire existed for over three hundred years. It was the greatest empire then known to the Western world. It sprawled across the map from California, New Mexico, and Texas to Florida. It included Mexico and Central America. It reached to the southernmost tip of South America, where the waters of the Atlantic rush to meet the Pacific. It included the Philippine Islands. The Caribbean was a Spanish lake. In all, this empire covered some 10 million square miles. It was, indeed, an empire on which the sun never set.

For over three hundred years the King's galleons plied the Pacific and Atlantic oceans and the Caribbean Sea. Cargoes of silver from Mexico and of gold from Peru were hauled across the Andes to Lima for transport to Panama to await convoys to Spain. Cargoes of sugar, cocoa, hides, spices, dyewoods, tobacco, and furs were shipped from the fortress cities along the Caribbean. From the Spanish ports of Cádiz and Seville, the Crown's fleets carried Cordovan leather, Malagan wine, Toledan steel, and Murcian silks to Havana, Vera Cruz, Cartagena, and Porto Bello on the Isthmus of Panama. From Porto Bello, the cargoes were hauled overland to the Pacific. They were then transported by another fleet to Lima for distribution throughout South America, as far as Buenos Aires on the Atlantic coast.

The condition of the conquered population was probably neither better nor worse than their centuries-old lot as serfs in the ancient Mayan, Aztec, and Inca civilizations. To the Indian victim, there was little difference between extermination in the murderous wars of their native *caciques* and death from starvation and exhaustion in a Mexican silver mine.

For more than three centuries Spain's empire achieved an impressive record of political stability. But Spain's legacy to the New World included much more than an organizational structure of political unity. Before the decay and rot of the Hapsburg empire set in, Spain planted in the New World the seeds of its own flickering efflorescence. From the Berber tribesmen of the Atlas Mountains on the northern rim of Africa (who found themselves at home on the parched, desolate, windswept plains of Castile) came the toughness of spirit, the resilient hardness which, like the famous Toledan steel, bends but does not break. From the blood of the Arab (who crossed over the natural highway of the Strait of Gibraltar into the Iberian Peninsula and left the indelible mark of his eight centuries of dominion) came an appreciation of the sensuous and a feeling for indolence. The Arab was at home in Andalusia, an Oriental garden in the south of Spain. It was in the south that the Moors built Seville, Córdoba, Málaga, Granada, cities of voluptuous splendor. The Spanish character is by nature incapable of accepting the Anglo-American ideal of work as an end in itself. It is repelled by the acquisitive instinct. "The grandest enterprises," Ángel Ganivet has Hernán Cortés say, "are those in which money has no part, and the cost falls entirely on the brain and heart."

From Spain's African heritage came the celebrated dispersive quality of the Spaniard, the fatal flaw of his character: the attraction for ideas but lack of interest in their execution. From the Sephardic Jewish physicians, scientists, philosophers, and financiers came the brooding discontent and the taste for reflective rationalism. Their expulsion by the Inquisition—that "cold and calculating instrument of God's terror" —deprived Spain of its finest intellects. From the provinces of Asturias and Galicia (which the Moors never subdued) came the valor, the fierce sense of independence, the Messianic pride, the lust for battle, the instinct for revenge, the impulse for rebellion.

From this amalgam of Iberian blood transplanted to America was derived Spain's most precious gift of all: the consecration of the individual and the respect for his dignity as a man.

Out of Spain's New World empire arose the cry for social justice which today echoes throughout the continent in a mounting crescendo. The struggle for justice was intensified by the polarization of the Spanish character. Cortés' old companion-in-arms, Bernal Díaz, gave classic expression to the Spaniard's dichotomy of motives when, with simple bluntness, he said: "We came here to serve God, and also to get rich." It was Bartolomé de Las Casas, soldier of fortune, capitalist-turned-priest, who first raised the voice of the Church in an impassioned appeal to the conscience of the Crown for justice to the despoiled Indian. It was a Spanish hidalgo, Don Luis de Velasco, a worldly man of affairs, the King's own viceroy, who wrote to His Catholic Majesty, Philip: "The liberty of the Indians is worth more than all the mines in the world, and the revenue which the Crown receives from them is not of such consequence that the Crown would on that account crush under foot human and divine law." More than three hundred years before Lincoln's Emancipation Proclamation, the Council of the Indies responded to the appeal of conscience by ordering the Indian slaves freed. Other nations have subsidized exploration and in the process acquired empires. Spain's obsession with justice for a conquered people was unique.

From the Council of the Indies emerged the earliest conception of regional economic planning for an entire viceregal area: roads, harbors, irrigation and drainage, a communications network of navigable canals. The Council nurtured the development of the mining industry and the promotion of exports and imports. The Castilian Crown united its New World empire in a trading system such as twentieth-century Europe is only on the threshold of realizing. From the Council of the Indies, too, came the conception of the continent as a single political unit—an idea that Latin American political leaders are asserting in our own time. In the eighteenth century, the King's minister, Don José Campillo, urged agrarian reforms that have a modern ring—distribution of land to the Indians without payment of taxes, training in the use of improved agricultural methods, and an ample supply of credit for the purchase of agricultural tools.

Spain's militant soldiers of the Cross—whose ranks contained the kingdom's best intellects and its most devoted servants, the hardy, tough Dominicans and the compassionate, practical Franciscans—built the first schools, introduced the first printing press, and fostered the earliest technology in weaving, dyeing, ceramics, masonry, carpentry, silk raising, and agriculture. The friars promoted the New World's earliest universities at Santo Domingo, Mexico City, and Lima; they preceded Harvard by a century. As Don Salvador de Madariaga reminds us, the constructive and civilizing work of the Jesuits was immense. From New Spain to Chile, there was hardly a city of importance in which they did not exert a powerful influence on education. In their missions along the Río de la Plata, illiteracy among the Indians was eradicated. One of their first books was a study of the Indians' language, the *Vocabulario de la Lengua Guaraní*. It was the Spanish genius for self-destruction—the Quixote complex—which led to the expulsion of the Jesuit Order from Spain and the New World. Daring, intelligent, resourceful, the Jesuits did not hesitate to criticize whatever and whomever they disapproved of, including the King himself. But they had become too powerful; they threatened the Crown's power. Even in a theocratic state, power was not divisible. If the City of God in the New World did not always correspond to the purity of the churchmen's dream, the Church and the universities in the twentieth century continue to be the fountainhead of reform and the voice of protest against man's inhumanity to man.

Spain gave to much of the New World its magnificent instrument of communication—a language that is clean and virile, an anvil upon which the tongue may strike its commands. Gabriela Mistral, the Chilean poet and Nobel Prize winner, once declared: "What unites us in Spanish America is our beautiful language and our distrust of the United States."

To its New World children, Spain left a heritage that is disdainful of the small truths but passionately committed to the big truths.

In the New World, history was in search of a role. Spain improvised brilliantly. Out of the fragments and debris of Europe's colonial past, Spain's contributions survive.

What this empire did not provide was the practice and habit of local self-government. It is an ironic footnote to the history of representative government that medieval Spain led Europe in civil liberties. As early as 1020, the Charter of León recognized the hereditary rights of the serf in the soil that he tilled and his freedom to change his seigneur. At that moment there developed in Spain a unique flowering of Spanish democracy through the famous rights, or *fueros*, of the cities and regions. From the rights of the community there developed that remarkable body the Cortes, to which the monarchs gave respectable heed, for it was the Cortes that sanctioned the right to levy taxes and appropriated grants of money—even the right to reign was within its purview.

The *cabildo abierto* was for the medieval Spaniard what the village green—the commons—was to become for the men of New England some centuries later. This springtime of popular democracy—the dawn of the common man's right to be heard—was swallowed by the movement for unification as Spain slowly but inexorably brought eight centuries of Moorish dominion to an end. Vigorous independent local governments did not fit into the collectivist ideas of that extraordinary conjugal political partnership of Ferdinand and Isabella. Their accession to the throne in 1469 consummated the centralization of power in Madrid. In their hands, Spain became a holy state.

Except as a formal tradition, the spirit of municipal independence and the democratic fervor of the ancient *cabildo abierto* were unable to take strong root in the colonies. In a passage describing the preparation for democracy in the northern British colonies, Clinton Rossiter, in *The First American Revolution*, points to the lack of such preparation in the south. He writes: "Before there could be a democracy there had to be liberty and self-government, and before Washington could make his revolution the men of the assemblies had to make theirs." To paraphrase Professor Rossiter, Bolívar had made his revolution, but Spain's colonials had not made theirs. That the ideas of the Enlightenment and the ideals of the American and French revolutions (which provided the intellectual foundations for Spanish-American independence) could have revived the *cabildo* was improbable in view of the power vacuum created by the removal of the Crown's authority. The forced withdrawal of Spain left three centers of power in the former colonies: the Church, the *criollo* aristocracy, and the military leaders of the victorious armies. This was not, however, a triumvirate that shared power equally. The *criollo* aristocracy had assumed power but was unable to rule. It had no base of popular support or popular allegiance. It had no experience with government. After fifteen years of warfare, the army could not be controlled by civilian authority. Juan Martín de Pueyrredón in Buenos Aires, O'Higgins in Santiago, San Martín's protectorate over Peru, and Bolívar's rule over Venezuela and Colombia were enlightened despotisms. The "generals" had been educated in the tradition of the French *encyclopédistes* and were among the most cultivated and enlightened men of their time. At heart, they were authoritarians who paid lip service to popular sovereignty.

The drafting of the new constitutions for the new American republics fell to the intellectual "doctors." They created magnificent documents replete with the noblest expression of man's hope. Modeled on the United States constitution or the republican institutions of France, they philosophized on the rights of man. They contained explicit guarantees of democracy: freedom of the press and assembly, trial by jury, universal suffrage. They promised democracy. In practice, the commitment was not fulfilled. Even to this day almost all the constitutions remain literary monuments. "Paper and ink," Bolívar contemptuously called them.

The generals and the doctors created governments "for" the people. They did not establish governments in Lincoln's meaning—of the people, by the people, for the people. Liberators who betrayed the liberated, constitutions that made a mockery of democratic principles—this was the legacy to the people from those who made a revolution. For more than one hundred and fifty years, Latin Americans have lived with a myth—the myth that their countries are democracies. In his penetrating essay on Mexico, *The Labyrinth of Solitude*, Octavio Paz describes this habit of living with an illusion:

> The political lie established itself almost constitutionally. The moral damage it has caused is incalculable; it has affected profound areas of our existence. We move about in this lie with complete naturalness. For over a hundred years we have suffered from regimes that have been at the service of feudal oligarchies but have utilized the language of freedom.[1]

Thomas Jefferson wrote to Edward Everett in 1824 that "the qualifications for self-government in society are not innate. They are the result of habit and long training." He prophesied that in Latin America the acquisition of this habit and training "will require time and probably much suffering." The conditions for the development of democratic habits and training were not supplied by Bolívar and his generals. Instead, they created an environment of chaos. The pursuit of unlimited and despotic power became the objective of every local and regional satrap. The power struggle generated anarchy. The impoverished people fought

[1] Octavio Paz: *The Labyrinth of Solitude: Life and Thought in Mexico* (New York: Grove Press; 1961), p. 122.

the Constitution." And his by the "Restorer of the Laws."
And so the dreary cycle starts all over again as exiles plot,
gather funds and arms, and await the *pronunciamiento* of
the Leader for launching one more *Putsch*.

The struggle for power is not merely a personal clash
between rival *caudillos*. The ultimate prize is possession of
the economic power base, euphemistically called "government." In his notable study *Arms and Politics in Latin America,* Edwin Lieuwen estimates that over a period of five
years (1954–59) six Latin American *caudillos* (several of
whom are still enjoying the fruits of their plunder) made
off with over $1 billion in personal loot and graft.
Some "sons of the Mexican Revolution" are known to have
retired from the presidency as millionaires. Politics in Latin
America can be a richly satisfying career, at one and the
same time fulfilling a revolutionary ardor and providing the
trappings and panoply of power, popular adulation along
with personal aggrandizement. Adhemar de Barros, a well-
known Brazilian politician, once expressed the same idea
more simply and with brutal candor, when he exclaimed to
the voters of São Paulo: "I steal, but I achieve!"

With some oversimplification, this is the game of musical
chairs that has characterized much of Latin America's political
movement—and still does. The revolutions are not comparable to the great crises of Europe in which a political system
disappears and a new social class emerges. In over a century, since the Wars of Independence, despite countless
civil wars and changes in the Palace, Latin America has witnessed only three social revolutions representing an upheaval in the existing economic and political structure: the
Mexican Revolution, the Bolivian Revolution, and the Cuban
Revolution.

"Latin American politics," Rómulo Betancourt once wrote,
"has always been characterized by violence." In the Latin
American political system, violence is an institutionalized
method for the transfer of political power. In Honduras, for
instance, from 1824 to 1950—a period of 126 years—the
executive office changed hands 116 times. Over a nine-year
period ending in 1940, Ecuador had fourteen presidents, four
of them during a single month. Since Bolívar's death in
1830, Venezuela has had twenty-six different constitutions. In
the present century, Venezuela cannot claim to have had
more than three honest elections, the last in 1963, when
Raúl Leoni was elected President. In the years from 1830

to 1900, there were at least fifty revolts. The central government was overthrown by violence on thirteen different occasions. For all but fifteen years of its more than a century of independence, Venezuela has been ruled by dictatorial *caudillos*.

With a few notable exceptions, the signal failure of the Latin American political system, as Frank Tannenbaum makes clear in his brilliant *Ten Keys to Latin America,* is its inability to provide for orderly and responsible transfer of power. The system is incapable of achieving this central political objective because accession to power is illegitimate. Thus political instability is endemic. The prolonged tenure by the *caudillo* does not signify the absence of political instability, but only the suppression of potential and incipient revolts by competing *caudillos.* The protracted tenure of a Vargas in Brazil (1930–45) or an Ubico in Guatemala (1931–44), the "single candidate" elections in Nicaragua and formerly in the Dominican Republic, and the "controlled opposition" in Paraguay are illustrations of governmental authority retained by force. In those regimes in which the military is the real power but operates behind the theatrical gauze of a civilian administration, there is only a deceptive appearance of political stability. The peaceful interlude of the *caudillo* is in reality no more than the calm found in the eye of the hurricane.

It was the hope that the democratically inspired revolts against the *caudillo* system—which began in Brazil in 1945 and continued in Argentina, Bolivia, Peru, Colombia, Venezuela, Costa Rica, Honduras, Guatemala, and Cuba—would usher in a new era of popular, representative government. A new generation and a new type of political leader had arisen. In Argentina, it was Frondizi, a lawyer-politician. In Costa Rica, it was Figueres, a planter-industrialist. In Brazil, it was Kubitschek, a physician-politician. In Bolivia, it was Paz Estenssoro, a professor of economics. In Guatemala, it was Arévalo, a professor of education. In Venezuela, it was Gallegos, a novelist. In Colombia, it was Lleras Camargo, a journalist. All had several traits in common: they were members of the intellectual community, and their political platforms were founded on social and economic reform. Some, like José Figueres and Juscelino Kubitschek, gave notable leadership to the democratic forces of their countries. Some, like Alberto Lleras Camargo, bound the wounds of their country and provided a sense of direction.

Others, like Víctor Paz Estenssoro, were the cement which held their revolutions together. Some, like Arturo Frondizi, failed in the struggle to achieve democracy.

The promise of political stability implicit in the postwar democratic surge was not fulfilled. The postwar revolution in communications struck Latin America with shattering impact. The American movie, the radio, and the airplane opened new horizons. World War II had idealized the Soviet Union. Communism became "respectable." The *campesinos* and Indian *peones* were stirred by the promises of democracy and the "news" of the "good life" of the Russian proletariat. The reform democrats were unable to meet the rising aspirations of the people. If an Alliance for Progress had existed at that juncture, it might have provided the economic underpinning for social reforms. But the United States was preoccupied with the recovery of Europe. The reform democrats were left to flounder in their own inadequacies. Vast intercontinental forces seized the hemisphere—a catastrophic decline in export prices; the cold war; the divisive effects of Castroism. They were beyond the political control of any individual. The new democrats were powerless to stay the tidal wave of migration from the countryside into the cities —a mass of humanity which, unable to find jobs or decent shelter, became the ideal breeding ground for social and political tensions. Paradoxically, by producing a fissure in their backward societies, the new democrats succeeded only in unleashing political and social instability. Dr. Castro has dedicated himself to exploiting each such crevice of unrest by terror, arson, and gunfire.

One of the serious limitations of the American mind is its lack of comprehension of the psychological attitudes of other societies. We delude ourselves into believing that we are in communication with peoples of alien cultures whereas in reality our ideas skim over their minds like a stone hopping across the placid surface of a pond. Despite our wide travels and outwardly cosmopolitan lives, the mainsprings of political behavior of other lands and people tend to elude us. One of the great American illusions is the assumption that if only other people would understand our point of view, they would adopt it readily. Hence our frustration and disillusionment when other societies do not adopt liberal, democratic governments, or spurn the market system of private enterprise in favor of centralized direction over economic activities, or do not reshape their shockingly mismanaged societies into neat replicas of ours. This conflict between illusion and reality lies at the root of our widespread disenchantment with foreign aid. Moreover, the notion of violence as an accepted technique for the alteration of the governmental structure is distasteful to us. We are prone to sublimate the presence of violence in our own social behavior. The folly and tragedy of this attitude is dramatically apparent in the Negro uprising that has created as grave an internal crisis as the nation has experienced since the Civil War. Our minds and emotions rebel against the existence of violence and its concomitant, political instability, as both uncongenial and dangerous to our own psychological security. When we witness the phenomenon on a continental scale in our own hemisphere, our reaction is likely to be traumatic. In the business community, we voice our "loss of confidence" in Latin America. On the legislative front, appropriations for the Alliance for Progress are cut to shreds by an embittered House of Representatives. It is a rare day when the press carries a "favorable" Latin American story. In many offices of the Washington establishment, Latin America is shrugged off as already "down the drain."

Heraclitus long ago observed that one does not bathe twice in the same stream. Change is the law of life. In our time, change is proceeding at a pace that is both dizzy and perplexing. It is shot through with the revolutionary ferment of a generation unwilling to accept the past as a condition of the present. In our search for political stability in this kind of world we are Don Quixotes charging windmills. In Latin America, especially, the pursuit of political stability is a chase after a will-o'-the-wisp.

CHAPTER THREE

Where the Soldiers Call the Shots

MILITARY INVOLVEMENT in politics is prevalent throughout much of the contemporary world. It exists in the Middle East, in sub-Saharan Africa, in Turkey, in Pakistan, in Southeast Asia. It is not unknown to the France of Charles de Gaulle. In Spain, the army has intervened in politics as a matter of "right" for almost a century. In Latin America, politics is the business of the military.

Although it is fashionable to criticize the Latin American military for using the *coup d'état* against constitutionally elected governments, it must be recognized that the military has also supported democratic elections. The armed forces of the Dominican Republic ensured Juan Bosch's election to the presidency in 1962. The Venezuelan military guaranteed the 1963 presidential elections. General Juan Carlos Onganía made it possible for Argentina to hold a presidential election in 1963. Having intervened to prevent Víctor Raúl Haya de la Torre from assuming the presidency, Peru's military secured a constitutional election in 1963 which placed Fernando Belaúnde Terry in the presidency.

It should also be noted that democratic politicians have not been averse to using the *coup d'état* when it served their own purpose. In 1956, Dr. Juan Manuel Gálvez, President of Honduras, engineered a *coup d'état* against himself so as to enable Dr. Julio Lozano to take over the Palace. A former President of Honduras, Dr. Ramón Villeda Morales, was the successful candidate through a deal with Colonel Hector Carraccioli, chief of the army. The price that Dr. Villeda paid for his election was an agreement that the armed forces of Honduras would be responsible only to the Congress (which in practice meant there would be no control over the military). An independent military ousted Dr. Villeda from the presidency in October 1963. In 1945, Rómulo Betancourt and Raúl Leoni conspired with a group of junior officers of the Venezuelan armed forces to oust President Medina because—as they charged—he was "planning" to rig the elections. Alfredo Vitolo, former Minister of the Interior during the administration of President Frondizi, coined the phrase *"elenco estable del golpismo"* ("permanent cast of the *coup d'état*") to describe those Argentine politicians who made a practice of knocking at the door of the barracks for help in overthrowing constitutional governments. Of the thirty-five attempted *coups d'état* against Frondizi, the majority were instigated by disgruntled politicians. The same can be said for the thirty coups attempted against Guido. Before becoming a member of the Illia regime, Vice-President Carlos Perette conspired with several, retired *"gorilla"* (colloquial for "reactionary") generals (who had opposed the return of civilian government) in a coup against the Chief of Staff, General Juan Carlos Onganía (who had supported constitutional government). The *coup d'état* that ousted Goulart in March 1964 was largely inspired and planned by several influential governors. Dominican politicians, notably Juan Bosch, conspired with the military to topple Donald Reid Cabral in the bloody revolution of April 1965. The point that should not be overlooked is this: democratic politicians have pulled the strings of more than a few Latin American military coups.

Although Latin America's armies have certain characteristics common to all military establishments—the authoritarianism inherent in a hierarchical structure; *esprit de corps;* technical specialization; an organization that can be deployed on command—there are, nevertheless, differences in attitude, function, and political style. These variations manifest themselves in differences concerning the conduct of inter-hemisphere affairs. For instance, at the Punta del Este Conference held in Uruguay in January 1962, the United States sought, among other things, a resolution excluding the Cuban regime from the Organization of American States. Argentina and Brazil were among the six countries in opposition. Upon his return to Buenos Aires, the Argentine Foreign Minister was rebuked for his stand by the Argentine military High Command. Two weeks later, Argentina broke diplomatic relations with Cuba. Upon his return to Rio de Janeiro, the Brazilian Foreign Minister was welcomed at the airport by the Brazilian Minister of War and high-ranking officers of the armed forces, who conveyed the full support of the Brazilian military establishment for the stand taken at Punta del Este. Brazil continued to maintain diplomatic relations with Cuba under the regime of President João Goulart.

In the military establishments themselves, there are sharp differences of outlook within the officer corps. Although the senior officers are in the main men of the people, their outlook is essentially conservative. They regard the military as primarily an instrument for the preservation of order. Politically, this means protecting the *status quo* and braking the revolutionary forces of the Left. In the junior ranks, among the *tenientes,* there are those who see Castro's way as the only way; others see "Arab Socialism" as the solution to the unrest of their countries. In the middle ranks—among the majors and colonels who are academy-trained—there is a strong sense of professionalism. Here, too, there can be sensed an uneasiness, some questioning as to whether the military has an effective mission. Their political sentiments are apt to be more conservative than those of the junior ranks. Families, promotion, retirement, create their own restraints. While there may be some emotional rapport with the yearnings of their younger colleagues, joining them involves too great a risk to career and security.

If there can be said to be any unifying thread which binds the officer corps, it is an instinctive hostility to the democratic processes. In part, this is an outgrowth of lifelong training in a hierarchical organization in which each element is subject to command—and obedience. In part—the greater part—it is the result of the conditioning process of belonging to an establishment that has been set apart, enjoys special privileges, and—in some countries—is the dominant power structure.

At one end of Latin America's military spectrum will be found a tradition of the military as a praetorian guard or shogunate. The striking characteristic of this type of military is that it considers itself a privileged caste. It is reminiscent of the German Reichswehr and the prewar Japanese officer corps, whose lower- and middle-class origins did not inhibit it from emulating the Samurai. Where praetorianism prevails— as, for instance, in Argentina, Peru, and Guatemala—the military establishments are in reality states within states. In these countries, the civilian state (when it is in existence) is permitted to exercise the formal trappings of government: it mans the departmental bureaucracies; it operates the foreign service; the nominal chief of state is a civilian. But no civilian president, cabinet minister, or ambassador ever forgets where the real power lies.

The popular notion that Latin America's armed forces intervene in politics because the civilian control has broken down—that once the governmental machinery has been repaired, the military returns to its "normal" business—is a myth. The *normal* business of the military in these countries is politics. When, following the election of Dr. Arturo Illia as President of Argentina, an army colonel said to an American reporter: "Now we can go home," he was talking through his garrison cap. Although Dr. Illia is the constitutional President of Argentina, elected by the people through their Electoral College, his administration will stay in power by sufferance of General Juan Carlos Onganía—or his successor. This is an arrangement in which responsibility-without-power confronts power-without-responsibility.

At the other end of the scale is Costa Rica. Its army was replaced by a thousand-man police force in 1948, when José Figueres and his *figueristas* led the first defense in the Americas against an attempted Communist take-over. When the military sought to nullify the election, Figueres simply dissolved the army. "Why," he asked, "should a group of professional men assume the right to annul the popular will as expressed at the polls?" Don Pepe Figueres' question remains the most important unanswered question in Latin America.

Somewhere in the middle of the spectrum lies the tamed military, which is to be found in Mexico, Uruguay, Chile, and Colombia. One of the earliest efforts in this hemisphere to control the Latin American military predilection for politics was that of José Batlle y Ordóñez, Uruguay's greatest statesman and the creator of the first welfare state in the Western Hemisphere. Batlle believed that the excessive concentration of power in the hands of a president was an invitation to the *caudillo* instincts to set in motion the twin forces of *coup d'état* and dictatorship. At a constitutional convention in 1917, it was agreed that executive power should be divided between a president and a National Council of Administration. In Uruguay, the armed forces are under the direction of a civilian minister. Although the military is disciplined and plays a subordinate role in the affairs of the country, the infectious disease of military seizures of power spread to Montevideo. During the week of September 26, 1963, in which Juan Bosch's administration in the Dominican Republic collapsed, it became necessary for the Uruguayan National Council to reprimand a small group of officers against any further efforts to intrude themselves into the civil authority of the Council. The mere recital of this event scarcely conveys the shock felt in *colorado* political circles at this attempt at political involvement by the officer corps, whose removal from politics was thought to be absolute.

Until the overthrow of Paz Estenssoro in November 1964, the notorious praetorian tendencies of the Bolivian army had been progressively curbed. The army had been put to useful work in the construction of roads and rural schools, in furnishing medical services to remote villages, and in other public works of the type undertaken by the American Army Corps of Engineers.

In Mexico, the generals' tendency to act as *caudillos* was eliminated over a generation ago during the presidency of Cárdenas. It was accomplished by giving the military official representation in the Party of the Mexican Revolution. When critics objected, Cárdenas said: "We have not put the army in politics. It was already there. In fact, it had been dominating the situation and we did well to reduce its influence to one vote out of four." The Mexican military is still a powerful factor in the political life of the country. The Mexican army is tied closely to the political machines of the state governments, which exercise enormous political influence. But the army no longer dictates to the civil authority. It participates with the civil authority in the crucial political decisions. Since 1929, bureaucrats, white-collar and professional workers, trade unionists, and peasants have been integrated into the official party. They act as a counterbalance to the military. The military is, therefore, only one of the power blocs. Although no President of Mexico fails to consult the army chiefs, the point is that the army exerts its influence within the framework of the official party. It is not an independent political force as in other Latin American countries.

The merger of the army with the civilian power blocs within the official party is an outgrowth of efforts by successive presidents. Mexico's postrevolutionary period (1917–29) was characterized by military *caciquismo*, with each of the former revolutionary generals in charge of a zone or district. In 1929, General Calles brought the former generals into the party.

There were abortive revolts by revolutionary generals in 1923, 1927, and 1928. Each revolt, however, enabled the President to purge the officer corps of dissident elements. Vacancies were filled by younger men, who were professionally trained in Mexico's own military schools or in European academies. By the end of World War II, the old-style political generals were largely retired. The new army was reduced in size and led by a new generation of military technicians. The Mexican army was fortunate, during this period, to have had as its Chief of Staff an extraordinarily gifted leader—General Tomás Sánchez Hernández. Educated at St.-Cyr—the elite French military academy—General Sánchez was astute enough to recognize that acceptance of obsolete military equipment from the United States would impair the technical efficiency of the Mexican army.

It has taken Mexico over forty years to rid herself of political domination by her generals. During this period, the Mexican people have been living with a myth—the myth of the "Revolution." In reality, the Revolution has evolved into a political formula that enables a consensus to be reached by the political power blocs of the country. The official party is the symbol of the Revolution. The electorate does not furnish a mandate to the political hierarchy, and the rank and file of the party have little or no voice in the selection of the candidates. Nomination is tantamount to election. The President selects his successor. Presidents are drawn increasingly from the bureaucracy or the party machine. This system is not representative government as it is known in Great Britain or the United States. But it is precisely the absence of representative government which has made it possible to subordinate the military to the civil authority. Popular democracy could lead to the selection of presidential candidates whom the military could not tolerate. Political parties competing in popular elections might espouse policies inimical to the military. Differences between the military and the civilian politicians would be magnified. Under the Mexican system, the President resolves conflicts within the party structure,

Party decisions reflect the balance of power among the blocs. The unique Mexican political system probably holds the solution to the problem of securing the military establishment's allegiance to the civil authority.

Since the early part of the nineteenth century, the Chilean armed forces have intervened in the political life of the country only once—in 1925, not a chapter in which the Chilean military takes pride. Not only are the Chilean armed forces under civilian control, but the officer corps is probably the most professional-minded of any Latin American military establishment. The prophylaxis of noninvolvement may have worked too well on the Chilean officer corps. A Chilean officer will invariably find a polite excuse to avoid being drawn into a political discussion. The Chilean armed forces are so completely divorced from politics that it is probably the only military establishment in Latin America which would obey a constitutionally elected Marxist president. Had the presidential elections of 1964 been won by the Marxist coalition, FRAP (Frente de Acción Popular), the Chilean Chief of Staff would undoubtedly have pledged the support of the armed forces to Dr. Salvador Allende.

In Colombia, in 1953, the military intervened in the seemingly irreconcilable fratricidal strife between the Liberals and Conservatives with the promise to end the widespread banditry in the rural areas. This led to a savage dictatorship under General Gustavo Rojas Pinilla. By 1957, Rojas Pinilla had quarreled with businessmen. He antagonized the Church by trying to centralize all social welfare activities and to capture the Church-supported labor union. In May 1957, Rojas decided to arrest Guillermo León Valencia, the candidate of the Liberal and Conservative parties. This ignited a student riot. For a whole day the students demonstrated in the streets of Bogotá while police and troops looked on. General Rojas moved 35,000 troops into the capital. But resistance spread. Former President Lleras Camargo organized a strike of the city's leading businessmen and bankers. Cardinal Luque issued a pastoral letter censuring Rojas. For the armed forces, the Cardinal's letter was conclusive. The Commander in Chief, General Navas, informed the President-General that he must go.

The military of Colombia is professional-minded. The Colombian army engages in a limited kind of Corps of Engineers activities—building roads, bridges, and water systems and furnishing medical assistance to rural inhabitants. Insofar as their own institutional activities are concerned, the armed forces are not under civilian control. As in other Latin American countries, there is a tacit agreement between the military and the civil administration that if the latter will keep its nose out of the military business, the soldiers will permit the civilians to go about theirs. Part of the understanding requires that there be no cuts in the customary military budget. The relationship involves a form of ransom. Colombia is confronted with critical economic and social problems. Banditry is widespread. Indeed, as previously noted, in a large area south of Bogotá there was no control until 1965 over at least five long-entrenched bandit zones that were virtually "independent republics," organized on Communist lines. An incipient Castro insurrectionary movement is making itself felt with sporadic bombings, killings, and gunfire.

Frente Nacional, a coalition formed in 1957 by the Liberals and Conservatives to end their internecine warfare, has disintegrated. The Government is immobilized. Unable to muster the requisite two-thirds legislative majority, President Guillermo León Valencia has declared a "state of siege," and governs by decree. Beset by the typical frustrations of the Latin American chief of state, Colombia's poet-President described his predicament in these pithy terms: "The political groups, the pressure groups, and the conspiracies have not let me govern."

The former dictator, General Gustavo Rojas Pinilla, has emerged as a potent political force. In the March 1966 congressional elections, Rojas's party, the National Popular Alliance, was catapulted into position as the chief opponent of the National Front's Liberal presidential candidate, Senator Carlos Lleras Restrepo. Though Lleras, a respected lawyer and economist and widely known public man, was the victor in the presidential election in May 1966, his politically unknown last-minute opponent selected by the former dictator garnered almost 30 per cent of the vote. This is a measure of the irreconcilable opposition the new President will face. Dr. Lleras does not come from the *oligarquía* or the industrial *nouveau riche*. Born into one of Colombia's most illustrious families, whose distinguishing characteristic for a century has been its penury, Lleras is dedicated to social change by democratic methods. Rojas Pinilla has nothing to offer to the Colombian people except demagogic prom-

ises. Embittered and frustrated by the lack of social progress, Colombia's urban workers and rural peasants have forgotten what Rojas was and have chosen to ignore what he is.
An authoritarian and *golpista* at heart, Rojas is likely to attempt a *coup d'état*. He has threatened to substitute "the
dialectic of the dagger for the tyranny of the hated ballot
box." Mounting political and social tensions may compel intervention by the Colombian armed forces.

Significantly, where the military is responsive to the civil
authority, its budget is substantially less than the 21 to 27
per cent normally taken by the praetorians. It is 12 per cent
in Mexico; in Uruguay, 11; in Venezuela, 9; and in Costa
Rica, 3. The Chilean armed forces received 22 per cent of
the national budget, but this can be explained by Chile's
special big-power relationship to Argentina (21 per cent),
Brazil (28 per cent), and Peru (23 per cent).[1]

The role of the military in Venezuela is an anomaly. Over
a century ago, Bolívar referred to Venezuela as "a barracks."
Until the advent of the administration of Rómulo Betancourt, the Venzuelan armed forces were like a foreign army—
forces occupying their own land. The Venezuelan military
illustrates the development of Latin America's armed forces
from guerrilla fighters to professional soldiers. It was only
thirty years ago that General Juan Gómez, dictator of Venezuela, began the modernization of the military forces by
building *la ciudad militar de Maracay,* a specially constructed
headquarters for a modern army. At the turn of the century,
a typical Latin American "army" was led by a "general"
whose rank was conferred by the *caudillo*. He was known as
el general de dedo—general by courtesy. His command was
an *ejército de montoneros*—a band of guerrillas, a ragged
company of "revolutionary" soldiers armed with obsolete
rifles and machetes. Their encampment was not unlike a
scene from a film depicting Pancho Villa, the Mexican revolutionary bandit.

General Juan Gómez was himself a product of the school
of guerrilla soldiers. Having made himself dictator of the
country, he began the liquidation of *los generales de
montoneros* by centralizing military power in the new city of
Maracay. Gómez never lived in the capital at Caracas. As
an old *montonero,* he regarded Caracas—situated in a valley

[1] Gustavo Lagos: *International Stratification and Underdeveloped
Countries* (Chapel Hill, N.C.: University of North Carolina Press;
1963), p. 106.

surrounded by hills—as a natural ambush. He chose to live at Maracay. A shrewd guerrilla fighter, Gómez understood that Caracas could not be captured without first destroying Maracay. He appointed General Eleazar López Contreras as his Minister of War, with command of the forces stationed at Maracay. The old *caudillo,* however, continued to maintain his personal army. In his *El triunfo de la verdad,* General López Contreras observes that it was not until 1921 that the provinces were expressly prohibited from raising their own armies and that the dictator had his own personal army until 1937. In the same year, a War and Navy Ministry was established with control over the air corps. The first modern airplane purchased by the new ministry was destroyed in a crash, in which the pilot was killed. General Gómez concluded that God did not look with favor on airplanes. The development of the Venezuelan air corps languished.

Venezuela's military development also illustrates a glaring weakness in Latin American military establishments. Except in Peru, Brazil, and Argentina, there are no schools of higher learning comparable to our National War College. Talented officers are therefore unable to expand their intellectual horizons through study of contemporary economic, political, and social problems. For most Latin American officers the *cuartel* is the outer limit of their world. Today, the *coup d'état* provides relief from the boredom of garrison duty in the small towns in the interior. Changes in the Palace generally result in promotions and pay raises.

I once attended a lecture on geopolitics by my friend Dr. Víctor Goytía, former Justice of the Supreme Court of Panama, to the officers of the Dominican air force. This was a unique experience for these officers. As with most of the Latin American military establishments, the Dominican armed forces have not been given the opportunity to study modern history. Some of our American universities can make an invaluable contribution by offering to provide courses for some of the Latin American military academies in the physical and social sciences, economics, and other fields. Among the smaller countries, particularly, such an offer would be welcomed.

One of the best investments that the Agency for International Development can make for the long-term political development of the Dominican Republic is to underwrite a modern curriculum for the service academies to which graduate cadets of Batalla de las Carreras are assigned. Junior officers could benefit by exposure to a seminar which demonstrates that violent revolution cannot alter the Dominican Republic's captivity to world prices for sugar and coffee, that social reforms cannot be accomplished without technical skills and lots of money, that the role of a twentieth-century Dominican military establishment is to help the country modernize itself.

The United States Department of Defense could place its superb educational facilities at the disposal of the Latin American military establishments. The Defense Department conducts the largest "university" in the world for its military personnel. It has more than 300,000 full-time students and almost 1,000,000 correspondence-school students. According to Teachers College, Columbia University, the educational system of the American armed forces is well equipped with modern teaching aids and the instruction is given by highly competent "professionally trained" military and civilian instructors. Many of the subjects taught are technical, but at least 60 per cent of the instruction is applicable to civilian occupations. This type of educational training, combining university courses and subjects potentially useful for civilian jobs, would serve Latin American junior officers far better than some of the academic courses in "counterinsurgency" now offered at the School of the Americas at Panama.

A military career is likely to lose its attraction if there are no sharp distinctions between the educational qualifications of the business manager and those of the army officer. Except in Brazil and Argentina, the Latin American officers do not receive the technical education needed for positions in industry. By narrowing the gap in technical knowledge, it may be possible to draw increasing numbers of officers into industrial careers. This problem deserves greater attention on the part of the Latin American military and Latin American businessmen.

The Venezuelan military gave its support to Betancourt and suppressed incipient revolts by junior officers who had come under the Castro-Communist influence. That the Venezuelan army's proclivity to engage in politics has been submerged, if not extinguished, is due to Betancourt. He paid the military appropriate deference. Their perquisites were not eliminated. He established an intimate relationship with the senior officers. They were encouraged to come to Miraflores

Palace each Monday to discuss their problems with the President. Betancourt took the officers into his confidence by discussing state problems with them. He fostered professionalism in the military establishment and extolled the officer corps as guardians of the Constitution. In turn, they respected Don Rómulo's political sagacity and admired his coolness under fire. Betancourt had an instinct for sensing the military's breaking point, and the ability to relieve the pressure—as in outlawing the Communists—before an explosion occurred. Betancourt's handling of the military was perhaps his outstanding achievement.

"Our national history, like that of ancient Rome, is essentially military." So wrote an Ecuadorean general and historian in 1930. Like the praetorian guards of Rome, the military forces of Ecuador have intervened repeatedly to make and break presidents and governments. Their latest intervention was in July 1963, in a *coup d'état* that removed from the presidency Carlos Julio Arosemena Monroy, a man of "masculine passions and vices"—in Arosemena's own phrase—and a legendary capacity for whiskey. Only twenty months previously, Ecuador's military forces had intervened to remove another president, José María Velasco Ibarra, a demagogic *caudillo* who had dominated the political life of Ecuador for thirty years. ("Give me a balcony," he once declared, "and I will become president.") Like other praetorian military establishments in Latin America, the Ecuadorean military receives a disproportionate share of the national budget—about one third. No accounting is rendered to the public on the uses of the military appropriations. Although there has been a civilian Minister of Defense since 1948, he is a figurehead. No National Congress has overlooked the military's budgetary demands. Not even Velasco Ibarra, who in his heyday was a popular idol, was able to force the military to relinquish its grip on the national treasury.

The most recent military junta was distinguished from its innumerable predecessors by its declaration of intent to transform Ecuador—economically, socially, and administratively—within a year. Washington officialdom was jubilant. Teodoro Moscoso, former Administrator of the Alliance for Progress, in hailing the junta said: "This government is getting on with reforms outlined under the Charter of Punta del Este."

Official enthusiasm might have been tempered had it been

familiar with the Ecuadorean military's last flirtation with social reform. Forty years ago, in July 1925, an idealistic group of young Ecuadorean officers, known as the Liga Militar, led a coup dedicated to a broad-based reform not unlike that which the recent junta proposed. It was not long before these youthful revolutionaries sold their idealism to the conservative elements and settled back to enjoy the fruits of political power. That was almost forty years ago. In the ensuing years, the Ecuadorean military has not shown the slightest inclination to take any leadership in the social or economic betterment of its country.

It would appear to be in order to entertain some skepticism regarding the staying power of the new social revolutionaries of Quito. The junta deserves credit for three accomplishments. It enacted an agrarian reform law to free landless *huasipungeros* (Indians who are attached to a hacienda and in exchange for their labor are provided with a shack and a small plot called a *huasipungo*) from virtual serfdom, established a merit-system civil service, and decreed a graduated income tax. That these laws will not be effectively implemented is suggested by an old Spanish precept: *se obedece pero no se cumplir* ("one obeys but does not execute the law").

The military junta also decreed that presidential and congressional elections were to be held on June 5, 1966. Former presidents were banned as candidates—a move to prevent Velasco Ibarra from running away with the election. (In 1960, he obtained the largest plurality in Ecuadorean history; within months of his election, Velasco Ibarra had managed to plunge the country into political chaos.) By eliminating the 73-year-old demagogue, the junta struck at the heart of Ecuadorean politics: none of the sixteen parties has anything approaching an ideology, and none has a leader with political competence. Few Ecuadoreans believe that the return of the military to the barracks will be anything but temporary. Indeed, the three-man junta was not even permitted to hold an election and to make a triumphal return to the *cuartel*. On March 29, 1966, the junta was forced to flee the country. Led by students, a weekend of violent demonstrations in a dozen cities persuaded the High Command of the armed forces that their colleagues had outlived their usefulness. They were told to resign. The military chiefs and the political leaders designated Clemente Yerovi Indaburo, 62, a businessman, and a political moderate, as Provisional President.

The proposition entertained by Washington that a reform-minded military regime would be able to modernize Ecuador's archaic economic and social structure will now go the way of other cherished illusions about Latin America.

(I have reserved discussion of the Brazilian military, the largest and in many respects the most unusual of the military establishments, for the section that follows.)

Political involvement by the Latin American military is neither transitory nor isolated nor exceptional. When it recurs so persistently for so long—it has been going on for a century and a half—it should be labeled as what it is: institutionalized political behavior. And it should be viewed as an independent political entity, a political force in its own right —one that frequently competes with other political movements. In this competition, the military political machine enjoys an overwhelming advantage: the ballot box cannot argue with the tank.

I have chosen to discuss in detail five countries—Brazil, Argentina, Peru, Guatemala, and the Dominican Republic— in order to draw a general profile of Latin American military establishments and to illustrate their differences.

Brazil

On August 25, 1961, the foreign offices and news centers of the West received the flash that Jânio da Silva Quadros had resigned the presidency of Brazil. I recall vividly my own amazement and disbelief when I heard the news in London. Jânio—as all Brazil knew him—had won the largest vote in the nation's history. Virtually the entire political spectrum had rallied around his candidacy. With his horn-rimmed glasses, scraggly mustache, and careless dress, he looked as unimpressive as the short-handled broom that he used as his political trademark, the symbol of what he intended to do with Brazil's inflation, corruption, and mismanagement. In barely ten years he had risen from a position as an unknown city councilor in São Paulo to the presidency of the Republic because he maintained direct contact with the people, dispensing with political parties, trade unions, and other organizational support. As governor of São Paulo—Brazil's richest, most highly developed, most industrial, and most populous state—his record had been impressive. The vast majority of Brazilians believed that Jânio would give Brazil its long-awaited reforms in land and in taxation; that he would be able to lead Brazil into the promised economic take-off by accommodating the Left without sacrificing the Right; that he could steer Brazil's orientation toward Europe, Asia, and Africa without wrenching the country away from the United States. Jânio generated the excitement of a New Deal for Brazil. Yet, barely seven months after he had taken office, he set sail for England and exile.

Some in Brazil thought his flight from the presidency was the result of a failure of nerve. Others have thought that Quadros sought to become a tropical Charles de Gaulle, an elected dictator, and that he had anticipated that his resignation would be rejected by the Chamber of Deputies, supported by popular demonstrations in the streets calling for his return. Ironically, at the new capital of Brasília, his resignation was received by virtually an empty Chamber, the majority of the members having already departed for their weekend. By the time the news reached Rio de Janeiro and São Paulo (where Quadros in his private plane at the airport awaited the anticipated tumultuous protest of the crowd), the ploy had backfired: the crowd reaction had failed to materialize; his resignation had been accepted.

Whatever the true reasons for Quadros' precipitate abandonment of his office (they remain shrouded in mystery), his stated reasons are not without interest. With characteristic ambiguity, Quadros charged that he had been "smashed by the forces" aligned against him. Perhaps what Quadros really had in mind was that after the euphoria of his election had evaporated, Brazil's own version of "checks and balances" began to operate against his presidential action: his tightening of credit, reduction of the military budget, legislative measures for land reform and higher taxes, opposition to the isolation of Cuba, a neutralist foreign policy. To co-ordinate conservative fiscal policy, nationalistic foreign policy, and socialist reforms called for greater political skill than Quadros possessed. Quadros also blundered when, in his bid for popular nationalist support, he conferred a high decoration on Major Ernesto Ché Guevara. This antagonized the conservative centers of power—the military, the Church, and the industrial and financial establishment of São Paulo. In my own view, Quadros was emotionally unstable; he lacked the toughness to stand up to a recalcitrant and hostile parliament. He was temperamentally incapable of operating under a system where he did not control *all* the levers of power.

Now we turn to the second act of this Brazilian play. The Vice-President under Quadros was João Belchior Marquês Goulart. At the moment of the presidential vacancy, Goulart was in Singapore, returning from an official visit to Peking. Forty-five, a wealthy cattle rancher, a *gaúcho* from Rio Grande do Sul, Brazil's cattle country on the borders of Argentina, "Jango" Goulart was a protégé of Brazil's last benevolent dictator, Getúlio Vargas, who dominated the Brazilian political landscape for a quarter of a century. Goulart is a short, heavy-set man, and walks with a noticeable limp to the left. Politically, too, Goulart leans to the Left. His appearance belies his wealth; he looks like a working man dressed in his Sunday clothes. His wife, Teresa, is one of Brazil's most beautiful women. Goulart is a tough politician. He understands power and the uses of power, but the responsibility of power has eluded him. The darling of the captive trade unions, which he largely controlled, distrusted by the intellectuals, suspected by the military, feared by the business and financial community, Goulart was something of a political chameleon and a political opportunist.

As Vice-President, Goulart would automatically have succeeded to the unexpired term of the presidency—except for the veto of Brazil's military establishment. As events have demonstrated, the instincts of Brazil's military were right: "Jango" Goulart was not the man to take over the presidency of the continent's biggest country. Despite the widespread misgivings that Goulart aroused, there were, nevertheless, many in Brazil who believed that under the Constitution he should have assumed the office vacated by Quadros. The Third Army, headquartered in Rio Grande do Sul (Goulart's home state), let it be known that it was ready to march on the capital to enforce Goulart's constitutional right to assume the presidency. The High Command at Rio de Janeiro was equally determined that Goulart should not be permitted to take his oath of office. In the South, armed militia were organized. Leonel Brizola (Goulart's fire-eating brother-in-law, and at the time governor of Rio Grande do Sul) indulged in flamboyant theatrics. He ordered barricades erected around the city. The harbor of Pôrto Alegre was blockaded to prevent naval landings. A threatened strike by the unions in support of Goulart was averted by an eleventh-hour appeal from Serafino Romualdi, AFL-CIO Inter-American Representative. Goulart, winging his way home from Asia, landed in the safety of his own state.

What might well have turned into an ugly, bloody, fratricidal civil war was averted through that special genius possessed by the Brazilians—a sense of timing, an appreciation for balance, and the capacity to reach an accommodation with the realities. The Brazilian compromise was to alter the Constitution from an executive system (in which power resided in the President) to a parliamentary system (where power was vested in a Prime Minister), with the President reduced to a ceremonial figurehead.

Such was the shortened mantle with which Goulart was invested. Then followed four months in which for all practical purposes there was no functioning government in Brazil. The parliamentary system did not function in large measure because Goulart was determined that it should not work. Goulart designated Tancredo Neves as his Prime Minister. A small-town politician whose counterpart would be readily familiar in the United States, Neves reigned but did not rule. Determined to vindicate himself, Goulart insisted upon a plebiscite to determine whether the parliamentary system should be abandoned in favor of a return to the executive system. On January 6, 1963, 10 million of Brazil's electorate voted for the abandonment of the parliamentary system.

That Brazil was able to resolve this crisis without undergoing a bloodbath is a tribute to the maturity of the Brazilian people and to the restraint of its military. Although the military intervened to prevent Goulart from exercising his constitutional prerogative—a right that it traditionally assumes—once a formula had been evolved for resolving the constitutional crisis, the military accepted the decision. It did not attempt a naked seizure of power. On the contrary, it acted as a corrective balance in a situation which conceivably could have torn the nation apart.

The Brazilian armed forces regard themselves as custodians of the nation. Their duty, they believe, encompasses the right to exercise a veto when a decision of the civilian authorities jeopardizes the interests of the nation. Indeed, Article 177 of the Brazilian Constitution is interpreted by the armed forces as their authority for intervention. As a moderating power, the armed forces do not merge with the civilian authority. They maintain a separate existence. The contention that the military acted unlawfully by its intervention may be sound academically, but it is politically irrelevant—for Brazil. The Brazilian military is the only institution in the country whch has continuity and stability and which regards the country as a nation rather than as disparate regions. It did not seek to usurp power, but to prevent—as it feared —the abuse of power.

Politically, the Brazilian military is unquestionably the most potent independent political entity in the country. In times of crisis, the chief of state will consult with the military High Command more earnestly than with the civilian political leaders, for the position of the military will be the determining factor.

Unlike other military political entities in Latin America, the Brazilian military traditionally has been a progressive force in the life of Brazil. Until the coup against the Goulart regime, the Brazilian military establishment was careful to remove itself from the political scene once it had moved to "protect" the Constitution. This occurred in 1932 after a revolt in São Paulo, in 1935 when the Communists revolted, and in 1938 when the *integralistas* attempted a *Putsch*. It is to the credit of the military that in 1955 it blocked an attempt to prevent Juscelino Kubitschek, the elected President, from taking office.

The Brazilian military establishment is not a caste. Nor is it the instrument of the Brazilian plutocracy. The attitude of an overwhelming preponderance of the officer corps was expressed by General Humberto Alençar Castelo Branco, the new President, in a letter to the armed forces on March 20, 1964, in which he said: "To defend the privileges of the rich is to follow the same anti-democratic line as serving Fascists or Communists." General Castelo Branco, who spent much of his career in the poverty-stricken Northeast, once remarked that the most distasteful side of army life was "having to protect rich landowners who treat their peasant workers like slaves." Army officers are recruited largely from the upper bourgeoisie of the cities and the small landowners. Many of the officers are sons of noncommissioned officers. Vice-Admiral Candido da Costa Aragão, the former Marine Corps Commandant, had been an enlisted man. It is not an uncommon sight in Brazil to see an officer traveling by bus to his suburban house. In Argentina and Venezuela, officers have chauffeur-driven cars and live in the most exclusive section of Buenos

Aires or Caracas. An Argentine lieutenant receives a salary equivalent to that paid to a Brazilian general of a division. On the average, Argentina's officers receive in pay four times as much as the equivalent Brazilian rank. Of the three services, the army is considered the most democratic. Brazil's naval officers are drawn largely from the traditional families. Their political views are generally conservative. The air force has the exuberance characteristic of similar establishments in other parts of the world. The armed forces reflect the social mobility and what Gilberto Freyre calls the "racial democracy" of Brazil. They mirror the political tensions of the country and the sharp cleavage between the political Left and Right.

The third and final act in this Brazilian play is almost a repetition of the second act, in which the military sought to prevent Goulart's accession to the presidency. In the dénouement, the military revolted against him.

There is a striking parallel between the regime of Juan Bosch in the Dominican Republic and that of João Goulart in Brazil. Each touched a hidden nerve of violence in his countrymen. Dominicans and Brazilians are remarkably alike: They are easygoing, tolerant, and not addicted to bloodletting. By their demagoguery, Bosch and Goulart unleashed class conflict; in the Dominican Republic it verged on racial conflict. Goulart and Bosch polarized the political Left and Right. In both countries, hate, fear, and dissension poisoned the air. In Brazil, it needed only a lighted torch to ignite the country.

João Goulart was forced into exile for two reasons: (1) he was incapable of governing in a democratic framework, and (2) he sought to destroy the discipline of the armed forces. Under his regime, Brazil was bordering on political and economic chaos. Goulart's acts of desperation were motivated in part by the economic deterioration of the country —to which his own incapacity to govern contributed. Prices rose in 1963 by more than 80 per cent. The rate of growth dropped to 2 per cent from 8 per cent in 1961. A population increase of about 3 per cent wiped out per capita income gains. Despite soaring coffee prices—the highest in fourteen years—Brazil was bankrupt: she was unable to meet her short-term commercial and government debts. The federal deficit for 1964 was estimated by Interim President Mazzilli at 1.5 trillion cruzeiros. At the current free rate of exchange for the dollar, this amounts to $1.36 billion. Goulart lacked the courage and the will to deal resolutely with a ravaging inflation that consumed Brazil's economy. The manner in which he defaulted on his agreement with the United States Government to carry out stabilization reforms was typical of his *modus operandi*. He sent his Finance Minister, San Tiago Dantas, to Washington to obtain sizable loans. With Goulart's knowledge and approval Dantas signed an agreement with David Bell, Administrator of the Agency for International Development, whereby in return for United States financial assistance Brazil agreed to carry out a series of stabilization measures for the control of inflation. Upon his return to Rio, Dantas was denounced as a traitor by Goulart's demagogic brother-in-law, Leonel Brizola. Goulart promptly fired Dantas. And that was the end of any attempt to control inflation.

He manipulated disorder, and then sought authority to declare a "state of siege." He fed the fires of political tension by failing to act decisively to halt a wave of strikes, work stoppages, and public disorder that paralyzed the country. Under the guise of "social reform" he practiced a strategy of deception. Although Goulart is not a Communist his use of the extreme Left, particularly the Communist-dominated Comando Geral dos Trabalhadores (CGT), made it a Trojan horse within the democratic citadel. He declared cold war against foreign and domestic private business. For instance, he ordered the Bank of Brazil to deny discount loans to banks he considered unfriendly. To court favor with *yanqui*-baiting extremists, he encouraged the enactment of a law relating to the remittance of profits by foreign corporations which struck at the heart of private investment. Hypocritically (for, since his rise to the presidency, he had continued to become the largest landowner in Brazil, with holdings of almost 2 million acres) he attacked the national legislators as a "Congress of Privilege" for refusing to enact his land-reform proposals—proposals that were so vague they could not possibly be passed, even if the deputies had been disposed to do so. He asked that expropriated land be paid for in bonds, rather than in cash as the Constitution required. (In Brazil, where inflation grows at the rate of 7 per cent monthly, payment in bonds— even bonds and cash—is tantamount to payment in wall-paper.)

As opposition to his regime mounted, Goulart began a series of maneuvers that appeared to have as their objective the creation of a radically different political power base. He asked Congress to extend the right to vote to illiterates, to legalize the Communist party, and to allow military personnel to run for public office while on active duty. Had the Chamber of Deputies been so foolish as to enact these measures, they would have handed Goulart a golden opportunity (1) to employ the consummate skills of the Communists, (2) to organize, with their help, vast numbers of slum dwellers and illiterate peasants, and (3) to obtain a solid core of Leftist supporters among noncommissioned officers, who would be immune from regular military discipline. Goulart threatened that, if these measures were not approved, the people would take matters into their own hands. Interestingly, if the Partido Social Democrático—the party of former President Kubitschek, Goulart's political ally—had combined its voting strength (115 votes) with Goulart's Partido Trabalhista Brasileiro (122 votes), they could have mustered a sufficient majority (237 votes) to carry Goulart's proposals. Brazil's political parties are no more monolithic than ours; in practice, they are shifting coalitions. Moreover, even Goulart's congressional allies were unwilling to commit political *hara-kiri*.

To overcome the refusal of Congress to enact his proposals for land reform, he resorted to land expropriation by decree. He announced that privately owned land up to six miles on either side of federal highways, railroads, and waterways would be seized. Landowners in the backlands, who are about as enlightened as Middle Eastern sheiks, hired professional gunmen to protect their property. The governor of São Paulo was reported to have distributed machine guns and rifles to landowners. Goulart also signed a decree expropriating privately owned (Brazilian) oil refineries.

At a mass meeting in Rio on March 13, 1964, held to commemorate these expropriation decrees, Leonel Brizola—Goulart's political stalking horse—was wildly cheered when he called for the dissolution of Congress and its replacement by one composed of workers, peasants and "lots of nationalist sergeants." At this same rally, Goulart called upon noncommissioned officers and enlisted men to support his regime, implying that they were to do so even against the orders of their superiors. After this speech the then Chief of the General Staff, General Humberto Alençar Castelo Branco, characterized the Goulart regime as one in which "insurrection now is a legitimate action by the people."

Many thoughtful Brazilians feared that Goulart's real objective was to establish a syndicalist Congress, to cancel the presidential elections, and to hold power as a dictator in the manner of Vargas or Perón. To the military High Command, it was increasingly apparent that Goulart was unwilling to play the game according to the rules. Both military and civilian political leaders were convinced that he was deliberately trying to subvert constitutional government as a *caudillo* of the revolutionary Left.

In brief, this is the backdrop against which the army uprising should be viewed. The military revolt was triggered by two incidents that occurred toward the end of March 1964. On March 26, 1,425 sailors and marines locked themselves in the Rio headquarters of the Metallurgical Workers' Union in protest against the arrest of a marine corporal, who was charged with violating navy regulations against political activity by naval personnel on active duty. With overtones of the Kronstadt naval base revolt at the time of the Russian Revolution, a group of sailors abandoned the aircraft carrier *Minas Gerais*, anchored in Guanabara Bay, to join the mutineers. Shooting occurred in the compound of the Naval Ministry as sailors sought to desert. Incidents were reported aboard warships. The Minister of the Navy, Admiral Silvio Borgos de Souza Mota, resigned after failing to persuade the rebels to submit to arrest. The Marine Corps Commandant, Vice-Admiral Candido da Costa Aragão, was relieved of his command because of his sympathy with the mutineers. The acting Commandant of the Marine Corps, Rear Admiral Luiz F. Sinai, threatened to resign because of the use of force in the arrest of the rebellious marines and sailors. Terms for their surrender were arranged by the Comando Geral dos Trabalhadores. Amnesty was granted to the mutineers after a conference between Goulart and the new Minister of the Navy, Rear Admiral Paulo Mario da Cunha Rodrigues. As Congress prepared to investigate the rebellion, influential newspapers became critical of the dilatory handling of the affair. High-ranking naval officers protested the government's failure to punish the rebels. The Military Club, through its president, Marshal of the Army Augusto Magessi, announced the army's support of the naval officers in protesting the failure to discipline the rebellious enlisted men. The General Workers' Federation threatened a general strike "if an attempt at a coup against President Goulart [was] made."

As if to thumb their noses at the military hierarchy, the amnestied sailors and marines paraded through the streets of Rio, Adding insult to injury, the triumphant sailors and marines carried on their shoulders Admiral Aragão, the Marine Commandant (who had been restored to his command), and his Chief of Staff, Admiral Susano. Naval officers protested that these admirals "shared a victory that meant destruction of discipline for the navy." Under heavy pressure, Goulart reopened the case, but also characteristically ordered an investigation of the officers who demanded disciplinary action and who called on the nation to defend itself against "Communization."

Four days later, on March 30, Goulart delivered an impassioned speech to a meeting of noncommissioned officers; he pleaded with them to be loyal to him rather than to their regular officers. This speech was the proverbial straw that broke the camel's back. The following day, March 31, an army unit stationed in Juiz de Fora in Minas Gerais declared itself in revolt against the President and his regime.

It is a mistake to assume that the uprising of the army in Minas Gerais was spontaneous. No military coup is spontaneous. In Latin America the steps leading to an actual coup are as formalized as those in the ballet. They may be described as: (1) the *trabajos,* or tentative testing of opinion among other army units; (2) the *compromisos,* or agreements or commitments, by other military groups regarding their participation; (3) the *acción,* or actual uprising by a garrison, a barracks, or a larger military unit; (4) the *pronunciamiento,* or proclamation, by the "Revolutionary" High Command; (5) the march on the capital, the seizure of communication and transportation centers; (6) the announcement that the military is in complete control of the government; and, finally (7), the appointment of a military junta to take over the government apparatus, the promise that there will be elections in the future (or as originally scheduled prior to the coup), and the arrest of the opposition —in Brazil, all suspected of being "Communists" or members of the extreme Left.

A few trusted colonels were sent to test army opinion in the various commands as early as October 1963. The understanding reached among the supporters of the projected uprising was purely defensive—the military would act only under prescribed conditions. The Second Army, stationed in São Paulo under the command of General Amaury Kruel, would march on Rio, and other commands would announce their adherence to the revolt. Actually, the revolt at Juiz de Fora was premature. The other formalized steps were followed ritualistically. There was, however one variation: before proceeding to execute their plan, the High Command conferred with the governors of the three most important states—Magalhães Pinto of Minas Gerais, Adhemar de Barros of São Paulo, and (on the night before the uprising) Carlos Lacerda of Guanabara.

Goulart had very few known supporters within the military establishment, but they were strategically placed—the commander of troops at the port of Santos; the commander of the Fifth Division of the Second Army; the chief of army communications; the commander of the First Division at Rio; and, most important of all, the commander of the Third Army in Rio Grande do Sul, Goulart's home state. (The Revolutionary High Command subsequently removed from the active-duty list 122 officers, including 16 army and air force generals and 5 admirals.) When the military struck, enlisted men and noncommissioned officers did not turn against their officers. Military support for Goulart collapsed within forty-eight hours.

Popular support for Goulart was virtually nonexistent. In the Northeast, the peasant leagues were not led by Francisco Julião, a disciple of Mao Tse-tung and Fidel Castro, into militant protest—Julião went into hiding. In the big cities, the denizens of the slums did not erupt into the streets to fight with whatever was at hand. Not a single worker turned out in Rio de Janeiro to defend Goulart, although the unions had plenty of arms. The Moscow-oriented Communists understood better than Goulart's rabid nationalist supporters, the Peking Communist wing, the CIA and the American Embassy that there was no broad-based popular support for a Leftist take-over—they did not even attempt to lead the mobs into the streets. "As far as we are concerned," said one Communist leader, "Jango is dead. He was a stupid man." In Rio and São Paulo, the end of the Goulart era was greeted with wild rejoicing, parades, and carnival-like celebrations.

The military moved with cold efficiency. Preserving the fiction of constitutionalism, they quickly made known their desire that the President of the Chamber of Deputies, Paschoal Ranieri Mazzilli (next in line of succession, there being no Vice-President in office), should take the presidential oath. Mazzilli had scarcely finished taking his oath, and Goulart had not even fled the country, when, with unseemly haste, Washington sent congratulatory cables to the new "constitutional" government—a diplomatic blunder which would cost the United States dearly. In less than a week the High Command discarded any pretense of operating under the Constitution. In a radical departure from its traditional style of political involvement, the military took direct control of the apparatus of government: Brazil became a totalitarian state under military rule.

On April 9, the military proclaimed an "Institutional Act" in which the High Command announced that "the revolution is not seeking to legitimize itself through the Congress." On the contrary, it was stated that the Congress obtained its legitimacy from the military High Command. For all practical purposes the Brazilian Constitution was replaced. At least the position of the Revolutionary High Command was honest. It was not attempting to masquerade behind a papier-mâché constitutionalism, which has characterized so many Latin American seizures of power. Promulgation of this act marked a complete reversal of the historic role of the military in avoiding usurpation of the civil authority. One can only speculate about the reasons for this extraordinary turnabout: A realization that the political parties were incapable of leading Brazil out of her economic and political morass? that the country could not be allowed to drift aimlessly (without fatal consequences) until the presidential elections were concluded in 1965? that, unless the sharp turn toward the Left was reversed, Brazil would be in critical danger? that Goulart's attempt to destroy military discipline had weakened the foundations of the military establishment?

Under the act which established this authoritarian state, the Chiefs of Staff of the armed services were empowered to oust members of Congress, the judiciary, state governors, state legislators, civil servants, and municipal councilmen on "suspicion" of being Communists. The right to judicial appeal was rescinded. The power to suspend political rights for ten years—including the right to vote and to hold elective office—was assumed by the military. Legislative and judicial immunity and academic tenures were lifted for a period of six months.

The Revolutionary High Command ordered the federal legislators to "elect," within forty-eight hours, a new President. Bowing to the inevitable, the civilian leaders chose

Castelo Branco because "he thinks like a civilian." The High Command preferred an orthodox military type. For two months the three chiefs of the armed services would share the executive power with the President; thereafter, it would be exclusively in the hands of President Castelo Branco.

Under the Institutional Act, the President was authorized to declare a state of siege; Congress was forbidden to alter his budget bills by voting more money than he requested; Congress was required to vote within thirty days on any constitutional amendment submitted by the President; other presidential bills would automatically be considered approved if Congress had not acted on them within thirty days; and the margin for congressional approval was reduced from two thirds to a simple majority.

On April 11, *The New York Times* reported (on p. 1) that forty members of Congress had been expelled because of Communist or extremist activities endangering the state. Subsequently, four other men met the same fate. About half were members of former President Goulart's Labor party. Left-wing nationalist writers and newspaper publishers sought asylum in foreign embassies. Brizola, who had fled to his home state of Rio Grande do Sul, was hunted by the military police. Purges were mounted against state legislators and municipal councilmen. Thousands of real or imaginary Communists were placed under arrest. In Guanabara Bay, a luxury liner and a navy transport ship were pressed into service as temporary jails. The sun-drenched, beach-loving *cariocas* of Rio had never experienced such a Red hunt, as soldiers and policemen invaded homes and private clubs. As the purge spread, tight censorship was imposed; long-distance telephone calls were monitored; and offices of the wire services were occupied by armed troops. The Revolutionary High Command dismissed two university presidents. The Higher Institute of Brazilian Studies was abolished on the ground that it was a hotbed of Communist activity. The residence of Dom Helder Camâra, Archbishop of Recife, was invaded by soldiers searching for the secretary of Miguel Arrais, governor of the state of Pernambuco, who had sought asylum. The political rights of sixty prominent Brazilians, including Goulart, Brizola, Prestes (the Communist party leader), and Francisco Julião were suspended for ten years.

Brazilians were shocked out of their euphoria when they learned that the High Command had stripped of their political rights former President Jânio Quadros (who, whatever his culpability for Brazil's plight, had not been labeled "Communist" even by the extreme Right), Celso Furtado, the internationally known economist (whose dedication to the ideals of the Alliance for Progress had made him something of a hero to the New Frontier and to many of the younger generation of Brazilians), and former President Kubitschek (under whose administration Brazil had achieved her spectacular growth).

Among those in the United States who admire Brazil and her people, there was also a feeling of shock and sorrow at the spectacle of soldiers attempting to save democracy by destroying it.

The bishops of the Church were moved to petition the Revolutionary High Command to exercise moderation. Among the responsible centers of public opinion there were second thoughts about where Brazil was heading.

In his inaugural address the new President stressed Brazil's alignment with the West and repudiated the "reactionary Right" as an alternative to Communism. He endorsed orthodox economic development through private enterprise, but admonished Brazil's businessmen that their sacrifices would have to be greater than that of any other sector. He has moved toward a reduction in public spending and the swollen government payrolls by appointing as his Finance Minister Octávio Gouvêa de Bulhões, a highly regarded, internationally known financial authority.

Under the leadership of the former ambassador to the United States, the respected economist Roberto de Oliveira Campos, as Minister of Planning, reforms were undertaken in tax collection, public administration, agricultural production, and housing. Inflation was braked. The country's international financial credit was improved. Foreign private investment, which under Goulart had come to a standstill, was encouraged to return. The São Paulo establishment, as the power center of the country, supported the revolutionary regime by abandoning subsidies, embracing austerity, and demonstrating a willingness to unleash social reforms which were politically frozen under Goulart.

That Brazil had not succeeded in evolving a viable political formula after eighteen months of military rule was evidenced by the tensions engendered following gubernatorial elections early in October 1965. The victory at the polls of candidates linked with the party of Juscelino Kubitschek (who returned after sixteen months of self-imposed exile), and

the defeat of National Democratic Union candidates in
Minas Gerais and Guanabara, sharply divided the military
establishment. High-ranking influential officers, who opposed
the holding of elections on the grounds that "pro-revolu-
tionary" candidates would be defeated because of the un-
popularity of the regime's austerity program, contended that
Kubitschek's return and the large popular vote received by
his party and the party of Goulart justified their misgivings.

Frustrated in his own presidential ambitions by the defeat
of his hand-picked gubernatorial candidate, Governor Carlos
Lacerda, who has been described as Brazil's "only active
volcano," erupted into a bitter denunciation of the President
as "the betrayer of the revolution." The Chief Justice of
Brazil's Supreme Court, Alvar Moutinho Ribeiro da Costa,
accused the military of interfering with the independence of
the judicial system. "It is time," the Chief Justice publicly
stated, "that the military realized that in democratic regimes
it is not their role to act as tutors to the nation."

In a stormy session the Congress—representing in the
main the old Vargas clans and Kubitschek's party—attacked
the federal government's request for special measures to control state governments. The governors-elect resented the
threat to their powers. Castelo Branco was unable to muster
sufficient votes to overcome congressional opposition and to
exercise a moderating influence between the military "moderates" and "radicals" (who favor the hard line). On October 27, 1965, he promulgated Institutional Act No. 2,
which restored to the President the power to rescind popular
elections and to assume control over states determined to be
in a "state of internal commotion."

Acting under this decree, Castelo Branco abolished all
political parties, enlarged the Supreme Court—from eleven
to sixteen members to offset the influence of Kubitschek and
Goulart appointees—and established indirect presidential
elections by the Congress. By the same decree, Castelo
Branco removed himself from a new term of office.

The contest between the "hard line" officers and Castelo
Branco centered on the seating of Francisco Negrão de
Lima, Governor-elect of Guanabara State. A military board
of inquiry requested his arrest on the grounds that he was
implicated with the Brazilian Communist party. Castelo
Branco staked his own reputation and that of the revolutionary government on the installation of Senhor Negrão
de Lima, candidate of the proscribed Social Democrat-Labor

coalition. To President Castelo Branco, the taking of office by Negrão de Lima was the test of his own authority and a demonstration of the restoration of the democratic processes. A former military man, the President left nothing to chance. His trusted friend General Jurandir de Bizarria Mamede took over the command of the First Army, headquartered on the outskirts of Rio. His strong right arm at the barracks, War Minister General Artur da Costa e Silva, held earnest conversations with the obstreperous colonels. As a final precaution, 3,000 troops were deployed at the inauguration of Governor Negrão de Lima. President Castelo Branco's victory over the military radicals was symbolized by a unanimous decision of the Supreme Military Court. It rescinded a military order for the governor's arrest.

The extinction of Brazil's thirteen political parties opened the way for a "party of the revolution"—the National Renovating Alliance—that will support the government's candidate, General Artur da Costa e Silva, to succeed President Castelo Branco. It may also mark the beginning of a profound transformation of the former political clusters, which were merely vest-pocket, *ad hoc* opportunistic coalitions, without constituencies, devoid of modern ideas, and representing only the ambitions of their leaders. An opposition party, the Brazilian Democratic Movement, will field a candidate against General Costa e Silva, but this is merely a gesture as the party's candidate is given no chance to win.

Brazil is desperately groping for the right political formula —and it will be a Brazilian formula—by which to govern the world's fifth largest country with the techniques of an open society. Another political failure in Brazil will inevitably produce extremist solutions.

Revolutions never stand still. Brazil's revolution will also change its course. The Brazilian tradition of intellectual and creative freedom is too strong, the Brazilian people are too civilized, the preponderance of the military is too firmly rooted in a liberal tradition, to sustain a Brazilian version of McCarthyism.

The greatest contribution that the United States can make in helping Brazil in her travail is to exercise a dignified and restrained diplomacy. Eager-beaverism is not diplomacy. North Americans who admire Brazil and the Brazilian people can contribute by their compassionate understanding.

Brazil is a country with a future, but she lacks an essential ingredient to realize her potential as one of the world's great powers—capable and responsible democratic leadership that can transform the vision of her greatness into reality.

Argentina

The cult of arrogance is an acknowledged national trait of Argentina. As early as 1824, when Bernardino Rivadavia, one of Argentina's ablest leaders, sought England's intervention in an impending fight with Brazil, Foreign Secretary George Canning expressed his annoyance with Rivadavia's arrogance, saying that he "demanded as a right that which he was entitled to only as privilege." In the Argentine classic *Life in the Argentine Republic in the Days of the Tyrants,* Sarmiento writes: "Argentines of whatever class, civilized or ignorant, have a high opinion of their own worth as a people. The other American peoples throw this vanity in their faces and act offended at their presumption and arrogance. I believe that the charge is not unwarranted, but I am not concerned about it."

Argentinians were wont to joke about their big Brazilian neighbor to the north as a people who had just fallen out of the trees. As for the Indian countries, they were outside the pale of civilization. Argentina's manifest destiny was to be Latin America's leader. Her attitude toward the rest of Latin America was that of a superior power. The United States was a rival, viewed with suspicion at international or hemisphere assemblages.

Argentina was potentially one of the world's richest countries. From her fertile pampas came the supplies for England's larder. In the 1920's, the Argentinian worker was as prosperous as his North American counterpart. Argentina enjoyed the reputation of being the most sophisticated country in South America. Buenos Aires was the Paris of Latin America. The rich Argentine playboy was known internationally. Children of the *estanciero* families were raised by English nannies.

An older generation of Argentinians must look back upon this world with nostalgia. Today, Argentina is bankrupt. In a very real sense, she has lost her political moorings and has demonstrated an incapacity to govern herself democratically. In half a century—from 1916 to 1966—Argentina has had only three free elections. Argentina has shown herself to be precisely what she used to boast she was not—"South American."

To understand Argentina's sickness, some of her history must be recalled. Since the last quarter of the nineteenth century, Argentina's central problem has been how to reconcile the tradition of *caudillismo*—the rule by the gauchos of the pampas—with the requirements of a highly literate Europeanized middle class—the only true middle class in Latin America—composed of immigrants from Italy, Spain, Germany, France, Switzerland, England, and Austria. Argentina's modern era of government, the period roughly from 1890 to 1930, was divided between twenty-six years of rule by an oligarchy of the great *estancieros*, bankers, lawyers, and merchants—the *distinguidos*—and some fourteen years, beginning in 1916, of government by "Radicals," the party of the new middle class. (In Latin American political nomenclature "Conservative" means precisely what the term implies. "Liberals" are conservatives and "Radicals" are liberals but never radical.) The Radicals failed in their attempt at governing largely because they were victims of both the world-wide depression of the thirties and their own ineptness. "The brief period of Radical rule . . . demonstrated that Argentina was not prepared for democratic government of the British or North American kind." [2]

The year 1930 witnessed the overthrow of Hipólito Irigoyen, who had grown senile in the presidency. Corruption was rampant in the government departments; the workers were disillusioned and blamed Irigoyen for the rise in living costs and unemployment. Although the revolution which overthrew Irigoyen was a popular uprising supported by the old conservative families as well as by the opposition parties, students, and the discontented masses, the real organizers were a group of military officers (among them a young captain named Juan Domingo Perón) whose leader was General José Félix Uriburu, an extreme conservative. He immediately declared a "state of siege" and proposed the abolition of universal suffrage and the secret ballot. Once again government was restored to the old regime, a group of conservative generals and *estancieros*, supported by bankers, merchants, and the hierarchy of the Church.

In 1943 the era of Perón was ushered in through a *coup*

[2] George Pendle: *Argentina* (2d ed.; London and New York: Oxford University Press; 1961), p. 71.

d'état by another group of army officers, known as the Grupo de Oficiales Unidos, or GOU. The leader of the GOU was none other than Juan Domingo Perón, now a colonel. Colonel Perón's military followers did not come from the old landowning families; they were middle class in origin. Since their abortive coup in 1930 this military group had come to realize that the *estanciero* class could no longer satisfy the requirements of a modern state. Indeed, the old landowning aristocracy refused to share its political power despite the shift that had occurred in the sources of wealth. Of the one hundred persons who in 1941 paid the highest income tax, only ten were *estancieros*. Industrialists, bankers, importers, motion-picture executives, and radio-station owners now formed the moneyed class. More people held jobs in industry than in agriculture or cattle raising. Yet the landowning aristocracy continued to hold a monopoly of political power as if this radical shift in wealth and employment had never taken place.

The comments of the British ambassador, Sir David Kelly, on the situation in Argentina in 1942, the year preceding Perón's seizure of power, are illuminating. Writes Sir David: "When I returned [to Argentina] as Ambassador in June 1942, the outstanding phenomenon for me in the Argentine situation was that the group of great *estancieros* and lawyers, known collectively as the *distinguidos*, who had, when I was there in 1919 and 1920, formed the opposition to the radical demagogue President Irigoyen, were in 1942 apparently firmly in the saddle again and had been for many years. The Jockey Club and its more select and more expensive inner circle, the Círculo de Armas, were again, as before the days of Irigoyen, the great centers of political gossip and the power behind the scenes." [3]

Basically, therefore, the 1943 coup led by Perón was motivated by the conviction of the younger officers that the balance of political power had to be redressed and the promise of the 1930 revolution redeemed. In his classic *A History of Latin America*, Hubert Herring observes: "The prosperous upper classes had themselves to thank for the latest turn of events. They had controlled Argentina, with one brief interval, for ninety years; they had named presidents and had often contributed to the building of the nation. But they had failed to serve the Argentine people; they had denied them free political institutions, monopolized the land, and per-

[3] Quoted in Pendle: op. cit., p. 88.

petuated the colonial abuses of the workers. The middle class had also failed. . . . The oligarchy and the Radicals shared responsibility for the emergence of Perón and *peronismo.*"

With overtones of Mussolini's corporative state (Perón had studied in Italy) and Hitler's "wave of the future" (the military were convinced that German arms would triumph over the Allies), this military coup anticipated Nasserism. Perón, its leader, moreover, had great personal charm, exuded *machismo*—the special vanity of Latin American masculinity —and was the embodiment of the *caudillo*.

The details of Perón's Argentina need not detain us. In brief, his objective was to organize a social and economic revolution that would convert Argentina into a modern industrial state. The revolution was carried into every branch of national life. If Perón did not succeed in breaking the back of the *estancieros,* he rendered them politically impotent. The *descamisados*—the "shirtless ones"—were enthroned by Perón and his glamorous, energetic, and shrewd wife, Eva, through higher wages, holidays with pay, a forty-hour week, minimum-wage laws, pensions, and a host of social welfare schemes. If Perón was greatly admired in the *caudillo* tradition, "Evita" was worshipped as a goddess by the working classes. Her Fundación Eva Perón was a bottomless cornucopia of charity for the widows and orphans, for the sick, the lame, the halt, and the blind. That Perón was short-changing the country, that he was a buffoon, a scoundrel, a sybarite, a thief—these things mattered not at all to the *descamisados:* for them all that mattered was that Perón and Evita had made them *somebodies.*

Evita's death in 1952 was the beginning of the end for Perón. By 1955 the once-rich Argentine economy was in critical straits. Perón's fatal blunder had been to upset the balance between agriculture and the rest of the economy in his frenzied drive for industrialization—an error that had plagued other nations, notably the Soviet Union and China. By controlling prices for the state's purchases of beef and wheat (the profits on which were used to finance industrialization and the sprawling welfare state), Perón destroyed the incentive to increase agricultural productivity. Exports of wheat and beef dropped by 50 per cent from their pre-World War II level. The foreign debt exceeded more than a billion dollars; the domestic budget showed a heavy deficit.

Opposition to Perón hardened among the old landown-

ing aristocracy, the business community, and the Church.
The military, who had lifted Perón to power, had become
thoroughly disenchanted. The deluge was not far distant.
The navy and the air force were the first to strike. But their
plot foundered. Perón let loose a reign of terror in retaliation. *Peronista* gangs set fire to churches, smashed statuary,
and destroyed sanctuaries. The era of Perón ended as it
had begun, with a revolt at the barracks. Another general
was in charge as receiver for the nation.

In February 1958, Argentina held its first free election
since 1916. Arturo Frondizi, representing a sector of the
Radical party, became President with the support of the
peronista vote, a feat accomplished in large measure by
Rogelio Frigerio, a multimillionaire industrialist, who was
to become the *éminence grise* of the Frondizi administration and on whose person the militarists would later vent
their bitter hatred. It was Frondizi's aim to bring the
peronistas back into the community of government. Shortly
after his inauguration, he granted amnesty to *peronistas*
who were in prison or in exile for political offenses. He
enabled them to regain influential positions in the trade
unions and the judiciary. The military leaders objected to
these concessions. Frondizi found himself caught in a vise:
if he appeased Perón's followers, the military would crack
down; if he made concessions to the military, workers
struck; if he neglected the *peronistas*, he forfeited his political base. Frondizi performed something of a political miracle
by his skill in threading his way between these conflicting
pressures. With candor he told the Argentine people that
"Argentina has been living an economic fiction." He sought
economies in the swollen bureaucracy. With great courage, he
introduced exploitation of Argentina's oil fields by foreign
capital, mainly from the United States, so as to reduce Argentina's $300-million expenditure on oil imports. Argentina's
economic predicament was so grave that even the nationalist-
minded military hierarchy felt obliged to go along. Frondizi
did not obtain the approval of Congress in awarding contracts to the foreign oil companies. He believed that the
emergency was too critical to permit an interminable debate
by nationalist-minded deputies. (The bypassing of Congress
was used by Dr. Arturo Illia as a campaign issue in the 1963
presidential election. Significantly, the candidates of the
other major political parties—General Pedro Aramburu and
Dr. Oscar Alende—did not raise the issue in their bid for

popular support. As the combined vote of Aramburu and
Alende exceeded Illia's, the subsequent annulment of the
contracts would not appear to have been responsive to the
majority view of the Argentine electorate.)

Frondizi had so far retreated from his nationalist campaign electioneering as to have embraced in January 1959
an austerity program sponsored by the International Monetary Fund. As was to be expected, the program was unpopular. Nevertheless, by May 1960, Frondizi was able to
report to Congress that the economy was in a reasonably
satisfactory condition owing in large part to the austerity
program.

Still desirous of bringing the *peronistas* into the community of the nation, Frondizi persuaded a skeptical military that the *peronistas* should be allowed to run for office
in the March 1962 state and congressional elections. To
Lord Acton's famous reminder on the corrosive effects of
power there might be added a footnote that power also
creates political astigmatism. Frondizi may have lost touch
with the political realities and assumed that *peronismo* was
on the wane, or he may have mesmerized himself into believing that his political dexterity would enable him to handle it. Whatever the true reasons, Frondizi's confidence in
the outcome of the elections was such that he was prevailed
upon by his Minister of the Interior, Alfredo Vitolo, to
accede to the demand of the military High Command that
he execute a written agreement to the effect that, if the
misgivings of the military proved to be correct, Frondizi
would "intervene"—that is, nullify the elections. Frondizi
thereupon departed for Tokyo and a tour of the Far East.
Three months after his return to Buenos Aires, he learned
with shocked amazement that the *peronistas* had captured
ten governorships in twenty-two states and had won half the
congressional seats. To the military, the *peronista* triumph
was the straw with which to break Frondizi's back: not only
was he forced to abide by his agreement to annul the elections, but also, within a fortnight, on March 29, the constitutionally elected President of the Republic of Argentina
was arrested. Like a common felon, Frondizi was hustled off
to the prison on Martín García Island in the River Plate.
There, Arturo Frondizi savored the bitter truth of the Spanish
proverb: *El que fué a Sevilla perdió la silla.* Not to be in
the right place at the right time is to lose everything. His
trip to Tokyo had cost him the presidency.

An obscure country lawyer, José María Guido (selected by Frondizi to serve as President of the Senate because he was not a political threat), was literally dragooned by the military into the Casa Rosada as successor to Frondizi. Under a thinly disguised civilian regime in which Guido became a puppet in the hands of the military, the economic and political bankruptcy begun by Perón was completed. Argentina staggered from one crisis to another. It was not long before even the thin gauze of civilian administration was torn away as the generals and colonels moved into one ministry after another. Politically, the nation was in a state of paralysis; governmentally, it was a void. The military engaged each other in bloody conflicts. Attempted revolts by dissident elements of the military, who favored an outright military dictatorship with a period of military tutelage to "educate" the voters, were crushed. A bloody engagement led by the navy, which sought the overturn of the Guido regime, was struck down by elements of the army led by General Juan Carlos Onganía, leader of the "Blues," who sought a return to civilian government. Onganía agreed that a new election for the presidency should be permitted to take place on July 6, 1963, provided that none of the avowed *peronista* leaders was allowed to appear on the ballot. Thoroughly dissatisfied with life in a political limbo, *peronistas* and *frondistas* alike disregarded the instructions of Perón at Madrid and Frondizi at San Carlos de Bariloche (the mountain resort town to which he had been removed from his island prison in the River Plate) to cast blank ballots. Together Frondizi and Perón were supposed to control 45 per cent of the vote. Actually, of the nearly 10 million votes cast, only 18 per cent were blank. The remainder of the votes went to three candidates. Dr. Arturo Umberto Illia, an elderly country doctor but a practicing politician (who had split away from the old Radical party of which he and Frondizi had been members), received 26 per cent of the total vote, entitling him to 169 electoral college votes. Heading an anti-Frondizi wing of the Radical party, Dr. Oscar Alende received 17 per cent of the vote, with 109 electoral votes. The third of the presidential candidates, retired army General Pedro Aramburu (Provisional President following Perón's demise) received 15 per cent, the equivalent of 74 electoral votes. Although he received the largest popular vote, Illia lacked the necessary electoral college majority of 239 votes. However, through switching and jockeying of votes by the electoral college representatives of the minor parties, Illia was assured the requisite majority to be elected President of the Republic on July 31, 1963.

Although an elected President again occupies the Casa Rosada, Argentina's troubles are far from ended. The Illia government, lacking a clear majority, has to function through a coalition, at best an unstable political arrangement. The People's Radical Civic Union party, which rode to power with Illia, had had no experience in governing. President Illia's major policies still require the concurrence of *las bases* of the military commands. The cancellation of the United States and other foreign companies' oil contracts by the Illia regime demonstrates that the democratic politicians of Illia's generation, like the Bourbons, neither learn nor forget. For thirty years Argentina's state-owned oil company, Yacimientos Petrolíferos Fiscales (YPF), has tried to make Argentina self-sufficient in oil, and has failed. The foreign companies virtually succeeded in three years. Argentina desperately needs foreign investments to stimulate her stagnant economy. By cancelling the oil contracts the Illia administration has frightened foreign investors. The economy will remain depressed. As the London *Economist* (May 23, 1964, p. 827) said, "Argentine society [has] all the characteristics of a stagnating economy rather than a newly developing one." Argentinians have lamented the turbulence created by military rule, yet the first act by a civilian government has renewed military unrest. The officers led by General Juan Carlos Onganía supported the return to constitutional government because they believed that the country would achieve political stability and economic revival under civilian rule. The critical foreign reaction to the cancellation of the contracts undermined General Onganía's ability to control the dissident "Red" generals, who never had any confidence in the ability of the patriarchs of the Radical party to govern a modern state. The annulment of the oil contracts reflects a political leadership which is unaware of the significance of world opinion—a leadership whose intellectual horizon is circumscribed by the pampas.

The three main groupings of Argentina—the *estancieros,* the middle classes, and the working people—are opposed to one another. The middle classes (who could dominate the country politically) have been unable to coalesce. Like Banquo's ghost, the aging Perón from his exile in Madrid continues to haunt the scene. His followers constitute 35 per cent of the voting population. They refuse to lie down and die. Nor can they be waved out of existence by a political or military wand. Since their defeat in the presidential elections, the *peronistas* have split into three warring factions. The "moderates" seek integration into the democratic order; the "semi-extremists," under Andrés Framini, call for opposition short of violence; and the "extremists" are aligned with the Castro-Communists in an incipient campaign of terror. The military has been torn asunder on the question of the future of the *peronistas*.

Argentina is a fragmented and frustrated society. She suffers from the disease of military praetorianism. Surrounded by the ruins of *peronismo*, Argentina does not know how to rebuild herself. Indeed, she lacks the cohesiveness and the national will to create a new political order. The Argentinian melting pot, unlike its North American counterpart, has not produced an Argentinian identity or an Argentinian consciousness. In less than a century, between 1830 and 1921, about 40 million immigrants came to the United States. They represented enormous diversity in cultural heritage. Yet within two generations they were merged into an American identity. Take what would appear to be the most difficult case of absorption—the first-generation Japanese, the Nisei of World War II fame. In one generation they have become completely American in manner, attitude, style, and outlook. Their break from the mores of the Japan of their parents is total. Arturo Frondizi is himself a symbol of the difference in the absorptive capacity of his country and ours. The son of immigrant Italian parents, Frondizi is completely un-Spanish. He has the manner and style of a Florentine. Indeed, in his political style he reveals a discipleship to another gifted Florentine—Niccolò Machiavelli.

In a soul-searching essay written after the overthrow of Perón, a perceptive Argentinian, H. A. Murena, put his finger on the cause of the chronic Argentine sickness: "There is no community in Argentina. We do not form a body . . . we behave as if each one were unique and as if he were alone. . . . Argentina has rancorous, factious chaos, periodically illuminated by *coups d'état*. It is not an organism of which all feel themselves a part. Each organ believes itself the whole, and functions as if it were more important than the whole. Is there any more succinct definition of sickness?"

Despite her deep trauma, Argentina is shedding her cocoon of isolation. She no longer looks exclusively to London and

Paris for orientation. She no longer broods morbidly over the hegemony of the United States; in fact she is eager for the friendship of the United States. The old *estanciero* class has lost much of its former political power. A new generation of gifted Argentinians can provide democratic leadership. Until his retirement as Commander in Chief of the armed forces on November 22, 1965, the leadership of General Onganía offered some encouragement for believing that, if the Argentine military is not yet sufficiently mature to accept civilian control, it may be on the threshold of exercising a more restrained type of veto. General Onganía's departure has again thrown the military into turmoil, High-ranking officers are angered over what they consider to be the government's failure to take forceful action against Communist subversion—in Argentina and the hemisphere. They are concerned by the reluctance of the Illia administration to support the Inter-American Peace Force at Santo Domingo. The appointment of a Brazilian general as commander of the Peace Force rankles. General Onganía's criticism of his government in advocating an alliance between Brazil and Argentina to combat Communism, and his raising of the issue at a conference of hemisphere military officers at Lima, Peru, in November 1965 led to resentment by civilian members of the government who had expressed their disapproval of Brazil's military regime.

Argentina's tragedy is the absence of a statesman who can serve as a bridge between the Onganías of the military (who are not averse to civil government), the *peronistas* (who live on nostalgic memories of a faded and shabby revolution), and the middle-class politicians (whose ambitions are too parochial). Although an elected President again occupies the Casa Rosada, Argentina's anguish is not yet ended: it must still meld its disparate social and economic groups. The Argentinian melting pot must begin by creating an Argentinian identity and a sense of national purpose. And it must find a way to rid itself of its military caste.

Peru

At 3 a.m. on July 18, 1962, a Sherman tank under the command of Colonel Gonzalo Briceño, a graduate of the United States Ranger School at Fort Benning, crashed into

the presidential palace. Manuel Prado, Peru's constitution-
ally elected President, was placed under arrest. In the classic
Latin American tradition, a *coup d'état* had taken place.
Peru's military had moved from the *cuartel* into the *palacio*.
To understand this military take-over in Peru, it is necessary
to understand the significance of APRA (Alianza Popular
Revolucionaria Americana), and to grasp the significance of
APRA, one must understand the role played by Víctor Raúl
Haya de la Torre in Peru's contemporary political life. Both
the man and the party must be placed against the backdrop
of Peru—the land, the people, and its problems.

Peru is the classic example of a Latin American country
which is more royalist than the king, which is to say that in
Peru feudalism and the feudal mentality are probably more
prevalent than they were in medieval Spain. Lima, the "City
of the Kings," despite its modern, garish overtones of neon
lights, still retains an atmosphere of the colonial viceregal
splendor. Ten per cent of Peru's population of 11 million
people live in Lima. Lima is home for Peru's aristocracy, the
famous "forty families" who, it is said, control the country's
economic, political, and social life. Some 4 to 5 million Indians live on the *sierra*—no one knows precisely the exact
number. Statistics are a form of poetry in Latin America. In
any event, it depends on your definition of an Indian.
Whether or not he is included in the official census, the presence of the Indian is pervasive.

In the aftermath of revolutionary fervor following the liberation of Peru from Spanish rule, General San Martín declared in 1821: "Henceforth the aborigines shall not be called
Indians; they are children and citizens of Peru, and they shall
be known as Peruvians." Francisco Pizarro's companions and
Bolívar's and San Martín's lieutenants had other ideas.
*Latifundia*s worked by Indian serf labor and *gamonalismo*
became the norm. The latter term has been defined as "the
condition of inequality of the Indian with respect to the other
social classes . . . it is colonialism and clericalism projected
through a century of independent life; it signifies spoliation
. . . the connivance of the authorities in exploiting Indians
without conscience and without scruple." [4]

The first serious modern critic of Peru's feudal system was
José Carlos Mariátegui. After several years of study in

---

[4] Thomas R. Ford: *Man and Land in Peru* (Gainesville: University
of Florida Press; 1955), p. 111.

Europe, he published his *ensayos de interpretación de la realidad peruana* in 1928. He exposed the great problems of his country—the miserable condition of the Indian, *latifundia*, the political power of the Church, regionalism, and the inadequate educational system (which ignored the Indian completely). Although Mariátegui's approach was Marxist, he eventually left the Communist party. Among the reforms which he urged was a return to the Inca system of communal use of land. Peru must find its own political solution, he believed, without copying Europe or the United States.

Among Mariátegui's ardent student disciples at the University of San Marcos was Víctor Raúl Haya de la Torre. Descended on his mother's line from one of Francisco Pizarro's lieutenants, Haya de la Torre has the face of an Inca carving. Exiled from the University and Peru by the dictator Leguía, Haya fled to Mexico. There in 1924 he announced the formation of APRA. For almost forty years he has been the bogeyman of Peruvian politics. Haya de la Torre is the key not only to an understanding of the political events in Peru but also to the whole set of principles that are at the core of Latin America's democratic parties of the Left. Betancourt of Venezuela, Figueres of Costa Rica, Paz Estenssoro of Bolivia, indeed the once youthful and ambitious Perón, have all dipped into the thinking of Haya de la Torre and borrowed from his ideas.[5]

Heavily larded with Marxian idiom, Haya's program called for the nationalization of land and industry, a united front of workers and intellectuals, and—what was to become the central idea for the disciples of APRA—the unity of Indo-America (Haya's term for Latin America) against Yankee imperialism. Borrowing from Mariátegui, Haya's program turns on the need for Latin America to find its own political life free of European or North American influences. He has urged that Latin America's economic development be free of an exclusive dependency on external capital, but he has never said that foreign capital should be spurned. Haya has stressed the need for hemispheric unity and the abolition of frontiers, political as well as spiritual. The contemporary

[5] I am greatly indebted to Robert J. Alexander and Harry Kantor for my own understanding of the philosophy of Haya de la Torre. See Robert J. Alexander: *Prophets of the Revolution* (New York: The Macmillan Company; 1962), pp. 75–108, and Harry Kantor: *The Ideology and Program of the Peruvian Aprista Movement* (Berkeley: University of California Press; 1953), *passim*.

movement toward economic and political union is the flower of Haya's seed.

From its inception, APRA was a magnet which attracted Peruvian intellectuals, middle-class professionals, students, and the more advanced of the working class. Many of Peru's most dedicated and intelligent citizens were deeply convinced that "only *aprismo* can save Peru." To the Indians on the *sierra*, Haya de la Torre was the reincarnation of the Inca. To the army and the conservative ruling and governing group, APRA and Haya de la Torre smelled of revolution. They were both anathema. So they have remained to this day. Haya de la Torre was exiled. His followers burrowed underground and extended their influence in the trade unions, in the government bureaucracy, among the junior officers of the military, among the intellectual and professional classes.

In 1931, Haya de la Torre returned from exile to become the candidate against Sánchez Cerro, a Peruvian *caudillo*. Idolized by the students, the city workers, and the Indian peasants, Haya de la Torre won the election, in the judgment of impartial observers, with an electrifying campaign in which he held his audiences spellbound whether he spoke in Spanish or in the ancient Quechua tongue of the Indians. Haya de la Torre's victory at the polls was rewarded by imprisonment. APRA was outlawed. Leaders of the party were exiled. In the spring of 1933, the dictator Sánchez was assassinated. It was claimed that an *aprista* had been the assassin.

In 1939, Manuel Prado, a conservative banker and one of Peru's wealthiest men, assumed the presidency. In the benign aura of the World War II years, Prado permitted Haya de la Torre to return to Lima. Far from being moribund —as its enemies assumed—APRA was still a dynamic force and its influence was still pervasive. Peru went through the motions of an election in 1945. The progressive groups rallied behind José Luis Bustamante y Rivero, a respected lawyer and diplomat. APRA supported Bustamante. He was elected. Having made Bustamante's election possible *apristas* were given active roles in the administration. *Apristas* sat in the Cabinet, presided over the Senate, the Chamber of Deputies, and the University of San Marcos. Three years later APRA's brief day in the sun was over when the murder of an editor of an anti-APRA newspaper was blamed on the *apristas*. APRA members were forced to resign from the government administration. A revolt by sailors at Callao was laid to

APRA. The inevitable *coup d'état* against Bustamante occurred and General Manuel Odría became the new *caudillo*. Some *apristas* were jailed; others fled. Haya de la Torre sought the sanctuary of the Colombian Embassy, where he remained for five years, until 1954. Odría quickly put an end to the liberal-progressive APRA "nonsense" in Lima as the government resumed its traditional character with the army in charge.

The end of the Odría dictatorship saw a peculiar turn in the Peruvian political jockeying for the transfer of power. APRA was actually courted by the opposing factions. It was in this campaign that Ramiro Prialé, the Secretary General of APRA, emerged as one of the outstanding organizational leaders of the movement. Prialé and the other APRA leaders agreed to throw their support behind Prado, who had been persuaded to run for office for a second term. The *quid pro quo* for this backing was Prado's commitment to legalize the APRA party. For the *apristas* this objective, together with a reasonably democratic regime over the ensuing six years, was of supreme importance because the 1962 election was universally regarded as APRA's year to win. Prado kept his word. APRA was again a legal party. The exiles returned. Organization of the party machinery was placed in high gear. *La Tribuna*, the official party newspaper, reappeared. And Víctor Haya de la Torre himself came home to receive a tumultuous welcome. By the end of Prado's term, the Peruvian economy seemed prosperous; the superficial trimmings of democracy were in evidence; the *apristas* were no longer persecuted. By 1961, plans were being laid for the presidential elections to be held the following year. The candidates were the same men who ran in 1956. Fernando Belaúnde Terry, educated in Paris and the United States, an architect by profession, a university teacher, had barely lost the 1956 election. In his appeal to the younger progressive elements, he represented the most serious threat to APRA in its quarter-century of existence. There was also the old dictator, General Odría, who was attempting a comeback; and the perennial stalwart, Haya de la Torre.

This election was undoubtedly the most significant in APRA's history. During the preceding decade the APRA philosophy had undergone a fundamental change, particularly with respect to its position toward the United States. The rise of Nazism in Europe and Franklin Roosevelt's Good Neighbor Policy were determinative influences for Haya. But more significantly, new men were at the helm—men such as Prialé, who had carried on the hard, tough work of organization and negotiation while Haya was in exile. The new leaders had none of the old APRA romanticism in their approach to winning the coming election. They could speak calmly of the need for foreign capital in Peru's development. They thought the Alliance for Progress was a good idea. A quarter of a century had mellowed APRA. Nineteen sixty-two was to be APRA's year for enjoying the sweet taste of victory. Haya would be the candidate, although there were those who wondered if the Old Man still had the magic touch, whether his long years of exile might not have blunted his "feel" for the campaign. There were some in the party's hierarchy who believed that Haya was too "controversial" and that a respected *aprista* such as Manuel Seoane would clinch the victory. The doubts were quashed, if not completely dismissed, in the feeling of loyalty to Haya.

I recall a Saturday afternoon in September 1961, when I visited Ramiro Prialé at his party headquarters in Lima. Prialé paid me the compliment of saying that I was the first North American businessman passing through the area who had ever asked to see him. As I studied Prialé across the table, I could sense that his manner of speaking and his confidence were those of the professional politician. He would have been perfectly at ease with a Mayor Daly or a James Farley. Tough, shrewd, realistic, Prialé told me he had spent thirteen years in the jails of Peru's dictators. Yet the idealism came through as Prialé talked of the things which desperately needed doing in the most feudal country in Latin America. There was no doubt in Prialé's mind that his chief would win. He described in masterly detail the logistics of the campaign, the areas where the big vote was expected, where APRA would be in trouble, the marginal spots. And then came my question—to me it seemed the central question: Would the army allow APRA to take over the reins of government? Prialé smiled and replied that the question did not take into account the nature of the new Peruvian army. This army, Prialé went on, was essentially middle-class. Its officers had been exposed to economics and technology. They understood that reforms could no longer be delayed. They would support APRA in its effort to undertake reform measures peaceably and democratically.

Later that evening I thought again of Prialé's response. Was it the answer of a professional politician who could say nothing less to a visitor? Or was it true that the Peruvian army had undergone a metamorphosis?

Haya did not win a clear majority, although he led the other two candidates. Had the Congress been permitted to select the victor—as the law required—there is no question but that Haya would have been declared President-elect. It was this commanding strength of APRA which caused the military to charge that the voting had been fraudulent—a charge which was denied by the respected members of the National Electoral Court. For the second time Víctor Raúl Haya de la Torre was cheated by the Peruvian military of his earned right to the presidency of his country. By its action, Peru's military revealed with brutal clarity that the APRA leaders had been indulging in a pipe dream in their belief that the "middle-class" character of the officer corps would lead them to respect the people's choice of a government to carry out democratic reforms. A moderate reformist party (which might have spared Peru a repetition of what the Indian peasants had done through the violence of revolution in neighboring Bolivia) was not permitted to exercise its popular mandate by the modern *conquistadores* of Peru. Ironically, Manuel Prado, scion of wealth, member of the oligarchy, was routed from his bed in the early hours of the morning and deposed as the constitutional President of Peru. A military triumvirate took over the Palace with General Ricardo Pérez Godoy as the chief of the military junta.

General Pérez (who was shortly removed as *Presidente* of the junta for entertaining, according to his colleagues, dictatorial ambitions) promptly announced that new elections would be held June 9, 1963. Continuing, he said: "We of the armed forces are middle-class. . . . There will be land, houses, work, and food. . . . We will decrease the cost of living. . . . We will do all this in twelve months, not one day more." Even the llamas—beasts of burden on the *altiplano* since before the days of the Inca—joined in the hollow, mocking laughter which echoed through the land at this theatrical bombast.

The military did accomplish something during the year in which it held the levers of power. It reorganized the National Housing Institute; issued a decree for a land-reform program (which the Intelligence Unit of the London *Economist* reported as not having caused a ripple of concern among the *haciendados*); drew up Plan Peruano for the development of the east-central and southern Andes region, including a new 600,000-kilowatt electricity plant, new railways, high-ways, and ore refineries; and prepared a ten-year Economic and Social Development Plan. It did all this and raised its own pay by some $20 million (so that 35 per cent of the national budget is now siphoned off by the military establishment). It did something more: it kept its word and permitted the presidential elections to take place precisely on the day on which the army had stated they would be held—June 9, 1963. As knowledgeable and shrewd politicians, the military did one thing of considerable political significance: they changed the electoral laws so as to make it virtually impossible for a political party to win a congressional majority in a competitive three-cornered race. This alteration of the electoral law was designed to obviate a repetition of the pattern of the preceding year, in which, it will be recalled, Haya de la Torre's election was thrown into the Congress, where the APRA party had a majority of the votes.

Fernando Belaúnde Terry won handily. Out of a total 1,815,067 votes, Belaúnde received 708,931; Haya de la Torre, 623,532; and Odría, 463,325. Mario Samamé Boggio and his Unión del Pueblo Peruano party received 19,279 votes. Haya carried only nine departments out of twenty-four, and lost Lima (where the heaviest vote was concentrated) to Odría and Belaúnde. In a situation reminiscent of the 1960 presidential election in the United States (in which John F. Kennedy's personal margin was minuscule but the Democratic party in many parts of the country received strong endorsement), the APRA party showed a greater popular vote than its leader. To what extent Belaúnde's victory was the result of a widespread feeling that a vote for Haya was a "lost" vote is difficult to say. The fact that Haya was unable to carry many of the traditional APRA strongholds suggests that a good number of *apristas* had reached the reluctant conclusion that Haya's cause was lost because the army would under no circumstances allow him to wear the jeweled red-and-white presidential sash. That the vacillations and compromises of the APRA leaders and their preoccupation with the techniques of politics had disenchanted many of the intellectuals among the *apristas* was evident long before the election. That this vote was transferred to Belaúnde is quite probable. To what extent the psychology of wanting to be on the winning side influenced the outcome is again a matter of conjecture. A Peruvian businessman acquaintance of mine probably expressed the prevailing popular view when he said: "No matter who gets the votes, Belaúnde is going to win." The suspicion did exist that Belaúnde was the "official" candidate of the army officers and that he had made a deal with them. The APRA leadership believed this to be true and so charged during the campaign. Belaúnde was known to have the backing of many of the army's younger officers. (After his election, the Chiefs of Staff publicly showed their friendship for Belaúnde by making him an honorary member of the Orden Militar de Ayacucho.) Whatever the facts —they must await the research of the political scientist— Belaúnde's margin of victory was supplied by the Christian Democrats (with whom he had formed an alliance), the splinter parties of the Left, and the Communists (whose support he had welcomed in the past, but disavowed in the 1963 campaign).

Belaúnde's own party lacks a parliamentary majority, the voting control resting with the opposition parties. An embittered APRA and an opportunistic Odría party, although they have given Belaúnde's program temporary support, could eventually deny him their full political backing, or they may for their own reasons push him too far too fast.

I myself have thought that Belaúnde's principal difficulty lay within himself—his fascination with the faraway (colonizing the inaccessible forest shelf on the eastern slopes of the Andes and building roads across the top of the Andes to connect Colombia, Ecuador, Peru, and Bolivia, a re-creation of the ancient Inca highway system) rather than with the here and now (bulldozing some of the worst slums in the Western Hemisphere, not more than a ten-minute taxi drive from his official residence).

The facets of the mind are rarely disclosed in a single meeting between strangers. In a discussion with Belaúnde my instincts may well have deceived me. Power has a habit of destroying as well as transforming. Vested with the responsibilities of his office, Fernando Belaúnde Terry may yet succeed in being the first President to impose reforms on Peru. His administration enjoys the support of many in the professional, managerial, and intellectual classes, including men of the renown of Ciro Alegría, the novelist. Belaúnde has acted with political shrewdness in sending doctors into the Amazonas, where the presence of a doctor was unknown in all of Peru's history. He has restored the *cabildo abierto* in the townships and municipalities, allowing the people to elect their own *alcalde,* or mayor, instead of having him appointed by the central government at Lima.

Although Belaúnde's hand was forced prematurely on land-reform legislation when the Indians seized estates in the *altiplano,* land reform will be the crucial and ultimate problem which could break his administration. So long as land reform is confined to "colonization" on the other side of the *cordillera,* the Peruvian oligarchy will remain quiescent. But the moment Belaúnde attempts to buy or expropriate idle *hacienda* lands, the issue will have been joined. Indeed, the rumbling of the opposition can already be heard in the campaign begun by the big landowners attacking the constitutionality of Belaúnde's plan for payment in bonds in lieu of cash.

However Belaúnde moves, he will require money—lots of it. His program for reform could become stuck on the fly-paper of Washington's unwillingness to underwrite costly, diversionary colonization schemes or other plans which, although they look good on paper, may raise more questions than they answer. As much as I should like to see Belaúnde succeed, I have gnawing doubts. If I may be permitted an instinctive thrust into the future, my fear is that Fernando Belaúnde Terry may well be Peru's Kerensky. For reasons which will be apparent in a moment, he is not cast for the role of a General Naguib. Peru is beyond the stage where reform plastering can any longer hold the feudal structure together. Haya de la Torre has run his last race. The existing moderate APRA leadership may be displaced by younger men who are unwilling to follow the middle of the road; they may push APRA over to the Left. The Indians on the *sierra* are restless. They are susceptible of organization. They are discovering that direct action through seizure of land brings fast remedial action from Lima. They may be unwilling to wait a decade for land on the other side of the *cordillera.* The Indian youths who have served their time in the army, who have been taught to drive a truck, and have tasted the glittering life of Lima, are no longer content with the dead-end life of their villages. Communist guerrillas have intensified their efforts to stir up Indian resentments. In July 1965, at the insistence of the armed forces, a state of siege was declared as a precaution against guerrilla terrorism, concentrated in an area less than 30 miles north of the celebrated Inca ruins at Machu Picchu and 80 miles northwest of Cuzco. The so-called middle class, who saw Belaúnde as a savior, may have other thoughts as they find themselves still without housing. If the moderate reform program envisaged by Belaúnde proves inadequate to satisfy the pressure for land, houses, and a better distribution of income, the younger elements of the army can be expected to add their vigorous pressure for the military to move to the center of the stage with the army's own version of a "planned economy."

There is considerable speculation that the adumbration of national development planning by the Peruvian military points the compass toward Nasserism. I believe the analogy is misleading. Colonel Nasser's "Free Officer Corps" seized power in 1952 following a disastrous and humiliating defeat at the hands of the Israelis for which Farouk and his corrupt entourage were made the scapegoats. The "Free Officers" who manipulated Farouk's overthrow were rabid nationalists. They were filled with class resentment at the effendi class who were their overlords. The Egyptian seizure of power was not a military palace coup in the Latin American tradition. It was a military revolution which destroyed the political power of the old pasha class, instituted a far-ranging land and housing program for the *fellahin* (one of the most wretched populations in the world), mounted a drive for industrialization, nationalized virtually every phase of business and banking (except for the small shopkeepers), and prescribed goals for increasing the standard of living. Colonel Nasser's officers manage and direct the Egyptian economy.

Nasser's dangerous adventurism in the Middle East can be deplored without denying the progress he has made in converting Egypt into a modern state and in giving the Egyptian people a sense of dignity, their first since before the time of the pyramids. The fact remains, however, that Nasser and his officer corps are exponents of revolutionary socialism. There is not the slightest evidence to suggest that the senior officers of the Peruvian military establishment have any emotional attachment to "Arab Socialism." That it may have strong adherents among Peru's junior officers is something else. Among the junior officers and at the army's Centro de Altos Estudios Militares (CAEM) at Lima there is unconcealed admiration for Colonel Nasser as there is for Kemal Atatürk. There is even a grudging admiration for Fidel Castro. There is study of the Meiji Restoration. Karl Marx is not merely a name. As with the younger officers in the other Latin American military establishments, there is enthusiasm for a "planned economy" in which all sectors of the population respond to a central direction without the delays, compromises, and negotiations involved in the democratic process. But junior officers do not hold the levers of command—in Peru or elsewhere.

To put it in its proper perspective, the economic and development planning of the Peruvian military is in reality an extension of the traditional "public works" activities of the Latin American military. Other than the Perón interlude, when the Defense Ministry was in charge of a large segment of the Argentine economy, and the abortive social revolution led by Colonel Jacobo Arbenz Guzmán in Guatemala, I know of no instance where the Latin American military has shown any disposition to embrace the kind of military socialism which obtains in Colonel Nasser's Egypt.

Among the older generation of Peru's senior officers who were trained under French military missions, there may be nostalgic memories of Liberty, Equality and Fraternity. But among those in command, now, who obtained their graduate training in Spain's military staff college, there is admiration for Franco and Franco's Spain. In its senior echelons, Peru's military has a long record of resistance to reform. Its political beliefs are rooted in Peru's feudal society and in a pathological commitment to preserving the *status quo*. Peru's military has no discernible social philosophy distinguishable from a preoccupation with political power and its perquisites.

Guatemala

Guatemala may be a political entity, but it is not a nation. A tortured land, it is divided into two cultures, Indian and white. Half of Guatemala's population of 4 million consists of Mayan Indians. They care nothing for the white man and his culture. The Indian continues to speak his ancient tongue with its many dialects and adheres to his Indian ways. The Indian population is largely outside—or on the fringes of—the money economy. It is organized in distinctive village communities, in a kind of classless society. In a land where the soldier is considered more important than the schoolteacher, illiteracy is about 80 per cent. The *ladinos* (the Spanish-Americans, predominantly of a mixed racial strain, cosmopolitan, at whose social apex are the numerically small and exclusive "old families") despise the Indian. He is regarded as a work animal.

Political and economic power has been in the hands of the coffee-growing aristocracy and the army. The Church in Guatemala has not been a member of the official power structure. In little over a century, Guatemala has been ruled by four despotic *caudillos*. They ran the gamut from an illiterate, ruthless Indian barbarian, Rafael Carrera (1838–65), to an intelligent, ruthless "presidential-style" dictator, Jorge Ubico (1931–44). An older generation of *guatemaltecos* retains affectionate memories of Ubico. Yet Germán Arciniegas observes that the Guatemalan tradition of despotism attained a "savage climax under the megalomaniac General Jorge Ubico." An uprising by university students, joined by lawyers, businessmen, and elements of the army, finally led to Ubico's surrender of power to a three-man junta.

Then came Guatemala's "social revolution" under Juan José Arévalo (1945–50) and Colonel Jacobo Arbenz Guzmán (1951–54). After Ubico's removal, the provisional government promoted the candidacy of Dr. Arévalo, a widely respected but politically unknown personality. A forty-year-old professor, Arévalo had spent the preceding decade lecturing in Argentina at the University of La Plata. His political advantage lay in his disassociation from the Ubico regime and the old-line politicos. Arévalo proved to be an effective campaigner and caught the popular fancy. His election to the presidency was overwhelming. He gave Guatemala her first vision of social reform. He abolished forced labor, promulgated Guatemala's first labor code, laid plans for breaking up the large landholdings, created a Social Security Institute, began a reorganization of the army in the direction of less authoritarianism, and started educational improvements. Under his guidance, the Indians began to participate in the government. On the ledger books of achievement, Arévalo's actual accomplishments did not total to a significant sum. However, with that special mystique of the born politician, Arévalo etched himself on the hearts of the ordinary people of Guatemala, who, after years of cruel tyranny, found in him the best years of their lives.

Externally, Arévalo's claim to fame may well rest on his authorship of *The Shark and the Sardines,* a bitter, impassioned, and historically distorted denunciation of American imperialism. It was a best-seller throughout Latin America, and probably constitutes his *apologia* for his failure to achieve a genuine social revolution. Arévalo's second claim to recognition turns on his having been the first political figure in the Western Hemisphere to employ the *apertura a sinistra*. Arévalo's opening to the Left occurred through his fatal acquiescence in the candidacy of Colonel Arbenz to succeed him in the presidency. Although not a Communist when he received the blue-and-white silk presidential sash on March 15, 1951, Arbenz later became a full-fledged member of the Marxist brotherhood. A naïve soldier, he was potter's clay in the hands of the professional Communist cadres who soon moved into Guatemala *en masse*. These were no home-grown Communists. They bore the label "Made in Moscow." Under the Arbenz administration, the Communist grip took hold on all of Guatemala—the courts, the legislature, the propaganda media, the public administration. The army itself was not immune. It was on this stage that an Argentine doctor and professional revolutionary—who would later achieve fame as Major Ernesto Ché Guevara—made his debut.

The enactment of an Agrarian Reform Law on June 15, 1952, embroiled the Arbenz regime in a bitter controversy not only with its own coffee aristocracy but with United States business and official diplomacy as well. In an atmosphere of virulent nationalism, resentment, and rancor over "Yankee imperialism," rubbed raw by incessant Communist propaganda, the government seized the United Fruit Company's reserve banana lands. The company contended that the banana industry—which was Guatemala's second largest source of export revenues—could not survive without reserve lands to provide for the shifts in plantings. Compensation of $594,-572 was offered to the company for lands which it valued at $4,000,000. The report given to the press by Secretary of State John Foster Dulles on May 17, 1954, that Czechoslovakian arms were being sent to the Arbenz government blew the fuse on this phase of Guatemala's social revolution.

In his *Mandate for Change: 1953–1956,* General Eisenhower has filled in the details of an episode which has been surrounded by suspicion and rumor. On May 23, General Eisenhower informs us, the United States airlifted about fifty tons of rifles, pistols, machine guns, and ammunition to Honduras and Nicaragua "to help counter the danger created by the Czech shipment to Guatemala." On June 18, a column led by Lieutenant Colonel Carlos Castillo Armas (an exile whose supporters were trained by the CIA in Honduras and Nicaragua) crossed the border from Honduras into Guatemala with about two hundred men. General Eisenhower reports the events: "Things seemed to be going well for Castillo's small band until June 22. On that date Allen Dulles reported to me that Castillo had lost two of the three old bombers with which he was supporting his 'invasion.'" General Eisenhower states that, at a meeting on the afternoon of June 22 with Secretary Dulles and Assistant Secretary of State for Inter-American Affairs Henry F. Holland, the question was raised whether the United States "should cooperate in replacing the bombers." General Eisenhower reports that "the country which had originally supplied this equipment to Castillo was willing now to supply him two P-51 fighter-bombers if the United States would agree to replace them." (The "country" to which General Eisenhower made reference was presumably Nicaragua. The P-51 aircraft was United States equipment.) The sense of the meeting, General Eisenhower informs us, was "far from unanimous" with respect to replacing the P-51 aircraft. Continuing, General Eisenhower states:

"What do you think Castillo's chances would be," I asked Allen Dulles, "without the aircraft?"

His answer was unequivocal: "About zero."

"Suppose we supply the aircraft. What would the chances be then?"

Again the CIA chief did not hesitate: "About 20 per cent."

General Eisenhower concluded that it would be contrary to the spirit of the Caracas resolution and in violation of his duty not to replace the airplanes. "Delivery of the planes," he continues, "was prompt and Castillo successfully resumed his progress."

When the Guatemalan army refused to support Arbenz, he announced that he was relinquishing control to a provisional government. Castillo Armas was brought into the ruling military junta and eventually became its chief. His government was incompetent, corrupt, and unpopular, and his rule was punctuated by bombings and rioting. Castillo Armas was assassinated by a palace guard on the night of July 27, 1957.

After a series of makeshift governments, a career officer, General Miguel Ydígoras Fuentes, with the support of the conservative elements and the army, was installed as President on March 2, 1958. An ambitious prototype of the *caudillo* military politician, Ydígoras had served under Ubico and had participated in the revolt against him. During Arévalo's administration, he had been conveniently "exiled," first to Washington and then to London, where he served as ambassador. He sought the presidency against Arbenz, but was unsuccessful. After Castillo Armas took power, Ydígoras was appointed ambassador to Colombia. (Ambassadorial appointments are the conventional Latin American technique for disposing of political rivals.) Ydígoras' regime was not characterized by the savage despotism of his predecessors. It was, however, the usual corrupt, graft-ridden police state in which the windows were opened just enough to permit a faint breath of civil liberties. As President, Ydígoras was unpredictable, cantankerous, and personalistic. If Ydígoras was not the Nero of the Caribbean, neither was he its Pericles.

By the early sixties, his regime appeared to be reeling from the onslaughts of a revolt by elements of his own officer corps and student-led riots in protest against the government's rigging of the congressional elections. The Castro revolution had barely established itself in Cuba when it began to export insurrection into the Caribbean. Guatemala was among the targets of high priority. Ydígoras articulated the sentiments of those in the region who believed that Castro had to be removed by force. Guatemala became a training and staging area for the ill-fated Cuban invasion.

The time was approaching for the December 1963 presidential election and the transfer of power to another administration. Ydígoras vacillated—alternately creating an impression that he coveted another term for himself, grooming a candidate as his successor, and flirting with Arévalo (who from Mexico City had announced his own candidacy as well as his intention to return to Guatemala in March to begin his campaign). The Ydígoras government allowed a political tract prepared by Arévalo—*Carta política al pueblo de Guatemala*—to be publicly distributed. A curious hodgepodge of philosophy, warmed-over revolutionary history, and egotism, Arévalo's "message" contained as much incendiary impact as a smoked-out cigar butt. Although he has been accused of being a Communist—a charge which

Arévalo has denied—in his campaign tract he specifically repudiated Communism as spiritually repugnant and opposed to his principles as a teacher and a political leader. He had indicated his support for the Alliance for Progress, and had voiced severe criticism of the Castro regime. This was not good enough for the Ydígoras regime.

The events which transpired at Guatemala City in the last days of March 1963 can only be described as a Class-B Hollywood movie. All foreign airlines were informed by the government that their landing rights would be lifted if any sold a ticket to Arévalo. On March 21, Ydígoras announced that he was in possession of Arévalo's "Communist party card number." University students called a strike and attacked the homes of government officials and Rightist candidates. Guerrillas began a series of attacks on army installations. Bombs were exploded in Guatemala City. Unable to obtain entry into Guatemala by plane, Arévalo crossed the border by car on March 26. He was recognized by a soldier on patrol who assisted him in reaching his brother's *finca* on March 28. On March 30, the government announced a twelve-hour curfew beginning at 8 p.m. Only persons bearing a Defense Ministry pass were permitted on the streets. Assembly of more than four persons was prohibited. Military censorship was imposed on all communications. Police were placed under military orders and permitted to enter private homes and to search cars without warrant. Not trusting its own air force, the army obtained three jet planes from its obliging friend, President Somoza of Nicaragua, to quash the "Castro revolt." Guatemala City assumed the appearance of a city under siege. Arévalo appeared briefly in the capital for a press conference and then disappeared. At approximately 10:15 p.m. on March 31, in the classic ritual of the Latin American *coup d'état*, an army tank smashed open the iron gates of the Casa Crema, the presidential residence. General Miguel Ydígoras Fuentes, President of the Republic, was taken into custody, driven to the airport, and placed aboard a plane for Nicaragua. Colonel Enrique Peralta Azurdia, Minister of Defense, immediately proclaimed the suspension of the Constitution and dissolution of the legislature, and announced that he would exercise the functions of government. In a formal bulletin, the army charged that government leaders had been preparing "to return the government to anti-democratic elements." Upon his arrival in Nicaragua, Ydígoras called the *coup d'état* good for Guatemala and the rest of Central America.

The trouble with this scenario is that the plot is too pat. There are too many "false scents" designed to throw suspicion on too many characters. Let us look for a moment at Ydígoras' own candidate, Roberto Alejos, a well-to-do coffee planter on whose *finca* a contingent of Cuban patriots had trained under CIA auspices. Had there been any intention to hold an election, Alejos could have been "elected" easily. In Guatemala, the government in power has always been able to supply the votes required to put its candidate into office.

Did Ydígoras have knowledge of Arévalo's crossing of the border, as was implied by Colonel Peralta in an interview with a *New York Times* correspondent? Was there in fact an "alliance" between Ydígoras and Arévalo as Peralta later charged? Had Ydígoras deliberately set a trap for Arévalo by luring him back to Guatemala? Did the Guatemalan Left play into Ydígoras' hands by erupting into open rebellion, thereby paving the way for the declaration of a state of siege? Did the Ydígoras regime really fear Arévalo, or was he used as a bogeyman to frighten the conservative elements and the American Embassy? Was there a conspiracy between Somoza and Colonel Peralta to oust Ydígoras, as the former President charged?

Perhaps now we should turn to Colonel Peralta. For if there is a "villain" in this melodrama, the evidence points to him. Peralta is known throughout the Guatemalan officer corps as a strict disciplinarian, a devout Catholic, and a thoroughly humorless man. In the infinite boredom of whiling away the years in a Central American army, Peralta's career could hardly be called distinguished. Those who have had the opportunity to know him marked Peralta as politically ambitious. For a man with his eye on the Palace, in control of the army, and with a sense of timing, all that was required was the proper setting. The maneuverings by Ydígoras and the use of Arévalo as a paper tiger to create a state of alarm provided the setting. The success enjoyed by the military fraternity in Buenos Aires and Lima offered an additional stimulus for action. It is difficult not to conclude that Peralta's *coup d'état* was a contrived affair, an elaborate piece of theater reminiscent of the rituals of the Chinese warlords of the thirties, in which they engaged in fake battles and fake surrenders, with the "vanquished" general exiled to a lush diplomatic post, preferably Paris.

Eighteen days after the seizure of power by Colonel Peralta—on April 17, 1963—the United States Government gave its diplomatic recognition to the military dictatorship, after, as *The New York Times* reported, "extracting a tentative promise to hold elections in 1965."

There is nothing of the make-believe about this military dictatorship: it exercises its power with the savagery for which Guatemalan dictatorships are famous. Anyone who incurs its displeasure is tried, sentenced, and shot by kangaroo military courts. It is all done "legally." There is even a "law" of authorization. With exquisite irony it is called "Law for the Defense of Democratic Institutions" (*"Ley de Defensa de las Instituciones Democráticas"*).

At the Tricontinental Solidarity Conference held in Havana in January 1966, the Communist leadership made no secret of its determination to regain a dominant position in Guatemala, a strategically situated country for launching "wars of national liberation" in other Central American countries. Two guerrilla bands operate in Guatemala. One is led by Marco Antonio Yon Sosa, who is known as *"El Chino"* because of his Chinese father. He heads the "Thirteenth of November Revolutionary Movement." The other guerrilla band, known as the "Rebel Armed Forces," is led by Luis Turcios Lima. Yon Sosa and Turcios are former army lieutenants, who participated in the 1961 officers' revolt against Ydígoras. They operate from mountain hideouts in the northeast of Guatemala, near Lake Izabal, close to the border of Honduras. Turcios has the support of the Moscow-Havana Communists. Yon Sosa adheres to the Peking line; he was denounced by Castro as a "Trotskyite." Colonel Peralta contemptuously regards Yon Sosa and Turcios as "bandits"; he has offered a reward of $25,000 for their heads. Yon Sosa, according to Guatemala City wags, has offered $50,000 for Peralta's head.

A new Constitution was scheduled to go into effect in May 1966. It echoes the high-sounding principles that no *guatemalteco* takes seriously. They have all been stated before and not respected. Each Constitution has proclaimed the army to be nonpolitical, but officers have intervened, directly or indirectly, in the country's political life for so long that Guatemalans find it difficult to believe that this will change. According to the new Constitution, elections were held in March 1966 for a President, Vice-President, Congress, and municipal officials. Three candidates stood for the presidency—Colonel Miguel Ángel Ponciano Samayoa of the ultraright National Liberation Movement, Colonel Juan de Dios Aguilar de León of the conservative Institutional Democratic party, and Julio César Méndez Montenegro of the center-left Revolutionary party.

Ponciano is a former Chief of Staff of the army. He was critical of Colonel Peralta for not having waged a more vigorous campaign against the guerrilla forces. He believed that he could do better. In December 1965, reports reached Washington that Ponciano was planning a *coup d'état* against Peralta. On instructions from the Department of State, it is understood that the American Ambassador in Guatemala City delivered a strongly-worded message to Ponciano. In essence, Ponciano was told that the United States could not stop him from making a *coup d'état*, but it would deny him recognition and financial aid if he moved against the Peralta regime.

Aguilar is a reserve colonel and an engineer who has held various government posts. The officer corps does not regard him as one of its own. Why Aguilar was chosen as the candidate of the Institutional Democratic party has baffled observers. Some believe that Peralta wanted Aguilar as his successor because he was less ambitious and controversial than Ponciano.

Méndez, a former dean of the law school of the University of San Carlos, is not a professional politician. He succeeded his brother Mario as head of the Revolutionary party. Mario Méndez Montenegro was found dead in his home early in November 1965. His Revolutionary party claimed it was a "political assassination"; the police, a suicide.

Few Guatemalans were confident that there would be an honest election. Colonel Peralta had peremptorily rejected supervision of the elections by representatives of the OAS. Both Méndez and Ponciano charged that there were irregularities in the counting of the ballots, and exploitation of illiterate Indians in the backlands to hand Aguilar the presidency. In his last campaign appearance, Méndez accused the Government of stuffing ballot boxes even before the day set for the election. Méndez threatened to send his followers into the streets if the Government "fixed" the election in favor of Aguilar. "It could be another Santo

Domingo," he said, "but we have no choice." Under the direct command of Turcios, Communist cadres of urban guerrilla warfare specialists were standing by to take advantage of any disorder. Acting with dispatch, the Guatemalan secret police defused this time bomb by arresting some 20 Communist leaders. (A short time later, in May, when Turcios offered to return two kidnapped officials in exchange for the captured guerrillas, the Peralta Government found itself unable to make the swap—the prisoners had "disappeared.") Aguilar's party attempted to nullify Méndez's electoral lead by charging there had been double voting, use of false identification papers, and other irregularities in Guatemala City and four other municipalities where Méndez had easily defeated the other two candidates. Since Aguilar's party had the backing of the Government which controlled the voting machinery, the charge appeared to be without any foundation.

It is now apparent that everybody guessed wrong as to the winner—Colonel Peralta, army officers, the American Embassy, the press, the Communists, and the three candidates. With the Government in control of the electoral machinery, it was assumed that Aguilar would win handily, Méndez would take second place, and Ponciano, third. Méndez not only swept Guatemala City but led his opponents in almost every other district. His 201,070 votes were short of the absolute majority required for election. That Colonel Peralta's election of Aguilar had split the Guatemalan Right is apparent from the votes received by the two military candidates: Ponciano, 110,145 and Aguilar, 146,085. Their combined vote (256,230) exceeded Méndez's 201,070.

As no candidate received an absolute majority, the newly elected Congress chose Méndez, whose party won 30 of 56 legislative seats, or two more than necessary.

Would the army permit Méndez to wear the blue and white presidential sash? This was the overriding question. Both Peralta and Méndez demonstrated remarkable maturity in effecting an orderly transfer of power. Méndez tempered his fiery campaign oratory and soft-pedaled the threat to send his partisans into the streets. With a flexibility uncommon to political men of the democratic Left, Méndez reached accommodation with the two defeated candidates, agreed to select the Minister of Defense and Chief of Staff from a list of candidates submitted by the military, and gave satisfactory assurances that his administration would not be a repetition of the Arévalo-Arbenz "social revolution." Having declared that the army would respect the results of a fair election, Peralta staked his reputation on restraining an influential sector of the officer corps from launching a coup aimed at denying Méndez the presidency.

If Méndez is allowed to become President, he will be taking over leadership of a country that cries out for economic, social, and political reforms. To be sure, Guatemala has special problems because of her large, unassimilated, and neglected Indian population. Guatemala is, however, no different from the rest of Latin America: her problems are greater than the political capacity to solve them.

The Dominican Republic

On December 20, 1962, the Dominican Republic held the first genuinely free election in her history. It was a model election. There was no intimidation, no bribery, no stuffing of ballot boxes, no dishonesty in tallying the votes, no disorder. For a people who had no experience with the electoral processes, this extraordinary performance will remain a tribute to their dignity, discipline, and innate good sense.

As members of the OAS Observation Mission which had been sent to the Dominican Republic at the request of the Council of State, I and my companion, Dr. Carlos Martínez Durán of the faculty of the University of San Carlos Medical School, Guatemala, observed the polling at nineteen precincts in Salcedo Province. One does not readily forget the experience of witnessing barefoot peasants who had walked long distances for the privilege of casting a free ballot for the presidential candidate of *their* choice. Nor does one easily forget the expression on the faces of those who, for the first time in their lives, exercised their franchise as citizens. I must state here the fact that there was an election at all is a tribute to the members of the Council of State and, especially, to the unflinching determination of three very great Dominican patriots: Dr. Rafael Bonnelly (President of the Council), Dr. Donald Reid Cabral (Member of the Council), and Dr. José Antonio Bonilla-Atiles (Secretary of State for Foreign Affairs).

Juan Bosch, candidate of the Dominican Revolutionary party, received 628,000, or 60 per cent, of the 1,055,000 votes cast. Dean Carl Spaeth of the Stanford University Law School, Dr. H. Field Haviland of the Brookings Institution—colleagues on the Mission—and I met with the President-elect on the night of December 21. Our appointment was for 10 p.m. At the precise hour, President-elect Bosch was at our hotel. We had scarcely seated ourselves when there was a knock at the door. Word of the President-elect's presence had spread among the hotel workers, several of whom asked if they might congratulate their new President. Between Bosch and his visitors there was a genuine flow of affection, and none of the contrived bonhomie of the professional politician. The incident seemed to underscore what Bosch's victory at the polls had already demonstrated: he possessed that unique charismatic quality which mesmerizes people. I remember the thought crossing my mind at the time: what if Bosch should be unable to deliver on his promises? They were big promises. This man was an idealist, a poet, a philosopher. With no political or administrative experience of his own, where would he find the technical and administrative skills for the enormous tasks which lay before him? We listened to his plans. They were exciting plans for a better life for his people.

As Bosch bade us good night, Field Haviland's last remark comes back to me. In retrospect, it was prophetic. He observed that political scientists rarely were given Bosch's opportunity to apply their lectures in the laboratory of government. Seven months after his inauguration as President of the Dominican Republic, Juan Bosch was a prisoner in the Palace at Santo Domingo.

Bosch's short-lived regime has the aspects of a Greek tragedy, with Bosch himself cast as its most tragic character. The man and his efforts were both doomed to fail. They were caught in a web of circumstances which, with an inexorable logic, moved to a preordained failure.

To appreciate this Dominican tragedy we need to understand the mind and person of Juan Bosch. A distinguished Dominican psychiatrist with whom I discussed Bosch's personality characterized him as a paranoid schizophrenic. Typically, Bosch suffered from a persecution complex and the delusion of intellectual omnipotence. Dominicans who shared Bosch's exile in Cuba and other countries of the Caribbean confirmed these traits. Bosch fancied himself an expert, among other things, on military strategy, finance, the operations of government, and politics. He once lectured a Dominican tobacco grower and cigar manufacturer (whose family had grown tobacco for over a century) on the proper cultivation of the plant. A specialist in veterinary medicine brought from Chile by the OAS left Santo Domingo in disgust after Dr. Bosch had subjected him to a "lecture." Bosch's "Papa knows best" attitude made intellectual collaboration virtually impossible; anyone who opposed his ideas was regarded as an enemy.

It is a paradox of contemporary Latin American politics that the conservative Right and the democratic Left need each other to survive. A democratic regime requires the support—or at least the benevolent neutrality—of the conservatives in order to accomplish the business of reform. A progressive, democratically oriented regime needs time to eliminate the Castro-Communist extremists. An intelligent, conservative Right needs the democratic Left to prevent its own liquidation through violent revolution. Bosch never understood this law of political survival. Actually, Bosch thought the Dominican conservatives posed a greater threat to his regime than the extremists (who, as it turned out, used Bosch for their own purposes). The Dominican conservatives in the main supported Bosch. The National Civic Union (UCN) campaigned under Dr. Viriato Fiallo with a promise, if elected, to purge the national life of Trujillo elements. It pledged full co-operation with the Alliance for Progress. Bosch's PRD called for national reconciliation instead of a purge. During his campaign, Bosch never mentioned the Alliance. Because of his moderate approach, Bosch drew support from *trujillistas,* the armed forces, and the business community as well as from peasants and city workers.

In his fear of the Dominican conservatives, Bosch was a prisoner of mythology. After living in exile for twenty-five years he was a stranger in his own country. Unlike Guatemala, Ecuador, or Peru, for example, the Dominican Republic does not have a traditional Latin American "oligarchy"—landowning aristocracy, Church, and army. History and geography saved the Dominicans from the grip of medieval oligarchy, for Santo Domingo was the staging area for the Spanish conquest. Hernán Cortés, Diego de Nicuesa, Francisco Pizarro, Vasco Núñez de Balboa, Pedro de Valdivia, Pánfilo de Narváez, Hernando de Soto, Ponce de León, Álvar Núñez Cabeza de Vaca, and the other *con-*

quistadores sailed from Santo Domingo to the Gulf of Mexico, the Isthmus, and the southern part of the continent. The Dominicans were not conquerors; they were a conquered people.

Christopher Columbus called the lovely Caribbean island which he discovered Isla Española. Santo Domingo became the administrative center of Spain's empire. "The Emperor Charles V was told that the palaces of his Governor-General and the Archbishop in Santo Domingo were far more magnificent than the imperial residences he possessed in many cities of his European dominions." [6] The imperial splendor, luxury, and administrative importance of Santo Domingo lasted a short time. For the *conquistadores*, El Dorado lay to the south—in Mexico and Peru. As the colonists followed in the train of the conquest, Santo Domingo was reduced to a port of call for the King's ships. An occasional galleon plying between the richer West Indian colonies and Cuba anchored at Santo Domingo. At the close of the eighteenth century, the colony's ruling group was so depopulated that it numbered only 40,000.

With the declaration of war against Spain by the French National Assembly on March 7, 1793, Santo Domingo became a theater of invasion by British, French, Spanish, and Haitian armies. The Haitian patriot Toussaint L'Ouverture invaded Santo Domingo in 1801. It was reconquered by the Haitian despot Jean Pierre Boyer, whose troops occupied the country for twenty-two years (1822–44). Under the Haitian occupancy "the Dominican Colony slept a sleep which was almost that of death," in the words of Sumner Welles.

The Dominican upper class—the *"primera"*—is not a plutocracy. As wealth is measured in South America, they are poor. The Dominican Republic is a microcosm in which to examine the erosion of the political and economic power of the traditional aristocracy—a development that has also occurred in other parts of Latin America. Although the traditional families retain social prestige, actual power has passed into the hands of a relatively new aristocracy—an aristocracy of business and finance. It has been in existence for perhaps sixty to seventy years. It consists largely of descendants of immigrants, each generation of which has married into the traditional families. Donald J. Reid Cabral —until the April 1965 Revolution President of the ruling

---

[6] Sumner Welles: *Naboth's Vineyard* (New York: Payson & Clarke, Ltd.; 1928), Vol. I, p. 4.

triunvirato, the government's executive body—is of English descent. John Vicini—scion of one of the island's most prominent families—is of Italian extraction. The influential Parra and Santoni families are of immigrant origin. In addition to this aristocracy of business and finance there is a *nouveau riche*—"political capitalists" who acquired their money during the Trujillo era.

Among the business aristocracy there are many who have a deep conviction that the Dominican Republic must undergo a peaceful, democratic social revolution. The Vicini family, for instance, helped finance and fought in the underground resistance against Trujillo. Many of the members of this aristocracy saw the inside of Trujillo's prisons. As late as September 21, 1963, John Vicini and other business leaders made a desperate plea to be permitted to help save the Bosch regime from imminent collapse. Bosch began his term as President with the enthusiastic support of virtually the entire conservative sector of the Dominican Republic. But he was incapable of collaborating with this group because at heart he is a romantic revolutionary to whom capitalists are anathema. It is not a coincidence that Bosch's first child was named Leon Trotsky Bosch.

The Dominican Republic is a Catholic country, and the people are deeply religious. Bosch was hostile to the Church. As an exile in Costa Rica, he once proposed breaking relations with the Vatican as a plank in his party platform. While in Rome (between his election and inauguration) he deliberately avoided requesting an audience with the Pope. He was divorced. The hierarchy of the Church may have had reservations regarding Bosch, but they were not hostile. During the last week of July 1963, the American-born Bishop Thomas F. Reilly spoke out in an attempt to save Bosch. At the same time, the Apostolic Nuncio, Emmanuele Clarizio, accompanied by the bishops of the Church, held friendly discussions with the President regarding measures which they believed were necessary for his regime to regain popular support. Unhappily, in the village parishes some Spanish-born priests sought to inflame the *campesinos* against Bosch. These latter-day Torquemadas saw Juan Bosch as the incarnation of the anti-Christ.

To the Dominican armed forces, Juan Bosch was not a Víctor Raúl Haya de la Torre. Overwhelming numbers of the military and their families voted for Bosch. The Dominican armed forces are not—as in Argentina, Peru, Ecuador, or Guatemala, for example—political-minded. Under Trujillo the armed forces were an obedient instrument of the dictatorship. The slightest indication of political interest on the part of an officer was ruthlessly extirpated. The military High Command of the Dominican armed forces were junior officers during the Trujillo era. Their hands are not stained by the brutalities of the dictatorship. They are politically astute, and have demonstrated greater responsibility and more political maturity than many of the civilian politicians. Their professional attitude represents an entirely new tradition in the Dominican armed forces. Without exception, they come from poor families. They are close to the people. They are not a military caste. In the fall of 1963, I discussed with General Víctor Elby Viñas Román, Minister of Defense, and General Renato Hungría, Chief of Staff of the army, their plans for the establishment of rural schools for teaching illiterates and the utilization of army facilities for vocational training. (During the summer of 1964 a school for training rural agricultural teachers was established at El Centro de Enseñanzas at San Isidro. The initial cadre of thirty students consisted of privates of the Dominican armed forces.)

Until the Revolution in April 1965, General Elías Wessin y Wessin was probably the key figure in the Dominican military High Command. He commanded the air force training center at the San Isidro air base. His professional career has been devoted to technical training for the Dominican air force. He has studied at Peru's general staff school. He was not a Trujillo man. "I kept my mouth shut," he told me wryly, "otherwise I wouldn't be here." As commander of El Centro de Enseñanzas he controlled the pivotal tank unit of the armed forces. (Under General "Ramfis" Trujillo the air force was built into an elite arm, with its own infantry and tank components.) General Wessin y Wessin is idolized by many of the younger officers. Of Lebanese extraction, he is deeply religious. He is convinced that Bosch's regime was turning the Dominican Republic into "another Cuba." He believes that Bosch created the civilian militia for eventual use against the armed forces. In lengthy conversations with me, he insisted that he had no political ambitions. Nevertheless, neither he nor any of the other military leaders will countenance a return to *trujillismo*—or a dictatorship of the Left. Bosch had the support of the Dominican armed forces when he assumed the presidency. He could have converted the Dominican military into a socially constructive force in the life of the people. But to a conventionally minded Caribbean revolutionary like Bosch, the Dominican armed forces were the "enemy."

For the demagogic Latin American politician an invincible oligarchy is a useful myth: it provides a visible target for political attack. In the Dominican Republic, Bosch used a fictional oligarchy as his political whipping boy. In reality, there is no single dominant power in the Dominican Republic. The strands of power are like the movement of a Swiss watch: each part is dependent upon another. When all of the Dominican power centers arrive at a consensus, the structure functions. Even the armed forces are not monolithic. They are held in balance by their own power centers. The cement which binds *la casa dominicana* is racial democracy. The Dominicans have never had a Gilberto Freyre to publicize their racial democracy: it was taken for granted. Yet Juan Bosch deliberately sought to foment racial antagonism. Illustrious Dominicans are proud of their Negro blood —Dr. Heriberto Pieter (distinguished Negro director of the Institute of Cancer at the University of Santo Domingo); the mulatto poet Domingo Moreno Jiménez; the mathematician-philosopher Andrés Avelino; Ramón Tapia (former member of the governing Executive); Donald Reid (former President of the Executive, whose blue eyes, fair skin, and blond hair are as English as his father's ancestry, but who is proud of his great-great-grandmother, a Negro slave); Dr. Nicolás Pichardo (a distinguished physician whose family includes men of Negro blood who served their country in the highest posts). Juan Bosch injected an alien substance into the finely meshed Dominican body politic. He produced chaos.

Perhaps to atone for the years it had supported the Trujillo dictatorship, the United States played a key but secret role in the conspiracy which led to Trujillo's assassination on May 30, 1961. The heroism of an American Foreign Service officer, an agent of the CIA, and an expatriate American flier and his Dominican wife (who were the nerve center of the conspiracy) is a tale of adventure still to be told. Of the company of seven Dominicans who were directly involved with the liquidation of the tyrant only one survived: Antonio Imbert Barrera, the driver of the car used in the ambush of Trujillo. He was wounded in the exchange of gunfire. His companions were killed. The only surviving member of another conspiratorial group was Luis Amiama Tío. Imbert once told me: "My position in this country is unique. No one can challenge it. To do so would require the reincarnation of Trujillo, or one of my companions who died in action. I am the only survivor of the action which freed my people from the Trujillo tyranny."

Bosch was among the first of the exiles to return to the Dominican Republic after Trujillo's murder. He grossly misjudged the temper of his people by announcing that democratic government could evolve under Trujillo's heir, the notorious playboy General Rafael ("Ramfis") Trujillo, Jr. Bosch's statement stirred public opinion into anger; a hostile crowd besieged his house. He appealed to the greatly respected physician Viriato Fiallo to rescue him. During the election campaign Bosch returned Dr. Fiallo's kindness by denouncing him as a *tutumpote* (a colloquial word meaning "reactionary oligarch").

Encouraged by the United States, "Ramfis" Trujillo planned to continue his father's reign but with a few superficial democratic trappings. Dominican patriots, who fought in the underground against the dictatorship and suffered unspeakable tortures in Trujillo's prisons, were in no mood for *ersatz* democracy. On August 16, 1961 (a national holiday commemorating the second Dominican republic), Dr. Viriato Fiallo left his old-fashioned house in the old quarter of Santo Domingo where he practices medicine. He proceeded along the narrow streets where, as in Calle de las Damas, it is said the ghosts of colonial Spain walk in the early hours of the morning. Standing beside the three heroes of the Republic—Durate, Sánchez, and Mella—in the Plaza Independencia, Dr. Fiallo galvanized his countrymen with his celebrated *grito: "¡Basta ya!"* ("We've had enough!"). With this cry the Dominicans began their anguished search for democratic government—a search which still continues.

In the turmoil that ensued after Trujillo's death, the island was the scene of burning sugar-cane fields, street riots, police brutalities, and political murders. On November 19, 1961, the last of the Trujillo family fled after an exercise in "gunboat diplomacy" by the United States Navy. On January 1, 1962, a seven-man Council of State took office as a provisional government until elections could be held and a permanent government installed. Joaquín Balaguer —a distinguished intellectual but an ambiguous political figure who had long served Trujillo—became President of the Council. Both Imbert and Amiama became members of the

Council. Upon their own insistence they were made generals of the army with the rank of brigadier, but without actual command because of the objections of the regular army. A connection with the Dominican armed forces was a shield for Imbert and Amiama against the danger of their extermination by hired killers in the employ of "Ramfis" Trujillo, who had sworn to avenge his father's murder. Imbert (who invariably wears a uniform) and Amiama (who prefers natty civilian attire) are never seen without side arms. Amiama carries a regulation army pistol on his hip. Imbert wears a Spanish gun with pearl handle and intricately carved barrel. The homes of both men are guarded night and day by armed troops.

The Council of State had barely set up its offices in the former Trujillo Palace when, on January 16, 1962, the secretary of the armed forces, General Rodríguez Echavarría, executed a *coup d'état*. His accomplice was Balaguer. The other members of the Council of State were placed under house arrest in the military club at the San Isidro air base. The Council was replaced by a *junta cívica militar*. Curiously, its membership included Amiama and Imbert. For the second time in this period of turbulence and violence, the United States reacted sternly, sharply, and promptly. It released a strongly worded note stating that it would move to reinstate economic sanctions (imposed by the OAS against Trujillo and lifted only shortly before) unless the Council of State was restored to its governing status. On January 18, 1962, a group of young air force officers led by the then Captain Elías Wessin y Wessin freed the Council, arrested their own commanding officer, and shortly thereafter sent him into exile. Balaguer found it convenient to leave the country and was succeeded in the presidency of the Council by Dr. Rafael Bonnelly, patriarch of the Dominican political structure. In passing, this action by Captain Wessin y Wessin in preventing an incipient military dictatorship won him the respect and high regard of the influential centers of Dominican public opinion and of the armed forces.

In the Greek drama the tragic hero enters the stage exalted by his fame and honors. He displays *hubris*—"the insolence of irreverence"—a sin condemned by the gods. The Dominican tragic hero, Juan Bosch, exhibited his *hubris*. Between his election and inauguration Bosch was warmly received in Washington by President Kennedy. Bosch was the chosen instrument for the Alliance of Progress in the Caribbean. The Dominican experiment would be the democratic answer to Castro and his revolution. In Paris, *le grand Charles* received Bosch at the Élysée Palace, an honor not usually conferred upon a President-elect of a Caribbean sugar republic. His return to Santo Domingo was a Roman triumph: thousands greeted him at the airport and in the city. On February 17, shortly after his triumphal return, Bosch spoke to the Dominican people over radio and television. His marathon speech, which lasted several hours, shocked the thoughtful centers of opinion. Juan Bosch the presidential candidate had campaigned on a platform of reconciliation of all sectors of Dominican society. Juan Bosch the President-elect spoke scornfully of the conservatives who had supported his candidacy. Gone was the humility of the candidate in search of votes. In his place was an arrogant *caudillo*. The economic program that Bosch unveiled to a startled people bore no resemblance to his moderate campaign speeches. This speech resembled, in its length and its content, the familiar television harangues of Havana.

The triumvirate of the Caribbean—Muñoz Marín, Betancourt, and Figueres—gathered at Santo Domingo on February 27, 1963, for Bosch's inauguration. Present, too, were Presidents Orlich of Costa Rica and Villeda of Honduras. Lyndon Johnson, then the Vice-President, represented the United States. Bosch shocked his compatriots by refusing to accept the presidential sash—the symbol of his office—from his predecessor, Dr. Rafael Bonnelly. He offended Don Luis Muñoz Marín—friend, mentor, and host during his exile in Puerto Rico—by refusing at first to invite him to the ceremonies. Betancourt was incensed that Bosch should peremptorily order him to recall the Venezuelan ambassador because—as Bosch charged—he had been partial to Dr. Viriato Fiallo, Bosch's principal opponent in the election campaign.

As the Greek tragic hero is powerless to resist his fate, Bosch, too, was caught in a web of doom. He had a premonition of the impending catastrophe. Shortly after taking office, he remarked to a colleague that he felt as if he were the protagonist in a Greek morality play. Bosch assumed the presidency in an environment poisoned by conspiracy. Life under Trujillo had been a perpetual conspiracy. Trujillo's murder was planned and executed by a conspiracy. Dominicans are incapable of functioning except by conspiratorial action. One of the most respected members of the former Council of State told me at a reception on the day

following Bosch's election that he had been approached by
trujillistas to join in a *coup d'état* to prevent Bosch from
taking office.

Someone has said that the trouble with Latin Americans
is that they are Latin Americans. Bosch embodied all of the
troubles in his own person. He could not tolerate criticism.
He was unable to delegate authority. He offended old and
tried friends. He preached democracy but practiced *caudillismo*. He dismissed the members of the Electoral Board,
the body that had made his own election possible, and replaced them with political henchmen. He packed the judiciary with party followers, thus destroying its independence. Bosch used his own party as a vehicle to accomplish
the "dirty work" of carrying out controversial Leftist reforms. At the same time, he was engaged in liquidating his
own party because at heart he was a *caudillo* who could not
tolerate the political discipline of party organization. It is
significant that at the moment when his downfall was imminent, his own party did not rise to defend him. This was
left to the Castro-Communists. Indeed, as recently as January 11, 1964, Ángel Miolán, then president of the
Partido Revolucionario Dominicano—Bosch's party—said he
was convinced that Bosch was trying to destroy him and the
party. He went on to say: "If the armed forces had consulted
the legislative members of the party, the *coup d'état* could
have occurred without interrupting constitutional succession.
We [the party] had ready a ten-point ultimatum for Bosch.
If he had not accepted our ultimatum he would have been
repudiated by the Congress. There was an agreement by the
majority of the legislators on this point." [7] He did not regard the presidency as a responsibility to govern in behalf
of all the people. Interestingly, less than a month following
the election, this identical observation was drawn to the attention of the Minister of Foreign Affairs of Venezuela in
a diplomatic report prepared by the *chargé d'affaires* of the
embassy of Venezuela at Santo Domingo. In his report, Don
Rafael A. León Morales said: ". . . in reality, Bosch will
not be the President of all Dominicans. Juan Bosch will govern with the PRD, and with an olympian disregard for the

[7] An interview with Ángel Miolán by Pedro Álvaro Bobadilla,
published in *El Caribe* (a leading Santo Domingo paper), January 11,
1964, p. 9.

views of the other parties, of the other sectors, of other Dominicans." [8]

The *éminence grise* of the Bosch regime was Sacha Volman. A Rumanian-born, naturalized United States citizen, Volman was nominally head of the autonomous Dominican agency for economic development—Centro Interamericano de Estudios Sociales. Responsible Dominicans believed that Volman was an agent of the CIA. When pressed for evidence they said their information came from friends in Costa Rica, who had known Volman intimately during the years when he was ostensibly an instructor (as was Bosch) at the Instituto de Educación Política, a school financed by the CIA for training younger Latin Americans for political action. Volman occupied the luxurious villa of Trujillo's daughter, Flor de Oro. Four other former Trujillo houses located in various parts of the country were also used as hideaways by Volman. Haina Mosa—"Ramfis" Trujillo's Lucullan villa with a swimming pool on its second floor—served as Volman's headquarters for training political students, and Volman had his own private security guards there.

Bosch violated the customary guarantees of freedom of assembly and due process of law. In retaliation for a nationwide shopkeepers' strike, he ordered General Belisario Peguero, chief of the national police, to deport fifteen foreign merchants of Santo Domingo—five Chinese, five Lebanese, and five Spaniards. Bosch was forced to abandon this operation when the Santo Domingo papers printed scathing editorials denouncing his arbitrary and undemocratic act. Because they were critical of his actions, Bosch arbitrarily shut down six privately owned radio stations and one TV station. He tried to bring *El Caribe* (which supported his candidacy but criticized his authoritarian methods when he was President) into line by withholding payments for the printing of official government notices and by intimations that the paper would be expropriated.[9]

Bosch demonstrated that professors are not politicians and that the political trade cannot be mastered overnight. In the naïve belief that his massive *campesino* support at the

[8] The confidential report was "leaked" to the press at Caracas and reprinted in *El Caribe* on March 23, 1963.

[9] The publisher of *El Caribe,* Germán Emilio Ornes, was for many years an exile after his newspaper was expropriated by Trujillo. After Trujillo's death and through the efforts of the Inter-American Press Association, he regained possession of his property.

polls had somehow already created a revolution, Bosch spurned political collaboration with the opposition leaders. He turned his back on Amiama and Imbert, both of whom had supported him in the election campaign. The magnitude of his electoral victory contributed to his downfall. The opposition parties were not afforded an opportunity to debate legislative bills. A bill to provide legislative sanction for a contract which Bosch had negotiated with a group of European financiers for $150 million of public works was scarcely debated before its enactment by the PRD-dominated Congress. (After Bosch's downfall, an analysis by a leading attorney of Santo Domingo and a financial expert of the World Bank revealed that Bosch's so-called contract was in reality a "brokerage agreement." It did not bind the European financiers to anything.) Another bill introduced by Bosch to recover concealed assets of the Trujillos and their henchmen was so loosely drawn as to pose a threat of confiscation for virtually any businessmen who had ever done any business under the Trujillo dictatorship. Labor was angered by Bosch's attempt to force all unions into a government-controlled confederation. Catholics were disturbed over the legalization of divorce and plans to extend government control over education.

Bosch's proposal for a new Dominican Constitution created widespread dismay and alarm among those who had supported his candidacy. It was not an instrument embodying basic democratic principles. It was a catalogue of economic and political nostrums and, like so many Latin American "constitutions," nothing more than a party platform. To silence opposition to his proposed Constitution, Bosch resorted to the demagogue's oldest and shabbiest trick: he used the invasion of the grounds of the Dominican Embassy at Port-au-Prince by Duvalier's strong-arm ruffians, the infamous *tonton-macoute*, as a pretext for creating public hysteria. He ordered the Dominican armed forces to the Haitian frontier. Over the radio he threatened to invade Haiti and to destroy its capital. In Santo Domingo, Bosch's "Haitian war" was referred to jokingly as *la guerra de la constitución*. Nevertheless, the confusion engendered by the Haitian "crisis" served Bosch's purpose—the Constitution was approved.

By spring 1963, public confidence in Bosch and his administration had virtually vanished as a result of a series of events involving the use of arms by civilians. The secret

service of the Dominican armed forces, I was told, learned
that a member of Bosch's cabinet had purchased a sizable
quantity of small arms in Venezuela. They were shipped to
Santo Domingo on a vessel owned by another member of
his cabinet.[10] Bosch placed an order with the American military authorities for 100 AR–13 rifles used by the United
States Army. When it was learned they were for use by
Bosch's own political party, the Pentagon canceled the order.
I was told that the Dominican military attaché in London
informed his superiors that a member of Bosch's cabinet was
negotiating for the purchase of small arms valued at 1 million pounds. At police headquarters I was told that over a
period of several months the supervisor of the government's
arsenal at San Cristóbal—Camilo Todeman, aged thirty-
one, a German who came to the Dominican Republic in 1952
from Stuttgart—sold at least 70 submachine guns and about
300 rifles to Bosch's party followers. According to the police,
30 submachine guns were found at a place called Loma
Cotui. (Early in December 1963, Todeman was captured
with a band of pro-Castro guerrillas who had been engaged
in armed insurrection in the mountains. He admitted his
complicity in the clandestine sale of weapons, but sought to
exonerate himself by claiming that he was a double agent
working for the Communists and the United States. He insisted that he had supplied information on the arms transaction to an attaché of the American Embassy. To prove
the accuracy of her husband's story, Todeman's wife delivered one of the attaché's cards, with his phone number
written on it, to a high Dominican official. Todeman maintained that, in return for his services to the American Embassy official, he hoped to obtain visas for himself and his
wife to travel to the United States.) In the Dominican
"cloak and dagger" game, it was virtually impossible to dis-
tinguish Communists from CIA agents. Frequently they were
identical. An honored and respected member of the foreign
colony in Santo Domingo informed me that when he showed
a list of well-known Communists to an officer of the Ameri-

---

[10] General Elías Wessin y Wessin has testified before a committee
of the United States Senate that arms were smuggled into the Dominican Republic on the freighter *Bordaco,* owned by Diego Bordas,
Secretary of State for Industry and Commerce in the Bosch cabinet,
and on Aerovias Quisqueyanas, an airline also owned by Bordas. See
Testimony of Brigadier General Elías Wessin y Wessin, Hearing before the Subcommittee of the Committee on the Judiciary, United
States Senate, 89th Cong., 1st sess. (October 1, 1965), pp. 122–24.

can Embassy, he was told: "Lay off those people! They're CIA."

These developments have a special meaning when coupled with two additional facts. Mysterious fires broke out in the sugar-cane fields. Many believed they were "Reichstag fires" to justify the organization of a militia to serve ostensibly as armed guards for the cane fields. General Wessin y Wessin told me there were at least forty training centers for the militia. Figures vary as to the actual number of *milicianos* in being and planned. Some officials thought there were 2,000 militia, with plans for an eventual 15,000 to 18,000. Others believed there were only 800 actual militia, with a planned expansion up to 20,000. The facts will probably never be known. The cardinal question is: Why did Bosch want a militia? The national police had 9,500 well-armed men— armed, incidentally, with the most modern "riot weapons" supplied by the Agency for International Development. The Dominican armed forces had about 20,000 troops. Surely this force was more than adequate to guard the cane fields against saboteurs. It is difficult not to conclude that Bosch's purpose in creating an armed militia was to provoke a conflict with the regular armed forces.

The dénouement was rapidly approaching. On July 14, 1963, the general staff of the armed forces invited Bosch to meet with them at San Isidro. The purpose of the meeting was to acquaint the President with the deep concern of the general staff over the creation of the *milicias,* with their Cuban overtones; the tolerance of his administration toward well-known international Communists in the government; and the growing public uneasiness over the administration's Leftist orientation. The Chiefs of Staff assured the President of their complete loyalty. Bosch replied angrily that the military were involving themselves in civil matters, that he knew how to handle the Communists, and that the meeting constituted a *golpe de estado* (*coup d'état*). Under the circumstances, Bosch said, he had no alternative but to resign.

Curiously, Manuel Tavarez Justo, president of the 14th of June Movement—a pro-Castro organization—was the first to learn of the San Isidro meeting. On July 15th, advertisements sponsored by the 14th of June Movement appeared in the Dominican papers with a warning of an imminent *golpe.* On July 16, Bosch addressed the country over radio and television. He denounced the military for its attempt at a *coup d'état.* Scornfully, he said any *golpe* would fail *"porque los militares saben que un golpe de estado durará en la República Dominicana lo que una cucaracha en un gallinero"* ("because the military knows that in the Dominican Republic a *coup d'état* will be crushed like a cockroach in a chicken yard"). All of the Chiefs of Staff told me of their shock and outrage at Bosch's deliberate distortion of the meeting of July 14. I have listened to a tape recording of this speech. It left me with the strong impression of a man delivering his own funeral oration. Bosch knew he had failed. The speech was designed to prepare the way for his exit. He concluded his swan song by exhorting Dominican youth to be on guard against enslavement of their country by foreign capital.

During August, tension reached the boiling point. A popular movement identified as a *movimiento anticomunista cristiano* electrified the country with its Sunday demonstrations. The first demonstration in Santo Domingo on August 4 drew an estimated crowd of 30,000. The man who led the movement, José Andrés Aybar Castellanos (Secretary of Finance during the Reid Cabral government), is an accountant whose family has been in the Dominican Republic for over three hundred years. From discussions with Aybar and others associated with the movement, I am satisfied it was not—as Bosch charged—a reactionary political movement secretly organized by the armed forces. On the contrary, the *movimiento* was inspired by fundamental Christian ethics: its objective was to create a renaissance of the humanity of Christ among all sectors of the population. It held *cursios*—gatherings at which rich and poor, master and servant, men and women of every rank and condition who were never brought together, shared a communion of spirit. The chaplain of the air force, Padre Marcial Silva, led the *cursios* among the armed forces. How well he succeeded is illustrated by an incident which I observed at the military mass to which I was invited by General Wessin y Wessin on the Sunday following President Kennedy's assassination. In the presence of civilians, officers and enlisted men together made their confession. This act of Catholic humility will not usually be witnessed among the armed forces of any other Latin American country. Padre Marcial became the object of Bosch's venom. In his broadcast on July 16 he demanded that Padre Marcial be fired.

To allay the explosive tensions, the Partido Social Cristiano selected three distinguished Dominicans—Dr. Ángel

Liz, Dr. Miguel Piantini, and Dr. René Puig—to serve as a committee of mediation between Bosch's regime and a disillusioned public. Bosch declined to hear their recommendations.

Bosch was aware of the gathering storm. During August he visited Santiago de los Caballeros, the island's second largest city. He announced that he would make a number of changes in his cabinet. It was soon apparent that Bosch either was insincere or lacked courage to make the changes. Individuals whom Bosch approached learned that he had offered the same portfolio to others. In any event, he did not change the composition of his cabinet.

On September 18 the storekeepers throughout the country closed their doors in protest against the government. (It was this strike which caused Bosch's order for the deportation of the fifteen foreign merchants.)

On September 23 at 6:30 a.m. Radio Santo Domingo—the government-owned broadcasting station—announced that Haitian armed forces had bombarded Dajabón, a frontier town. At 8 a.m., while still at breakfast, Bosch summoned the Chiefs of Staff to the Palace. He stated that a Dominican air base as well as Dajabón had been shelled and that he was endeavoring to place a call to Washington requesting immediate action by the OAS.[11] Bosch ordered the air force command to have an aircraft drop leaflets over Port-au-Prince, warning the inhabitants that the city would be bombed at 11 a.m. General Hungría, former Chief of Staff of the army, placed a call to his field commander on the Haitian frontier, who reported that Dajabón and the air base had not been shelled, that all was quiet on the frontier. General Hungría so advised President Bosch. He dismissed the report. (General Hungría told me that the Venezuelan and American military attachés, who had called on him during the day, both stated there was no truth to Bosch's assertions. They knew from their own intelligence there had been no bombardment.) At this juncture, Commodore Rib Santamaría proposed that before the air force bombed Port-au-Prince, an on-the-spot check be made by officers of the

11 Bosch sent a cable to his ambassador, del Rosario (who was not accredited to the OAS). Arturo Calventi, the ambassador to the OAS, a hold-over from the Council of State, was not informed. The cable is dated September 23, 1963, and was dispatched from Santo Domingo at 8:30 a.m. Although signed by Héctor García Godoy, Foreign Minister, there is no record at the Dominican Foreign Office to show that the cable was drafted in the Foreign Ministry.

general staff and the President be advised of their findings. Bosch agreed reluctantly. Upon termination of the conference with the Chiefs of Staff, Bosch summoned the diplomatic corps to the Palace and informed them of the "bombardment" on the Haitian frontier.

At 10 a.m., accompanied by three members of the Santo Domingo press, eight general staff officers left for the frontier. They reached the border at 12:30 p.m. They found no evidence of mortar shelling or artillery bombardment. They did find—on the Dominican side of the frontier—General Léon Cantave, the Haitian general, who supposedly was leading the Haitian forces of liberation. The official inspection report states that General Cantave was wearing a "gray cashmere suit, white shirt, and was carrying three suitcases." The report concludes: *"Estaba impecablemente vestido"* ("He was dressed impeccably"). Upon their return to Santo Domingo, the military informed President Bosch of their findings. Bosch appeared shaken by the report. His reply was: *"Está bien"* ("O.K.").

At 10:10 on the same morning, a spokesman for the Dominican Embassy in Washington announced that a cable from Santo Domingo had advised that the bombardment from Haiti was continuing and that the government was taking all necessary steps to protect Dominican lives and property. The president of the Council of the Organization of American States, Ambassador Gonzalo Facio, summoned an emergency meeting of the Council. Bosch dispatched an ultimatum to President Duvalier declaring that Port-au-Prince would be bombed unless the Haitian attack ceased within three hours.

Why did Bosch perpetrate this farce? Why did he seek to embroil his country in a meaningless war with Haiti? Why did he persist in this hoax after his own Chiefs of Staff knew that the "bombardment" was a figment of his imagination? Why did he deliberately embarrass the OAS? Why did he make a laughingstock of the international press who in good faith reported the incident as another "Latin American crisis"? The answer is clear: the classic textbook prescription for the revolutionary demagogue in critical straits is to create an "incident"—preferably with a traditional enemy. This transfers popular attention from a domestic crisis to a war crisis. This hoary device has been used time after time by Nasser, Sukarno, and other demagogues. Bosch's "incident" would have worked but for one fly in the ointment: the Dominican armed forces.

The climax of Juan Bosch's strategy of deception was reached on September 25, 1963. At 7 p.m. Manuel Tavarez Justo, "maximum leader" of the pro-Castro 14th of June Movement (who became a guerrilla early in December and was shot in an engagement with a military patrol near La Manacla in the island's central *cordillera*), addressed the country over the government radio facilities. His speech was a defense of Bosch's dismal record—a record of irresponsibility, international deception, and betrayal of democracy. A shocked Dominican public asked: why should the leader of the Castro-Communist movement be given radio time on the government-owned station to defend the Bosch regime? After this performance, even the die-hards wondered if Bosch—intentionally or unintentionally—was a puppet whose strings were pulled by a bearded showman on a neighboring island.

Later the same evening there was a reception at the Armed Forces Club for Admiral William E. Ferrall of the United States Navy. Bosch commented on the presence of only three air force officers. He stated that this was tantamount to insubordination. (I asked General Atila Luna, former Chief of Staff of the air force, why he was absent. He replied: "I was not invited by the President.") Bosch requested the Minister of Defense, General Viñas Román, to direct the Chiefs of Staff to appear at his house. General Viñas replied that he would accompany the President with those officers present at the reception. At his house Bosch insisted that the absence of General Atila Luna was an act of insubordination. Bosch suggested that the Chiefs attend a Mexican folk festival then performing in Santo Domingo, but that all Chiefs and Deputy Chiefs of Staff were to report to the Palace upon its conclusion.

Around one o'clock on the morning of September 26 the military arrived at the Palace in response to Bosch's request. Bosch demanded that Colonel Elías Wessin y Wessin be fired from the service because he was planning a *golpe*. General Atila Luna, when reached by telephone, declared the charge false. He defended Wessin y Wessin as a loyal, disciplined officer, and refused to obey the order. Colonel Marcos Rivera Cuesta stated: "Mr. President, it is too late to expect us to make changes that will destroy the unity of the armed forces." Commodore Rib Santamaría observed: "If you fire Wessin y Wessin, it will mean blood." Bosch replied: "Nothing will deter me from my course." Thereupon Bosch announced that unless Colonel Wessin was dismissed, he would resign. At this juncture, the military retired to the office of General Viñas.

After the departure of the military High Command (it was now about 3 a.m.), Bosch summoned Fabio Herrera, under secretary of the office of the presidency. (Herrera was until the April 1965 Revolution the permanent nonpolitical, career civil servant in the Dominican governmental hierarchy who provided administrative continuity between the successive regimes in power.) In the presence of Herrera, Dr. Miguel Domínguez-Guerra, Minister of Interior, Don Antonio Guzmán, Minister of Agriculture, and Colonel Julio A. Calderón Fernández, chief of staff of the office of the presidency, Bosch read the text of his handwritten resignation as President of the Republic. Upon concluding Bosch remarked: *"Esto se acabó"* ("This is finished"). He requested Herrera to summon a stenographer and to have the Chamber of Deputies called into session "at noon." Colonel Julio A. Calderón Fernández informed the Minister of Defense of the President's resignation. Shortly thereafter General Viñas Román appeared at the President's office. In the presence of the Minister of Defense, the Vice-President of the Republic, Licenciado Jacobo Majluta (Minister of Finance), and several other members of the cabinet, Bosch again read the text of his resignation. Sometime between 3:30 and 4 Imbert and Amiama arrived at the Palace. At approximately 4 a.m. General Viñas returned. Removing his service pistol, he entered the President's office. His statement to President Bosch, as it has been repeated to me by the only civilian member of the government who was present, was: "Mr. President, as you have chosen to resign from your office as President of the Republic it is my duty to invite your arrest." Continuing, General Viñas asked: "Where, Mr. President, would it be most convenient for you to remain under custody?" Bosch replied: "Here."

Before sunrise on September 26 the military requested a meeting of the leaders of all the Dominican political parties. They were asked to form a new government. By September 27, the political leaders had agreed upon three men to serve as a *triunvirato*—the Executive of the new government. Selected and willing to serve were: Emilio de los Santos (who had been deposed by Bosch as head of the Electoral Board) as President;[12] Manuel Enrique Tavares Espaillat, an engineer-industrialist; and Ramón Tapia Espinal, a prominent lawyer. Six leaders of the political parties and the military thereupon signed a formal document in which they agreed to give their support to the *triunvirato*.

Sometimes it takes a brilliant cartoonist to catch a tragic mood. Herblock of the *Washington Post* depicted the whole somber tragedy of the Dominican debacle with a few strokes of his pen. In the background of his drawing he shows the continent with a line of ragged people along its shores. In the foreground, in a glass coffin, lies the body of a *señorita* —"Dominican Democracy." A wreath has been placed over her body—"From the U.S.A." And then Block's biting caption—"Latin American Showcase."

In the world of mythology Juan Bosch is a martyr, sacrificed on the altar of democracy. But in the world of reality, his failure as a democratic political leader handed Castro a bloodless victory. The Cuban propaganda is making it clear, not only to the Dominican people but also to the already eager ears of Latin America's youth, that there is only one way to make a social revolution—the Cuban way.[13]

Bolívar's bitter and tragic legacy to Latin America was a military system which refuses to recognize the supremacy of the civil authority as it is known in Great Britain and the United States. The fundamental axiom governing the relation between the military and the civil authority in a democracy was once expressed by General Omar Bradley, one of America's very great soldier-statesman, with absolute finality in these words: "Economically, politically, and militarily the control of our country resides with the civilian executive and legislative agencies." Lest it be assumed that the doctrine of civil supremacy has not been challenged within the American military establishment, it is well to re-

[12] Don Emilio de los Santos resigned as President on December 22, 1963. He was succeeded by Donald J. Reid Cabral, a businessman who was a Vice-President of the former Council of State. He was Foreign Minister at the time of Don Emilio de los Santos' resignation. Dr. Reid was in Israel for the signing of the Treaty of Jerusalem when he was notified of his designation as President of the *triunvirato*. Dr. Ramón Tapia Espinal resigned in April 1964, and was succeeded by Dr. Ramón Cáceres Troncoso, former Dominican ambassador in Rome. Dr. Manuel Enrique Tavares Espaillat resigned on June 27, 1964.

[13] For a discussion of the April 1965 Dominican Revolution, see pp. 258 ff.

call the most celebrated example in contemporary times, that of General Douglas MacArthur, who said in 1952: "I find in existence a new and heretofore unknown and dangerous concept that the members of our armed forces owe primary allegiance or loyalty to those who temporarily exercise the authority of the Executive Branch of Government rather than to the country and its constitution which they are sworn to defend." President Truman resolved this threat to the civil authority by removing the most brilliant and probably the most colorful soldier of World War II. Secretary of Defense McNamara incurred the resentment of some of the Pentagon hierarchy because of his blunt enforcement of his own executive authority. President Kennedy reiterated the American doctrine in unequivocal language: "Our arms must be subject to ultimate civilian control at all times." What the American doctrine implies is not just "professionalism," but categorical acceptance of the supremacy of civil authority.

One of the most frequently raised questions regarding Latin America is: What can be done to eliminate its militarism or to curb the military's proclivity for politics? Implicit in the question is the thought that the Latin American military establishments ought to be remade in the image of the North American or British establishment. Someone once said that every American is a missionary at heart. This American propensity for wanting to make over the world in our own image can be both mischievous and frustrating. Much of the contemporary world is not eager to emulate the American experience. The emerging lands do not find our unique political democracy useful. Many of the developed countries have a historic relationship with the administrative powers of a strong central state and a conception of economic planning which makes the American market economy largely inapposite. The American system, therefore, is not necessarily the ultimate goal for the rest of the world. This may also be true of the unique development of the American military establishment, with its allegiance to the civil authority and its avoidance of political involvement. In short, the American experience is an island unto itself.

Octavio Paz, the Mexican poet and essayist, once described the difference in attitudes between us and Latin America this way: "The North American considers the world to be something that can be perfected . . . we consider it to be something that can be redeemed." It is precisely this difference in attitude which holds the key to a more fruitful approach in dealing with Latin America's militarism.

Before examining what might be realistically undertaken, it may be useful, first, to clear away some of the underbrush that obstructs our thinking and actions. The first point to be kept in mind is that the United States is largely responsible for having created the military Frankenstein in Latin America. Wholesale dumping of surplus equipment from World War II helped to produce Latin America's swollen armies. Aside from Cuba (which has the largest and most modern military force in Latin America), the armed forces of Latin America consist of about 650,000 soldiers, sailors, and marines. In addition, in most Latin American countries the police are a paramilitary force. It costs about $1.4 billion annually to maintain Latin America's military establishment.

Latin America's armies, navies, and air forces have no role to play in the defense of the Western Hemisphere against thermonuclear attack. As the Cuban missile crisis demonstrated, in a showdown the United States takes charge. The only legitimate mission of Latin America's armed forces is internal security. An annual expenditure of over $1 billion for a police force of 650,000 men makes no sense for impoverished countries hovering on the edge of bankruptcy. This is the core of the problem. When Latin America's intellectuals and *yanqui*-baiters complain about the supply of arms by the United States, they are using the United States as a scapegoat for their own frustrations arising from their inability to come to grips with their own problem—the disproportionate share of the national budgets siphoned off by their own military establishments. Against the $1 billion or more spent annually on obsolete armaments by Latin America, the $55 million of United States military assistance is really small change. What some of our Latin American critics ignore is the effort by the United States Government to dissuade some countries—Peru and Brazil are examples—from purchasing obsolete cruisers and aircraft carriers which they do not need and cannot afford to maintain.

Whether the United States Government approves or not, armaments will be sold to Latin American countries by British, French, Italian, and German manufacturers. What the United States can do in these circumstances is to sell cheaper, sell less, and keep sophisticated weapons off the market. This is precisely what the Pentagon is doing. As an illustration of the current practice, Argentina recently agreed to purchase 50 jet attack planes, the A-4B, from the Douglas Aircraft Company at a cost of about $170,000 each. Though this aircraft is considered to be a conventional weapon by the United States air force, it is for the Argentine air force an advanced weapon. The French were pushing their Mirage aircraft, which is reputed to cost up to $1 million. Fifty Mirages would have cost Argentina more than five times as much as 50 A-4B's. If a country beset by as many economic troubles as Argentina must have such advanced weapons, it has saved at least $40 million by purchasing American aircraft. In other words, if you can't abolish sin, you can keep it in check.

The inarticulated reasons for the supply of arms by the United States to Latin America's military establishments are political ones. In a continent racked by revolutionary ferment, Latin America's military forces are the only centers of stability. In the majority of the countries, they are the dominant power structure. With few exceptions, the military is for all practical purposes *the* government throughout the area. Its influence is determinative. This fact of life is the real reason for a United States military presence in Latin America. By supporting Latin America's military establishments, the United States buys a kind of insurance against repetition of Cuban-style revolution. Foreign aid under the guise of promoting economic and social development enables poor countries to support military establishments which they could not otherwise afford to maintain.

After the April 1965 Dominican Revolution, the effectiveness of the insurance coverage by Latin American armies against Castro-inspired revolutions may be open to question. The Dominican armed forces had the reputation of being a highly disciplined force. Yet Dominican officers took their own Chief of Staff prisoner, conspired with the Castro-oriented 14th of June Movement, and opened their arsenals to mobs and Communist paramilitary units. Attendance at the United States' School of the Americas did not immunize these officers from the Communist virus, nor instill in them respect for the civil authority.

Another myth tenaciously held onto by American liberals is that the United States Government should not grant diplomatic recognition to a military junta. If there is any lesson to be learned from our Latin American experience, it is that the withholding of diplomatic recognition of a military junta will not cause the system to roll over and die. The hard fact

of the matter is that the Latin American military is utterly
indifferent to whether Washington withholds or grants diplomatic recognition. For the Latin American military understands thoroughly—and recent diplomatic experience in Argentina, Peru, Guatemala, Ecuador, Honduras, and Brazil
serves only to underscore their assurance—that the United
States has no other alternative but to grant diplomatic recognition to a military junta whether it operates behind the
thin gauze of a civilian regime (as it did in Argentina) or
holds the levers of governmental power directly as in Brazil
(or as it did in Peru, Guatemala, and Ecuador). Implicit
in the attitude of the Latin American military is an instinctive sense that Washington understands where actual
power lies. In those countries where the military is in fact
the real power structure—Argentina, Brazil, Peru, and Guatemala are examples—the logic of *Realpolitik* would require
two sets of diplomatic representation: one to the nominal
civilian government at the *palacio*, the other to the actual
government at the *cuartel*. Latin Americans have long entertained the suspicion that in practice something of the sort
exists in the roles of the American ambassador and the head
of the American military mission. A gifted and imaginative
military aide can be an effective and influential diplomatic
representative to the armed forces as, for example, Marine
Corps Lieutenant Colonel Bevan G. Cass, former naval attaché in the Dominican Republic. Finally, in the cold war
climate which has enveloped the Western Hemisphere, there
is perhaps the further realization on the part of Latin America's military that Washington is unwilling to gamble with
the consequences of a military regime which is allowed to
fish in Soviet waters.

Still another approach which strikes me as likely to be
barren of results is that of asking the Latin American military establishments to disarm voluntarily. The various proposals for disarmament and arms limitation which have been
advanced at inter-American gatherings all have one glaring
weakness: in effect, they advocate technological unemployment. If there is one lesson to be learned from history it is
that, from the glass-blowers in the early days of the Industrial
Revolution in England to the railroad workers in the era of
automation in the United States, the forced displacement of
jobs is resisted fiercely.

It is a truism that in Latin America, as elsewhere in the
world, money talks. There isn't a Latin American colonel

or general who is not aware of the location of the honeypot.
If withholding of diplomatic recognition cuts no ice, withholding of aid money hurts: this is the kind of leverage
which the military mind understands. The United States, as
Latin America's principal banker, is in a position to control
the *quid* which can produce the *quo*. It would be entirely
within our rights to make American participation in commodity stabilization agreements (as well as other types of
economic assistance) contingent upon the deployment of a
specified number of troops for highway construction, sanitation work, school and hospital construction, the supplying of
teachers for illiterates, establishment of industrial training
schools, and other constructive works. This type of activity
fits into programs with which the Latin American military
is familiar. This is not an attempt to eradicate the disease—
that is beyond our power. It is an approach that would utilize
a technically trained resource for socially constructive purposes.

How, it may be asked, is this approach different from
what the United States is now doing through its "civic action"
programs, which utilize part of military assistance funds for
Corps of Engineer projects? The difficulty with the military
assistance programs conceived as "public works" is that they
attack only a small part of the problem. Whether or not they
are adopted and how extensively they will be utilized are
matters of grace. What I am suggesting is the large-scale ap-
plication of the ancient carrot-and-stick technique. Although
there are many dedicated officers associated with "civic
action," it lacks imaginative direction, high priority, and
enough personnel from the Corps of Engineers. The entire
program is budgeted at some $9 million, which is the best
indication that the program is not taken seriously.

A Frenchman once suggested that if the nation co-operates
with the army in time of war, it is only just that the army
should assist the nation in time of peace. Surely no Jesuit
missionary ever exceeded the work of that remarkable Brazilian officer General Candido Mariano da Silva Rondon in
pacifying and assimilating the Indian trbes of central Brazil
or in constructing railroads and laying telegraph lines in that
region. The present-day Bolivian and Peruvian armies, too,
are bringing their technically trained skills to the Indians
in the backlands. Public works, medical aid, education on an
undreamed-of scale, could be undertaken by Latin America's

armies. This would be the repayment to the people of a debt long overdue.

If the United States were to insist upon this kind of utilization of Latin American military power, it would give this country a moral standing with the ordinary people of the hemisphere such as we have never enjoyed.

Would not the hue and cry be raised that any such insistence by the United States was an affront to Latin America's precious sovereignty? I have no doubt that the cry would be heard. It ought to be dismissed out of hand. It has been said before but it bears repetition: the United States intervenes in Latin America as much by what it does as by what it fails to do. This is precisely what Talleyrand had in mind when he said that nonintervention is intervention by another name. If the proposal were considered unacceptable by a particular country, I see no reason why that country shouldn't be told to get its help elsewhere—or to continue to stew in its own stagnation. But would this not inevitably lead to that country's obtaining aid from Moscow? To my mind, the threat to go to Moscow is a bluff. The Russians have had their fill of adventurism in the Western Hemisphere. They are already heavily overextended in Cuba, which costs them $1 million a day. Cuba, as far as the Kremlin is concerned, is an accomplished fact. The U.S.S.R. is not eager for any further *faits accomplis* at this price. The need for a period of relaxation of tensions to promote internal development of the Soviet economy is imperative. The difficulties with Peking are much too grave to permit an embroilment in the morass of Latin America. Support for "wars of national liberation" is one thing; a major confrontation with the United States is something else. The Kremlin attaches infinitely more importance to the nuclear test ban treaty than it does to revolution in Latin America. This is a risk we can afford to take.

By steadily pushing the Latin American military establishments into useful, constructive public works of a type and scope with which they are historically familiar, I believe we would go far in providing their armies with a sense of mission—a mission which could lead them back to their people. Throughout the junior and middle ranks of the officer corps there is extreme sensitivity to the popular criticism that the armies of Latin America are not accepted by the people. Many officers know that Latin America's armies are not intended to be fighting machines in the thermonuclear age, and this lack of a true mission haunts them.

Who can say what sustained exposure to the people might do for Latin America's militarists? It might even lead to the rediscovery that Latin America's armies began their existence over a century and a half ago as people's armies. This is not the American way of seeking to perfect others in its own image—a course which inevitably leads to frustration and no results. It is, however, the Latin American way—the way of redemption. It could produce results.

CHAPTER FOUR

The Cry for Land

LAND IS the most explosive political issue in Latin America. And land reform is probably the most difficult and most complex single problem that confronts her progressive and orderly governments. It must be kept in mind that most of Latin America's population—60 per cent of the more than 200 million inhabitants—lives on the land and is largely outside the money economy, and that agriculture is the least productive sector in the individual national economies. It must also be remembered that any far-reaching program of land redistribution automatically involves a drastic rearrangement of existing property rights, income, and social status. Land reform, as John Kenneth Galbraith once observed, is not tantamount to giving "pensions to old soldiers." It is in itself a revolutionary process. The question which overshadows all others is: Can land reform in Latin America be attained by "methods short of revolution"?

Land reform has a direct relation to the success of the industrialization to which Latin America has dedicated herself. The industrialization program will, however, remain crippled unless the great mass of people receives a substantial improvement in nourishment. This is dependent primarily on greater agricultural productivity and a better utilization of food.

It must be remembered, too, that in Latin America good arable land is not a commodity in abundant supply, and that landholdings—particularly of the good land—are highly concentrated. Nor is redistribution of land everywhere an immediate, compelling necessity; for instance, *latifundio* is not a critical problem in Argentina, although a large part of the fertile pampas is made up of large holdings. It is not a critical problem because (1) the Argentine agricultural system does not follow the semi-feudal land pattern characteristic of other countries of Latin America, and (2) Argentina has for three quarters of a century used modern methods and modern equipment for large-scale production of grains and meat for its export trade. *Latifundio* is, however, of critical importance in such countries as Chile, Peru, Ecuador, and Brazil. In Brazil, a combination of large landholdings and obsolete agricultural practices keeps some 40 million of the country's 70 million people out of the cash economy. In Costa Rica— to take one of the smallest countries of Latin America—the land-tenure problem is not acute, most of the holdings being relatively modest in size. Costa Rica owes this piece of good fortune to the circumstance that the *conquistadores* found no Indians on the land. Without Indians there was no labor supply. Costa Rica was bypassed. In the early 1500's the central plateau of Costa Rica, known as the Valley of Desolation, was depopulated because of the spread of volcanic ashes —a phenomenon that has again occurred on the central plateau and threatened the existence of San José.

In El Salvador, to take another example, where landownership is heavily concentrated, the coffee aristocracy works its holdings intensively and, in the main, efficiently. Here the problem is to provide a better wage scale for the *campesinos,* decent housing, and other benefits associated with a rising standard of living. In Colombia, land reform is "respectable." As Albert Hirschman reminds us in his informative *Journeys Toward Progress,* the interest in land reform in Colombia did not come about as the result of a "sudden yearning for social justice." Spurred on by peasant squatters, land reform has been a developing process for at least thirty years. In Peru, President Fernando Belaúnde Terry, within two weeks of taking office, was forced into drastic land-reform legislation by Indian peasants who invaded rural estates, claiming the land as part of their Indian communities. In Chile, under the whiplash of a pastoral letter by Cardinal Raúl Silva Henríquez—Archbishop of Santiago and a greatly respected personage in Chile—political parties of all hues have begun to give major attention to reform, especially to the implementation of a land-reform measure enacted in 1962. President Eduardo Frei has made land reform a major goal in his program of peaceful revolution under Christian democracy. Venezuela began its land reform in March 1960, before the Alliance for Progress was conceived. In four years, Rómulo Betancourt's administration settled 60,000 *campesino* families on 3.7 million acres of land—land paid for in cash and bonds. As former President Betancourt is fond of pointing out, this is more land than Castro distributed under expropriation. Venezuela's land-reform law is probably the most carefully drafted legislation in all of Latin America. Its draftsmen included representatives of the peasants' federation, the landholders' organization, the Confederation of Workers of Venezuela, the four major political parties then in existence, government representatives, and technical experts on land-tenure problems. The significance of Venezuela's modest beginning in land redistribution becomes dramatically apparent when you pause to consider that in the sporadic guerrilla fighting now taking place in the Andean Mountains of Venezuela, it is the peasants who are bearing arms against the Castro-supplied and Castro-inspired insurrectionaries. Nowhere else on this planet is there a comparable example of peasants voluntarily fighting to protect *their* land against Communist guerrillas. With all his faults, which were legion, former President Goulart must ge given credit for having made Brazilians aware of the peasant and his feudal existence. Brazil's feudal landowners are doomed; they are fighting a rearguard action in resisting land reform.

These are some of the pressures and forces at work which are narrowing the problem of land reform. For the first time in Latin America's history, land reform is politically manageable.

Among the other problems in land reform which have to be surmounted are conventional attitudes and stereotyped thinking on the part of the reformers themselves. When Keynes said that "the difficulty lies, not in the new ideas, but in escaping from the old ones," he might have been talking of land reform in Latin America. A case in point is the notion that land reform, if it is to be successful, must break up the big estates. Actually, *latifundismo* is no longer even good politics; plainly, it is bad economics. Dividing up scarcity does not create abundance. The economic advantages lie with a greater technical development of the larger units. The available evidence does not support the political dogma that splitting up large landholdings into a fragmented individual peasant ownership will increase agricultural productivity. It has not worked in Mexico and in Bolivia. Interestingly, when the Algerian peasants took over the rich estates abandoned by the French *colons,* they recognized instinctively the folly of breaking up the large units into uneconomic fragments. The peasants chose instead to keep the estates as they were and to operate them through management committees.

Putting aside another piece of mythology regarding land reform—the Marxist notion that revolution is the only way to achieve a thoroughgoing redistribution of land—there remain, nevertheless, some hard, practical considerations which can slow down, or prevent the effective implementation of, the best-conceived agrarian program. Any ambitious land reform requires a great deal of capital. No other country in Latin America shares Venezuela's good fortune of floating on a sea of oil. Elsewhere, the quantity of money called for is simply not on hand. Moreover, the international banks have been wary of lending money for land reform. Bonds payable over ten to twenty-five years may be worthless at maturity. Under Latin America's political system there is no assurance that the government in power will recognize the "full faith and credit" of its predecessor. Land acquisition and development require great technical and organizational skills that do not seem to be available in Latin America. Such programs require political dexterity and consummate skill in compromising "irreconcilables," an art likely to be spurned by young men in a hurry, particularly if they happen to be of the Marxist persuasion. Land reform requires time and patience, both of which are running out.

The cardinal task of the political Center is to seize the initiative afforded by a changing climate of thinking now taking place in much of Latin America. If not universally, then in an impressive number of countries, it is feasible for the political Center and the conservative Right to communicate with each other. With the political skills that both sides possess, it should be possible for each to discern common interests and for the Center to relax the rigor of fear by the Right.

Before we go on to explore some practical ways by which land reform might be undertaken by methods short of revolution, it will be useful first to focus on the landscape and "get the feel" of the terrain.

Much of the tropics is useless for cultivation because excessive rainfall leaches basic plant nutrients out of the soil. Still other areas are too mountainous or too dry for normal cultivation. Of the more than 7.7 million square miles of Latin America's land surface, less than 5 per cent is actually cultivated. In the United States, 18 per cent of the land surface is under cultivation. Good land is not only in short supply in Latin America, it is also unevenly distributed. Five countries—Mexico, Brazil, Chile, Argentina, and Uruguay—have 47 per cent of the total arable soil. The remaining fifteen countries—containing 37 per cent of the population—have only 20 per cent of the arable land. In five countries—Paraguay, Bolivia, Peru, Venezuela, and Colombia—less than 3 per cent of the land is suitable for cultivation.

The reluctance of the Latin American governments to come to grips with land reform is readily understandable: it touches the sensitive nerve of the big landowners. For in Latin America 90 per cent of the land belongs to 10 per cent of the owners, a degree of land concentration "far greater than in any other world region of comparable size." [1] A revealing commentary on why land reform is approached gingerly may be found in the remarkably candid statement by the Chilean Government in its official reply to a United Nations questionnaire: "Owing to the economic and political structure of the country, land reform in Chile is difficult to carry out. Landholders who would be affected by an action of an economic, political, administrative, legal, or social nature will vigorously oppose its implementation, and their political and economic influence is very powerful . . ." [2]

A few figures will show the degree of land concentration in individual countries. In Guatemala, 516 farms (0.15 per cent of all farms) contain 41 per cent of the agricultural land; in Nicaragua, 362 owners control over one third; in Ecuador, 705 units (0.17 per cent) control 37 per cent. In Venezuela, 74 per cent of the farm acreage, comprising 6,800 units (1.69 per cent of all farms), is in holdings of over 1,000 hectares. In Brazil, half the farm land is in the hands of 1.6 per cent of the owners, while in Peru, 1.4 per cent of the landowners hold 62.8 per cent. In Chile, some 3,000 farms of

[1] Thomas F. Carroll: "The Land Reform Issue in Latin America," in *Latin American Issues* (New York: Twentieth Century Fund; 1961), p. 164.

[2] United Nations, Department of Economic Affairs: *Progress in Land Reforms* (1954), pp. 42–3.

1,000 or more hectares occupy almost 75 per cent of the farm land.

In most of Latin America, for historical reasons grounded in the land grants dispensed after the Spanish conquest and the Portuguese colonization, the best-quality lands are in the *latifundio*. This fact in and of itself serves to intensify land monopoly.

At the other end of the scale are the *minifundio* of the small landowners or squatters or landless ones, the vast majority of whom live a hand-to-mouth existence and are largely outside the cash economy. Here will be found the medieval Latin America which has scarcely changed since the Conquest and the Portuguese colonization. Throughout much of the backlands, mobility is restricted because of chronic indebtedness to the landowner. In return for a patch of land and a hut, all the members of a family are expected to provide the owner with free labor. In the *sierra* region of Peru an extraordinarily tense situation has resulted from feudal landownership and wretched working conditions. Here Indian *peones* earn the equivalent of one penny a day.[3] In his classic study of Brazilian plantation society, Gilberto Freyre describes rural Brazil in language which is a frightful indictment of the contemporary landowning aristocracy:

> . . . a latifundiary monoculture even after the abolition of slavery found a means of subsisting in certain parts of the country, with a more absorptive and sterilizing effect than under the old regime and with abuses that were still more feudal in character, through the creation of a proletariat under conditions of life less favourable than those of the mass of slaves.[4]

The panorama of misery, malnutrition, illiteracy, and semi-servitude in the backlands of Latin America is not exceeded by the shattering spectacle of the *fellahin* along the delta of the Nile, the peasantry on the plains of New Delhi, or the Chinese villagers on the Yangtze—in the judgment of so experienced a foreign observer as Gerald Clark, associate editor of the *Montreal Star,* who has seen the phenomenon

[3] Inter-American Development Bank: Second Annual Report (1962), p. 369.

[4] Gilberto Freyre: *The Masters and the Slaves* (New York: Alfred A. Knopf; 1946), tr. by Samuel Putnam; preface to the Second English-Language Edition, p. liv.

at first hand in all four areas.[5] And, as might be expected, it is the countryside of Colombia, Peru, Chile, and the Northeast of Brazil which is a prime target for Communist agitation. As an ideology, Communism is as meaningless to illiterate, diseased, and half-starved peasants as the dark side of the moon. But what they do grasp readily is the false promise that only Communism holds out hope for a quick change. They will follow a Francisco Julião—disciple of Mao Tse-tung and Fidel Castro—in the Northeast of Brazil, or a Hugo Blanco in Cuzco, Peru. *Who* the leader is and *what* he represents is of little importance. All that matters is that he promises to lead them to the promised land. If the landless peasants are inflamed by Communist agitators to take the land because it is "theirs," they will take it—as they have in Brazil and in Peru. And there will be bloodshed when the federal troops are summoned, as in Peru and in Brazil. Along the frontier between Bolivia and Peru, where the borders are meaningless to the migrant Indians, the descendants of the Inca in Peru are not unaware that it was the Indian who made a revolution and was responsible for the destruction of the *latifundio* in Bolivia. Celso Furtado, Brazil's well-known economist, says that if revolution comes to Brazil, it will be the peasants who ignite the spark. The Communists and the Church are in a race in Brazil—the one to be the first to throw the lighted torch into the tinder box; the other, by accelerating reform, to prevent the fire from starting.

Interestingly, Major Ché Guevara, in his manual *Guerrilla Warfare,* rejects the conventional Communist doctrine that revolution is to be carried out by the organized workers in the cities. To Guevara, the lesson of the Sierra Maestra should be clear to all of Latin America: revolutions are begun by small bands of dedicated revolutionaries who gain the sympathy and support of the peasants while an underground movement working in the cities acts through terror and sabotage. The Cuban recipe for revolution is being tested in Venezuela—in the trackless eastern provinces and in Caracas; in Colombia—in the "independent republics" of the bandit zones and in Bogotá; in Guatemala—in the mountains close to the border of Honduras and in Guatemala City. In Chile, the *inquilinos* are no longer willing to vote blindly for the conservative candidates of their *patrón*'s choice. Now they

---

[5] Gerald Clark: *The Coming Explosion in Latin America* (New York: David McKay Company, Inc.; 1963), p. 95. The reference to the Yangtze villagers is based on personal discussions with Mr. Clark.

vote for the Marxist Left. An incident I learned of in Santiago reveals with startling clarity the change that is taking place in the countryside. A woman came to the big house to ask the *patrón* for the use of a truck to carry her injured husband to town for medical help. Transportation was refused. The woman said she would send word to the local Communist deputy at Santiago. He would bring help for her man. She got the truck.

In many areas of Latin America, land is still cleared by the primitive slash-and-burn method. Thus it is quickly leached and eroded by rain, so that its working life span is limited. Farm implements consist frequently of stone-tipped sticks. The hoe and the machete are the standard equipment. In Honduras, for instance, five out of six of the small farms do not even possess a wooden plow. There is little or no use of fertilizer or insecticides. Scarcely any animal or traction power is employed. This is agriculture in the most basic meaning of the term: seed is sown and crops are harvested by the hand of man as in Biblical times.

In the Andean countries, stretching from Venezuela across the northern rim of the continent and down the west coast to Chile, peasants wring a precarious living out of the steep slopes of the mountains, on land which in other countries would not even be considered for farming. Because the methods of cultivation are primitive and wasteful, the yield is generally low—only 2 bushels of corn to the acre in Venezuela, for example, as compared with 64 bushels per acre in the United States. In Colombia, land utilization is thoroughly uneconomical. Indeed, the cattle herds probably have an easier existence than most of the farmers. The fertile, level valleys are used largely for grazing; the steep mountain slopes are reserved for agriculture. The poorer mountain lands are overpopulated in relation to the land resources, whereas the level land (except for areas planted to sugar cane, rice, and cotton) is in pasture. Large numbers of farm families eke out an existence on too little land, often on slopes of 45 degrees or more. Consequently, they exploit the land intensively, contribute to soil erosion, and create additional critical soil problems. Colombia dramatizes how a country can be squeezed in a vise between *latifundio* (too much land concentrated in too few hands) and *minifundio* (excessive parceling of too little land among too many people).

Throughout the Andean region, a substantial amount of hillside agriculture is probably inevitable. But what seems utterly absurd is that the best lands—the level lands—should not be cultivated intensively while the poorer hillside lands are. It makes no economic sense in Honduras, for example, that 90 per cent of the good flat land lies unused or that the landowners have sold or leased their poorest land to the small farmers who produce a major part of the crops grown in the country.

This pattern of uneconomical land utilization and antiquated methods of cultivation is probably the most important single cause of the low productivity of the agricultural worker and the resultant widespread poverty in the rural areas of Latin America. Throughout Latin America, the real problem is to increase the productivity of the arable land. For instance: in the United States, a single farmer is able to feed 28 persons. The reason, of course, lies in the mastery and utilization of modern agricultural technology, along with every conceivable form of assistance from the federal government and the agricultural colleges, access to markets, and so forth. In Latin America, on the other hand, one peasant has a backbreaking job to feed himself and his own family. With mechanized equipment, an American farmer works anywhere from 5 to 200 acres. The Latin American *campesino* with primitive tools works on a postage stamp—some 2 or 3 acres. American farming is so productive that it can—and does—feed a large part of the world. Latin America is so agriculturally unproductive that it can scarcely feed itself and must—in some countries—actually import food.

A good part of the failure of landowners to cultivate intensively is an outgrowth of their attitude regarding ownership of land. Land is not looked upon as a capital resource from which a proper return on investment is to be derived. On the contrary, landownership is expected to provide only a level of income adequate to the requirements of social position. Once this need is fulfilled, there is no particular incentive to increase productivity. In Chile, for example, large areas of the fertile Central Valley are removed from production by the large landholders because they have no real incentive to place more acreage under cultivation. This attitude contributes to chronic inflation by restricting agricultural output, limits the market for industry by holding back additional jobs for agricultural workers, and keeps a large portion of the population in perpetual hunger. Chile is now spending $140 million annually to import basic food.

Uncontrolled population growth and unproductive agriculture are the nemesis of the poor lands. As with other underdeveloped regions of the world, Latin America's population is growing faster than her production of food. Dr. Raymond Ewell, Vice-President for Research of the State University of New York at Buffalo, predicts massive famine during the 1970's throughout most of the world's poor lands and acute starvation in Latin America by 1980. If these trends continue, the Malthusian doctrine will be operative in Latin America in less than twenty years.

Latin America has within her grasp an unparalleled opportunity not only to avert an imminent catastrophe in food supply, but also to attain a permanent solution to her agricultural impoverishment by a resolute implementation of President Johnson's magnanimous offer to place the financial weight of the United States behind a Latin American fertilizer community. In his speech on August 17, 1965, commemorating the fourth anniversary of the Declaration of Punta del Este, the President said: "I hope the American nations will consider the establishment of a program—patterned after the European Coal and Steel Community—for the production and trade, on a continental basis, of fertilizer, pesticides and other products that are needed to increase agricultural production." Ernest Bevin, Britain's Foreign Minister, provided an immediate European response to General Marshall's historic proposal to help with Europe's reconstruction. Latin America's political leaders as of this writing seem to be unaware that the specter of starvation is staring them in the face. President Johnson's proposal appears to have been relegated to Latin America's *mañana*.

There is a managerial and administrative device, with proven success in the United States and Europe, which is made to order for a dramatic assault upon land reform and land development in Latin America—a device that can be the democratic answer to land reform by methods short of revolution. It is the Public Authority. Celebrated examples are the Tennessee Valley Authority, the Port of New York Authority, and the Port of London Authority. Europe used the Authority concept with signal success for the organization of its Coal and Steel Community. It was the Coal and Steel Authority, moreover, which provided the impetus for the broader political and economic goal of the European Common Market. Variations of the Authority concept have been used in Chile and in Colombia.

The Authority is essentially a device for the performance of specific functions and is designed to accommodate broad geographical areas. The Authority obviates the cumbersome and top-heavy bureaucratic structures typical of government departments. As an independent body, an Authority is removed from the political jealousies and overlappings of competing ministries. (In Venezuela, for example, no less than thirteen separate agencies are involved in land redistribution.) Free of the budgetary limitations of the government department or ministry, the Authority can establish pay scales that will attract men of high caliber and professional competence. Like any business corporation, the Authority may have its own capital structure and its own financial base. Because it is essentially a business corporation, it can command for its highest management respected public figures who are not political job seekers.

The Authority has the signal advantage of being able to work directly and closely with the people of the region— an ability that has contributed to the TVA's great success. This leads me to venture the further thought that being close to the people would enable the Authority to tap their manual labor on projects at a fraction of what it would normally cost. The French economist and civil servant Gabriel Ardant[6] has described experiments in Morocco, Tunisia, and Madagascar in which several hundred thousand peasants were put to work on small, local development projects such as water conservation, irrigation, reforesting, and dam construction. This is the type of work which country people can carry out with the means at hand—their own tools—and without costly equipment or foreign technicians. Because the peasants were working on their own land and profited directly from their own work, M. Ardant points out, it was not necessary to pay them more than a small wage in addition to some food. As an example of the low-cost expenditure for this type of operation, M. Ardant notes that in Madagascar, 100,000 peasants, utilizing less than $100,000, succeeded in a few months in irrigating 15,000 acres of land; if conventional techniques had been used, this project would have required several million dollars and four years' time. The unemployed and underemployed labor resources of Latin America's countryside run into the millions. The Au-

---

6 "Conquering Hunger by Utilizing the Unexploited Resources of the World," a paper presented to the World Food Congress, June 8, 1963, at Washington, D.C.

thority is a natural device for harnessing America's food surpluses to Latin America's untapped labor resources. Even if this labor force were only moderately efficient, it would still be able to accomplish at a fraction of the cost what the Alliance for Progress seeks to do with high-powered but scarce dollars.

The Authority can place under one managerial roof the whole sweep of operations required for a balanced agricultural economy—low-interest, long-term credits for the purchase of land, homes, seed, fertilizer, tools; storage and marketing facilities; penetration roads; mechanized farm equipment pools; irrigation, sanitation, and water systems; schools and hospitals.

By having both the power of decision and the purse, the Authority can undertake through the use of the radio the long, arduous task of wiping out the scourge of illiteracy to which Monsignor Salcedo in Colombia has applied himself with dramatic success. Here, the Japanese offer an instructive case study of the effectiveness of the radio as an educational device for teaching farmers new agricultural methods. The agricultural productivity of postwar Japan is so high that hunger has virtually been eliminated.

Among the peasantry the problem of agricultural education is especially acute, because of their innate conservatism. The peasant prefers to use the techniques of his ancestors and to continue with the crops which they grew. This is particularly true in the countries with heavy Indian populations. Without prolonged education in new agricultural methods, one of the fundamental objectives of agrarian reform—increased productivity—is unattainable. If one thing stands out clearly in the developmental process it is this: intelligent cultivation of the soil demands healthy farmers; and —as the Ford Foundation studies in India have shown— illiterate farmers are not healthy farmers. In Latin America— as, indeed, throughout the underdeveloped world—it is impossible for the advanced countries to supply enough teachers, agricultural advisers, and other technicians to increase the supply of food through improved agricultural methods. There is only one way this shortage can be overcome: training people to train others.

As an administrative instrumentality embracing an entire region, the Authority is an ideal medium through which land can be purchased from powerfully entrenched local landowners, or single corporate owners such as the United

Fruit Company, and distributed to rural people without re-
sorting to expropriation, as was done in Mexico and Bolivia,
more recently in Guatemala, and latterly in Cuba. The Authority can combine land acquisition and land redistribution
with the supporting measures of agricultural development
and co-operative marketing, all of which must be accomplished before any one of them can become effective. Backed
by an international guarantee, the Authority could ensure
that the bonds paid to the landowner will not so depreciate
in value as to make the transaction uninteresting. This is
the nub of the matter in getting landowners to sell. Many
have read the handwriting on the wall. The shadow of expropriation haunts them. If there is an opportunity to sell at
a reasonable price, with assurance that ultimate payment
will not be in "wallpaper," they will prefer the bird in hand
to the one in Castro's bush.

The essence of the proposal turns on the use of the carrot
and the stick. The Authority would offer to buy outright that
portion of an owner's land which lies idle. A condition of
the purchase of the idle land would be that the landowner
increase the productivity of the portion he retained. In this
way, the landless would be afforded the opportunity to acquire land, and by increasing the productivity of his own
holdings, the landowner would add to the employment opportunities and the economic stability of his particular region.

The Authority mechanism could operate regionally. One
such Authority could embrace Costa Rica, El Salvador, Guatemala, Honduras, and Nicaragua, for the underlying problems
throughout the area are similar. A regional Authority embracing Central America could become a significant instrument for supplementing the work of the Central American
Common Market. The Public Authority could eventually
eliminate the "Balkanization" of the area by straddling its
artificially created boundaries. We could name this instrumentality, as José Figueres has suggested, the "Lincoln-
Bolívar Authority."

Another grouping could be Colombia, Ecuador, and Venezuela. Still a third—or even a fourth—could take in the
southern tier of republics.

Although the capitalization of the Authorities would be
different in each case and could be determined only through
study, their stock would be subscribed by the principal
capital-exporting nations of Western Europe and by Canada,
Japan, and the United States. The participating Latin Ameri-

can countries in each of the Authorities would likewise subscribe. Inclusion of the members of the Atlantic Community and Japan is suggested because they have already embarked upon a joint enterprise of channeling capital to underdeveloped countries through the Development Assistance Group. Their participation in the Authorities would, therefore, be entirely appropriate.

If the stock were held jointly by European countries, the United States, Japan, Canada, and the other American republics, the management and administration of the Authority would become distinctly international. It would enable the Authority to draw upon the technical skills of experienced specialists from all of the subscribing countries—indeed, from every part of the world. It would have the salutary effect of subordinating United States participation, always a sore point in hemispheric relations.

Such an international organization offers the possibility of accomplishing one additional purpose of supreme importance: it would enable the Authority to issue its own securities, as do the World Bank and the Inter-American Development Bank. These securities could carry the guarantee of all of the participating governments. The ability of the Authority to issue its own securities backed by the world's leading industrial nations could make it possible for Latin America's ruling classes, who for centuries have been the big landowners, to sell parts of their vast holdings without having to put pistols to their heads.

With its operations extending over the entire Central American region, a Central American Authority could be the means of removing the United Fruit Company as a conspicuous target of anti-*yanqui* sentiment. It could do this by purchasing the United Fruit Company's abandoned banana lands (which amount to a considerable acreage) and, over a period of years, buy the actual banana-raising lands. Both could then be sold to small banana farmers with whom United Fruit would enter into contracts, as it has with conspicuous success in Colombia. United Fruit eventually could confine its activities to marketing, transportation, and the supply of agricultural technical services (which might not be an unpleasant prospect, considering United Fruit's political and other difficulties).

It would be fitting for the United States to take the initiative in the promotion of such regional Authorities for at least two reasons: (1) it is consistent with the support being given by the United States to the Latin American movement toward regional economic integration, and (2) the United States itself is no stranger to the problems of land redistribution and rural resettlement. Indeed, land distribution and land resettlement have been peculiarly American preoccupations since the days of the early Republic. As early as 1820 an 80-acre piece of land could be bought from the United States Government for $100. Long after the American occupation of Japan will have become a folk memory, General Douglas MacArthur's proconsulship will be gratefully remembered for the encouragement given to the Japanese reform effect in breaking up the big estates and redistributing land to a land-hungry peasantry. This was one of the most thoroughgoing redistributions of land the world has ever seen. A third of the total arable land of Japan changed hands. Thirty per cent of the population of Japan was affected. Its effects on the living standards of the former tenant farmers, on agricultural productivity, and—most importantly—on the political attitudes and activities of the agricultural population have been far-reaching. Today, the economy of Japan is consumer-oriented, with an emphasis on heavy engineering and chemicals. Television sets, washing machines, electric rice cookers, are no longer strangers to the Japanese farm family. It can be said that "Japan has now the things that truly 'underdeveloped' countries do not have—an educated and trainable labor force, efficient business organizations and management, comprehensive transportation and power systems, established world trade connections and ability to master and apply modern technology." [7] Although I do not wish to labor the point unduly—and I am aware that the Japanese themselves are prone to advance other reasons for their phenomenal growth—to my mind it is to Japan's massive land reform that a good share of the credit must go for what Japan is today.

It is worth remembering that the Mexican land reform, although it took a long and painful period for digestion (and is still not completely finished), is, nevertheless, in the judgment of students of Mexican agrarian reform a vital reason for Mexico's stable government, cultural renaissance, and spectacular industrialization.

History shows that, in every society, there is a margin of

[7] Research and Policy Committee, Committee for Economic Development: *Japan in the Free World: A Statement on National Policy* (Washington, D.C., 1963), p. 22.

safety with respect to social tensions which, if disregarded, leads to a social and political explosion. When this margin of safety is exceeded, it is no longer possible to buy time through reform. Although there are exceptions in particular countries, for much of Latin America the margin of safety is rapidly shrinking. There are, however, internal pressures at work which, as I have endeavored to point out, make the problem politically manageable. I share fully Professor Hirschman's view that Latin America's "reformers do not face a wholly hopeless task, and what would have required a major social upheaval thirty years ago may be achieved by methods short of revolution." [8] The experience of Colombia and Venezuela demonstrates that modest land reforms can be attained under democratic processes. Peru may be able under Belaúnde to make a dent in its critical land problem. The political climate of Chile is auspicious for carrying out long-delayed land reforms. Brazil, with its tradition of compromising the difficult, has the unique capacity to work out its immensely complex agrarian reforms without tearing itself apart.

The Authority—a proven managerial and administrative device—could be the means for the fulfillment of the promise of the Declaration of Punta del Este:

Land will become for the man who works it the basis of his economic stability, the foundation of his increasing welfare, the guaranty of his freedom and dignity.

[8] Albert O. Hirschman: *Journeys Toward Progress* (New York: Twentieth Century Fund; 1963), p. 274.

CHAPTER FIVE

The Curse of Monoculture

IF WE COULD POINT to any single symptom to describe Latin America's economic sickness, it would be its excessive dependence upon single commodities. Latin America's economic health depends upon its ability to export its commodities and foodstuffs to the industrialized nations at reasonable prices. For Americans who float on a sea of coffee—we consume each day 440 million cups—coffee is largely a matter of brand names. To more than half of the countries of Latin America, a one-cent shift in the price of coffee is literally a question of impoverishment or prosperity. Coffee accounts for over 23 per cent of the total export earnings of the 15 coffee-producing countries of Latin America. For individual countries it is higher. Fifty-four per cent of Brazil's foreign income comes from the sale of coffee. For Colombia, it is 67 per cent; for Guatemala, 52 per cent.

Just how lopsided Latin America's economies are can be seen from the extent to which export earnings are derived from one commodity. Bolivia relies upon the sale of tin for 73 per cent of her earnings. Chile obtains 61 per cent of her foreign exchange from the sale of copper. Uruguay looks to the export of wool for 51 per cent of her income. The Dominican Republic depends on sugar for 58 per cent of her foreign earnings. Ecuador receives 63 per cent of her foreign income from the sale of bananas. Cuba once earned 78 per cent of her dollars from the sale of sugar. Oil is

Venezuela's "black gold": 92 per cent of her revenue comes from the export of petroleum. Sixteen of the twenty Latin American countries derive more than half of their export earnings from one or two commodities.

These few statistics lay bare the whole problem of economic colonialism: They illuminate the motivation for Latin America's frenzied drive to industrialize. They help to explain the surge of xenophobic nationalism. They account in part for the irrational resentment toward the United States.

Latin America's monoculture has made her the captive of world prices. World commodity prices are notoriously unstable. Fluctuations of production and demand may cause earnings to swing up or down by as much as 50 per cent in a single year. Fluctuations in world prices raise havoc with national treasuries. A change of one cent a pound in the world price of copper spells a $7 million loss to Chile. A drop of one cent in the price of coffee means a $50 million loss to the fifteen coffee-producing countries. Between 1957 and 1962 (when the price of coffee fell from 52 cents to 35 cents a pound), Brazil alone sustained a loss of $1.2 billion.

Commodity prices fluctuate upward as well as downward. Price fluctuations can—and do—create tremendous windfalls. As Robert Heilbroner suggests,[1] a considerable part of the growth of the underdeveloped world during the first postwar decade was spurred by a commodity boom. William Butler, economist of the Chase Manhattan Bank, writes: "Over the past 60 years the less developed areas have gained more from the upward fluctuations than they have lost in periods of declining prices." [2]

Now, there is another side to the coin. Latin America is also an importer of machinery, fuels, foodstuffs, chemicals, iron and steel, and other finished goods. These are the goods and the raw materials needed for economic expansion as well as for the maintenance of existing plant—steel rails to replace worn-out tracks, milling machines for a new industrial factory. The bulk of these imports is paid for by the income earned from exports and not, as is sometimes assumed, with borrowed capital or foreign aid. Indeed, trade is much more important than aid for the underdeveloped coun-

[1] Robert Heilbroner: *The Great Ascent* (New York: Harper & Row; 1963), p. 125.
[2] William Butler: "Trade and the Less Developed Areas," *Foreign Affairs*, January 1963, p. 377.

tries. Total exports of the underdeveloped areas amounted to $35 billion in 1965; the total flow of aid (including private investment) was only $9 billion.[3] Moreover, export earnings are also the source for the repayment of foreign loans. The taxes levied on exporting companies help to support the operations of government.

Trade—the two-way exchange of goods sold and bought —is therefore still the main artery between the industrial North and the underdeveloped South. But it is precisely here that Latin America encounters serious trouble. Since 1937, the terms of trade—the ratio of export prices to import prices—have been unfavorable to the commodities that are the lifeblood of Latin America. The terms of trade for Latin America dropped by about 20 per cent during the eleven years after 1950. Indeed, the trade of the entire underdeveloped world has lagged. The underdeveloped lands' share of world exports has declined steadily, from 31.5 per cent of the total in 1953 to 24.7 per cent in 1960. Total exports of the underdeveloped regions since 1956 have increased only 2 per cent per year as against 6.5 per cent for the industrialized countries. In Latin America, the decline has been particularly severe. Excluding Venezuela, Latin America's exports have increased only 0.5 per cent per annum.

One of the reasons for the continuance of these trends is the shift in industrial uses of raw materials. In the United States—and to an increasing extent in Europe—industries are utilizing smaller quantities of primary products per unit of output. For instance, more telephone messages can now be transmitted per unit of copper wire, and copper can be replaced by aluminum if aluminum is cheaper. Less tin is used in each can manufactured; glass, plastics, and aluminum can be used as substitutes. And so it goes through the whole of the manufacturing process. In addition, advances in the reclamation of used materials and the reduction of critical raw material waste at the factory have worked to lessen demand. Radically new techniques for decreasing the size of electronic parts and components portend a revolution in manufacturing. This development bodes ill for primary-commodity producers. World War II forced the industrialized nations to find substitutes for raw materials. Synthetic rubber and nitrates became competitive with their natural counter-

[3] International Monetary Fund, *International Financial Statistics*, March 1966, p. 35.

parts. The development of nylon, rayon, plastics, and detergents is decreasing the dependency on and utilization of natural fibers. A synthetic coffee (which may not be far over the horizon) would of course have disastrous consequences.

Another factor which accounts for much of the decline of world trade in primary commodities is the growth among the industrialized countries, especially the United States, of price supports, export subsidies, and protection for domestic agricultural and mineral products. Preferences granted by the European Economic Community to the associated overseas territories in Africa and the traditional preferences granted by the United Kingdom to Commonwealth nations have had unfortunate consequences for Latin America.

The unfavorable balance between export and import prices has placed Latin America in an economic bind. While the prices for most of Latin America's exports have fallen drastically, the prices it must pay for its imports have remained fairly stable or have risen steadily. *In short, Latin America has been obliged to sell cheap and buy dear.* When a country lacks dollars, not only is it limited in its capacity to borrow from the international and private banks, but it also is unable to import capital goods and raw materials for its new industries. And without capital goods, economic growth comes to a standstill.

To make matters worse, the Latin American countries have experienced an unparalleled population expansion: it has been like the flow of lava after a volcanic eruption. Consider Mexico for a moment. Mexico now has a population about equal to the combined populations of New York, Pennsylvania, New Jersey, and Connecticut. Forty years from now—just a little after the year 2000—if Mexico's birth rate continues, she will have enough people to fill those four states *plus* all the rest of New England, the entire South Atlantic region, the entire West Coast, and Ohio, Indiana, Illinois, Michigan, and Wisconsin.

Latin America's difficulty (as, indeed, that of other poor lands) is that virtually all of the surplus national product is needed to feed the new mouths each year. Capital expenditures must be devoted to building schools, hospitals, roads, and other "nonproductive" services for mushrooming numbers of people. Thus little or nothing is left over for investment in new industrial facilities or improved agriculture. Hence it is difficult, if not impossible, to raise the standard of living. The result is economic stagnation.

This problem is not unique to Latin America. The under-developed countries can help themselves and plan intelligently for the future only if they are able to export their primary commodities to the industrial countries at prices which will earn sufficient income to sustain their population increases and to buy the capital equipment they require. *This is the crux of the problem of the poor lands of the world.*

Latin America's chronic balance-of-payments crisis (for which no end is in sight) was pointed up dramatically at the spring 1962 meeting, in Buenos Aires, of the Board of Governors of the Inter-American Development Bank by Dr. Jorge Mejía Palacio, Governor of the Bank for Colombia. After observing that "Latin America is in the throes of the worst crisis in its entire history," Dr. Mejía went on to say that, despite the generous assistance received by his country from the Alliance for Progress, "the losses suffered" through declining coffee prices were "two or three times greater than the special aid received." The former Brazilian ambassador Roberto de Oliveira Campos has made the same charge. He points out that the $2.6 billion lost by Brazil through declining commodity prices since 1959 exceeds the $1.6 billion of foreign aid allocated by the United States.

The cycle of "bail-out" loans to offset commodity losses points up sharply the dilemma the United States faces in its Latin American policy: Do we continue to pump into Latin America each year a billion dollars of foreign aid, which is insufficient to close the export-import gap? Or do we share with other advanced countries some of the responsibility for the commodity problems of the underdeveloped world? A report by the Chamber of Commerce of the United States puts the problem succinctly: "Aid to the developing nations may not only be a matter of loans and grants; it may also require the development of an effectively helpful attitude in regard to commodity trade, markets and prices." [4]

International commodity-stabilization agreements have been the most widely used technique aimed at insulating prices and production from the gyrations of the world markets. Commodity agreements have included wheat, sugar, tin, olive oil, and coffee. In some instances they operate through a mechanism under which supplies are purchased when prices are below a minimum figure and are sold when the price

[4] *Commodity Agreements: Their Role in the World Economy* (1963), p. 15.

exceeds a maximum figure. In other instances export quotas —or a combination of export and import quotas—are employed so as to control the amount that reaches the market. Regardless of the form which the arrangement takes, the purpose is to stabilize prices. Stabilization is accomplished either by the producing countries acting alone or by consuming and producing countries acting together. None of these agreements has been conspicuously successful. They can be used for only a few commodities. They will not work for products that are competitive with synthetic substitutes. It is not realistic to expect such agreements to be used for commodities exported by the industrial nations—vegetable oils and oil seeds, nonferrous metals, citrus fruits, and tobacco. Probably five commodities lend themselves to price stabilization: coffee, sugar, cocoa, tea, and bananas. Of these, as already noted, coffee and sugar are covered by international agreements. Recent negotiations for an international cocoa agreement were unsuccessful.

Commodity agreements ought not to be regarded as desirable ends in themselves: as such they would perpetuate "colonial economies." Moreover, if the benefits of price stability accrue only to the planters, the exporters, and the politicians instead of producing higher living standards for the mass of the people, the result is too limited to justify the financial cost. Such agreements can, nevertheless, serve as an effective device in a transitional period of crop diversification (from exclusive dependence upon, say, bananas to adding pineapples, beef, and tobacco), or for cushioning the transition from a situation of oversupply (coffee, for example) to a more balanced production or shifting into other cash crops such as cotton. They can become important tools in a change-over from heavy dependence upon agricultural exports to industrialization. Where the benefits of price stability are translated into education, health, housing, and better pay for the people, commodity-stabilization agreements can become vital instruments for the realization of social justice. Used for such purposes, commodity agreements should receive greater support from the United States and Western Europe. Although the United States has been reluctant to participate in such arrangements, it has, nevertheless, exercised leadership and initiative in the recently concluded world coffee stabilization agreement.

The French delegation to the United Nations Conference on Trade and Development, held in Geneva during March–

June 1964, proposed measures that go far beyond commodity price stabilization. They urged (1) organizing the world markets to prevent sharp rises and falls in commodity prices; (2) adoption of a plan to increase earnings of temperate zone products produced in the underdeveloped lands—wheat, for instance—to the same levels fixed for these commodities in the industrialized countries; (3) new international price-support agreements to lift prices of tropical commodities and raw materials; (4) preparation of a list of commodities whose prices can be raised without decreasing demand or encouraging the use of synthetic substitutes. This radical shift in international trade patterns would be financed by levying a tax on imports from the underdeveloped countries, the proceeds therefrom to be turned over to the exporting countries.[5] The French proposals bring to mind a passage in General de Gaulle's *War Memoirs,* in which he said: "Towards the complexities of the Middle East I flew with simple ideas. I knew that, in a welter of intricate factors, a vital game was being played there. We therefore had to be in it." [6]

It is difficult not to conclude that these "simple ideas" for changing the complex patterns of world trade were advanced by the French with tongue in cheek, knowing full well that they would be rejected by the industrialized North. With a touch of Machiavelli, the French poured gasoline over the fires of discontent raging through the poor lands in order to reveal the indifference of the other rich lands. The consequences of the Gaullist diplomacy are: (1) General de Gaulle will realize significant political mileage by posing as the only true friend of the poor lands. (2) France can exert leverage on Latin America because she can claim to hold the key that will open the door for Latin American exports to the European Economic Community. If France can in fact do that—a big "if"—a Paris-oriented "alliance for progress" will follow. (3) As the United States turned attention to Latin America only after the Castro revolution made it imperative, the trade crisis of the underdeveloped South will also compel constructive and realistic solutions by the United States. It is a pity that a world-wide conflagration is needed before the United States can act. The

5 *Memorandum Concerning Certain Items on the Agenda of the United Nations Conference on Trade and Development,* Submitted by France. E/CONF. 46/74, 27 February 1964, Eng. tr., pp. 11–14.

6 Charles de Gaulle: *War Memoirs—The Call to Honor: 1940–1942* (New York: The Viking Press; 1955), p. 167.

sensible reminder by Under Secreary of State Ball of the importance of private investment in economic development would have fallen on more receptive ears had it been placed in the broader context of bold solutions to the commodity predicament of the poor lands. But as one observer at the United Nations Conference put it: "George Ball was the only honest delegate at Geneva; he had nothing to offer, and so he offered nothing." Nevertheless, the sterility of the United States position at Geneva underscored Senator Fulbright's wise dictum: "An effective foreign policy is one which concerns itself more with innovations abroad than with conciliation at home."

A promising approach to Latin America's commodity-export plight may lie in the compensatory financing of declines in export revenues under a program sponsored by the International Monetary Fund. Under this arrangement, countries experiencing seasonal or long-range declines in the prices of their export commodities as a result of conditions beyond their control would automatically be granted assistance by way of loans. The IMF consented to Brazil's drawing $60 million to help meet its balance-of-payments deficit arising from a decline in export earnings of coffee and cocoa. The $60 million represents the difference in revenue between the value of Brazilian exports in 1962—a period of low coffee and cocoa prices—and the average of earnings of those crops during the years 1960–63.

This device of compensatory financing can be helpful in the sense in which a tourniquet is helpful in arresting the flow of blood from a severed artery. It is not, of course, a cure and was not intended as such.

Commodity-stabilization agreements and crop diversification are long-run programs. And over the short run, Latin America is stagnating. Such a situation is an ideal breeding ground for social tensions; it exacerbates political instability by polarizing the extremes of Right and Left; it is made to order for the local Pied Pipers of Castroism or the Military Man on Horseback.

While such long-range objectives are being explored, significant immediate relief should be provided for Latin America's stagnating economies by lowering or removing trade barriers to her exports to Europe and the United States. Latin American trade with the European Common Market could be expanded considerably were it not for high import duties, quantitative restrictions on imports, and internal consumption taxes. Coffee exports, according to the Organization of American States, could be increased by some $130 million yearly through the elimination of existing barriers. If the International Coffee Agreement is to be more than a device for "stabilizing hunger" (which some of its critics contend it is), European consumers—notably West Germany—will have to show some signs of willingness to lift restrictive taxes. In Germany a pound of coffee costs more than $2.00, of which about $.70 is tax.

The removal of trade barriers to the European Common Market is considered by Latin Americans to be of paramount importance because a sharp decrease in export opportunities is envisaged under the full operation of the European Common Market as a result of tariff preferences for tropical products—bananas, coffee, cocoa, and sugar—from the former African colonies. Indeed, the signing of a "convention of association" on July 20, 1963, between the European Economic Community and eighteen of the new African sovereignties has already inaugurated a system of free trade between the "Six" and its former colonies, to the further disadvantage of Latin America. The other problem that the European Economic Community presents, particularly for the South American countries, is its system of variable import duties which will keep import prices above domestic prices on temperate zone agricultural products—wheat, dairy products, fruits, vegetables, meat, and meat products.

It is the rare Latin American who does not resent the United States' discrimination against Latin American exports of grains, tobacco, cotton, wool, meat, zinc, lead, copper, and petroleum. Removal of those restrictions and quotas would, according to the National Planning Association, increase export earnings for the area from $850 million to $1.7 billion a year, roughly the amount of annual foreign aid committed to Latin America. Former President José Figueres of Costa Rica expresses the opinion of all responsible Latin Americans when he says that "reasonable prices for raw material exports would be worth much more to the economies of Latin America than the pump-priming efforts of the Alliance for Progress."

CHAPTER SIX

Industrialization: The
New Religion

WHAT ALCHEMY WAS to the Middle Ages, industrialization is to the underdeveloped world of this century—the magic elixir that can transform feudal societies. For Latin America, particularly, industrialization is the route to emancipation from exclusive dependency upon the exportation of raw materials. During the first quarter of this century, José Batlle y Ordóñez, the Uruguayan who must be placed at the pinnacle of the creative statesmen of the Western Hemisphere, was an early proponent of industrialization. During the twenties, Víctor Raúl Haya de la Torre, the Peruvian leader of the APRA party, gave industrialization a prominent place in his early Indo-Marxist philosophy. Perón made it the driving force of his ill-fated "corporate state." In Brazil, it was an integral part of Vargas' *estado novo*. The heavy emphasis upon industrialization by Mexico's revolutionary presidents beginning with Cárdenas has brought her into the forefront of development. The Great Depression of the thirties dramatized the urgency for building steel mills and factories for the manufacture of consumer goods. With the European and American industrial machine paralyzed, Latin America was unable to import consumer goods and capital equipment. World War II gave additional impetus to the Latin American desire for her own industrial plants. Latin America's supply of consumer and capital goods was rationed by the United States: Latin America was a client of the War Production Board. In Latin America, as in other underdeveloped regions, industrialization was the ideological focus of the revolution of rising aspirations. Heavy industry, technology, and the scientific knowledge which make them possible became part of the cult of economic nationalism.[1]

Industrialization became the new religion of Latin America. Its latter-day high priest is the distinguished Argentine Raúl Prebisch. A political economist in the English tradition, central banker, university teacher, international civil servant, Prebisch is a towering figure on the Latin American scene. A whole new generation of brilliant young economists —many of whom occupy high places in their governments' bureaucracies—has been profoundly influenced by his thinking. It was, however, Prebisch's direction of the United Nations Economic Commission for Latin America (ECLA) which produced the greatest impact on Latin America's younger intellectuals and the political leadership of the democratic left-of-center parties. For the ECLA studies not only articulated, but also provided the statistical "proof" to support, the long-smoldering resentment against what many believed to be a deliberate "conspiracy" by the industrialized nations to keep Latin America as a permanent producer of raw materials and foodstuffs.

The suspicion that a "conspiracy" actually existed was heightened by two sets of post-World War II developments. In the immediate postwar years, the economic policies of both the United States and Great Britain appeared to be insensitive to the aspirations of the underdeveloped countries. The goals of the postwar world were framed in terms that reflected exclusively the needs of the industrialized nations. Assistance for the underdeveloped world seemed to be an afterthought. To Latin America's leaders, who were primarily concerned with the *development* of their countries, an emphasis upon measures designed to assist the developed nations smacked of economic colonialism, another effort to keep Latin America in its prewar position as a supplier of raw materials and importer of manufactured goods.

The second of the conspiratorial circumstances was an economic doctrine much in vogue among the industrialized countries—the doctrine of "comparative advantage." Stripped of its verbiage, this was a conception of international spe-

[1] Arthur P. Whitaker: *Nationalism in Latin America* (Gainesville: University of Florida Press; 1962), p. 16.

cialization in which each country continued to do what it already did well. To the adherents of the conspiracy theory, the doctrine of comparative advantage was proof of the determination of the industrialized North to keep the underdeveloped South in a permanent status of a producer of raw materials and foodstuffs. It is one of the ironic twists of history that former Chairman Khrushchev, arch foe of "imperialism," should have embraced the doctrine of comparative advantage as the economic *modus operandi* for the nations of the Soviet bloc at a time when the doctrine has ceased to be fashionable among the West's economists. In the Western Hemisphere, whether from dire necessity—as is more probable—or as an echo of the voice of the Kremlin, Dr. Castro has announced that Cuba's role in the Soviet bloc is to be a producer of sugar cane and cattle—industrialization must wait. That the Marshall Plan was principally a European recovery program added grist to the mill. The suspicion was widely entertained in Latin America that this priority was determined in large measure by the desire of the United States to force Latin America to accept foreign private investments, a suspicion not entirely unsupported by the facts.

Economists in the United States have had critical reservations with respect to certain of the ECLA tenets, especially its generalizations regarding the inherent unfavorable trends in the terms of trade for Latin America. This skepticism was expressed as recently as January 29, 1963, by the then United States ambassador to Brazil, Lincoln Gordon, himself a distinguished economist. In an address to the Brazilian National Economic Council, Ambassador Gordon said: ". . . most serious scholars today are very skeptical as to the validity of any long-term generalizations about inherent trends in the terms of trade." As for myself, I have no professional competence by which to judge the merits of the controversy. Whether the ECLA's contentions are sound or fallacious seems to me beside the point. The ECLA studies strike me, a lay person, as having primarily a political significance. The economic studies are merely the latticework on which to train a sophisticated political argument.

To borrow Raymond Vernon's illuminating phrase, "countries upon whom history has imposed a sense of inferiority" have a deep, psychological compulsion to find a scapegoat for their resentments and frustrations. To Latin Americans, the feeling of "neglect" by the United States during the era

of the Marshall Plan and the accumulated exposure to the
vagaries of the world markets for their single-crop commodities left a bitter taste. It was as if they were beggars holding out a tin cup on a rainy day. It would be altogether
surprising if an organization—albeit an international organ
—consisting largely of Latin American intellectuals did not
mirror these emotions.

What the Fabian intellectuals did at the turn of the century for the nascent British Labor party, ECLA has done
for Latin America's democratic political leadership: provided
an ideological standard around which the political parties can
rally. If ECLA had not existed, it would have had to be
invented. The ECLA reports cloaked Latin America's nationalism with the respectability of its scholarship. With their
militant style, its studies became a "manifesto," a political
call for democratic action. They sought to mobilize Latin
America for the march to modernization.

To the ECLA ideologues, the way to redress Latin America's role as a second-class citizen in the world seemed to
be deliberately promoted government policies of forced-
draft industrialization supported by protective tariffs and import controls for infant industries. In this scheme of things,
the state was expected to take command of the scope, direction, and timing of investments. Capital formation
through the marshaling of savings was to be achieved by
state-directed measures aimed at cutting down the high-
consumption proclivities of the moneyed class. In the ECLA
view, Latin America's structural deformities—its class stratification, its unproductive and backward agricultural system, its landless peasantry—would not permit adherence to
the traditional conception of capitalism as a spontaneously
generated process in which *economic development* occurs
first and is then followed by *social development*, with a redistribution of income throughout the broad layers of the
population—the pattern followed in the United States, Great
Britain, and, more recently, Japan and Western Europe. In
the ECLA philosophy, as in the Indian Development Plans,
economic development and social development are to be
achieved simultaneously, in measured stages, through the
democratic processes.

A word should be said concerning ECLA's position with
respect to foreign private capital. I find nothing in the ECLA
writings to suggest that private foreign capital has no place
in Latin America's development. Raúl Prebisch has himself

made it clear that Latin America's capital needs are so enormous that it would be absurd to think of its development without the assistance of private capital from abroad. Prebisch quite properly insists that Latin America has no place for the obsolete, freewheeling, exploitive capitalism. He, like every other responsible Latin American political leader, welcomes imaginative, creative, and constructive foreign capital which, in the words of Gonzalo Facio, former Costa Rican ambassador to the United States, "will share Latin America's triumphs as well as its heartaches." Many of Prebisch's disciples, however, are hostile to private foreign investment. They prefer public loans from the United States or the international banks.

With the peculiar inconsistency to which American foreign policy is prone, ECLA was for years shunned as an international pariah. It was looked upon by official Washington as an organization whose philosophy was alien to the free-enterprise conception of economic development. This official attitude was inconsistent in the light of our support for India with her heavy emphasis upon government planning. Or our high regard for Japan, where government planning and control over business activity are inherent in the social structure. Or our admiration for the mixed economies of northern Europe, where Sweden, for instance, has experienced a decade without recession through a skillful combination of government short- and long-range planning, fiscal and monetary policies, measures for the control of investment and the shifting of manpower—all undertaken with the active support of Swedish industry, which under a socialist regime is 90 per cent controlled by private business. *Le Plan*, under which the French Government sets the targets for economic growth for both the public and the private sectors, causes not a ripple of concern. But when our gaze turns south of the border we recoil with horror at the very notion of government planning or interference with private business. Candor requires me to affirm that this astigmatism is not an affliction confined solely to the Department of State: it is also to be found in the American business community. Since the mid-fifties, our investment in the European Common Market has exceeded our entire Latin American investment. We clamor for admittance into Japan's lush consumer market. The Indian socialist ideology has not been a deterrent to private United States investments. When it comes to Latin America, however, we impose a different standard of values and react with entirely different reflexes.

Ironically, the Washington of John F. Kennedy spoke the language of ECLA whether, like Molière's Monsieur Jourdain, it knew it or not. There is something of a double irony in the circumstance that the dialogue should have commenced during the Eisenhower administration. The offer made at Bogotá on September 6, 1960, by President Eisenhower's Under Secretary of State, Douglas Dillon, to make $500 million of "social capital" available initially— with a commitment for large additional sums in the years ahead—represented a historic milestone in the United States' altered conception of how to assist Latin America's development. Just how significant a change in attitude this was may be gathered from a brief review of the recent past. In 1948, at another inter-American conference at Bogotá, General Marshall, then Secretary of State, bluntly announced that the celebrated plan which bore his name had no place or priority in Latin America's growth and development. Eisenhower's Secretary of the Treasury, George Humphrey, consistently refused to depart from "orthodox" international banking and investment practices insofar as Latin America was concerned. Robert Anderson, his successor at the Treasury, believed that Latin America's needs could be fulfilled through private investment and existing international and governmental banking channels. His opinion began to change only after Vice-President Nixon's disastrous goodwill trip in 1958.

What the pleas of Latin America's leading statesmen failed to accomplish over a decade, Dr. Castro and his Cuban revolution achieved virtually overnight. Twelve years after General Marshall turned his back on the hopes of Latin America for assistance through "social capital" for social development, Under Secretary of State Dillon, at Bogotá, bowed to the inescapable realities—in his phrase, "poverty, ignorance and lack of social justice."

When, in the summer of 1963, Dr. Raúl Prebisch relinquished his direction of ECLA, he must have taken deep satisfaction in seeing the fruition of much of his dream: the successful operation of the Inter-American Development Bank, the hemisphere's banker for "social capital," an institution respected by conservative banking circles throughout the world; and the beginning of a movement away from Latin America's closed economic system into the Central American Common Market and the Latin American Free

Trade Association. Finally, Prebisch must have taken quiet pleasure in the knowledge that the traditional patterns of international trade (which the ECLA school for so long had contended were obsolete) were being re-examined by the industrial nations of the North at the United Nations Conference on Trade and Development.

The question, however, remains: What has the thrust toward industrialization actually achieved? Indubitably, Latin America's policy of fostering local industry has worked. Her manufacturing industry now accounts for about 20 per cent of her aggregate gross product and employs about 15 per cent of her labor force. The rapid development of manufacturing has released exchange resources once required for the import of consumer goods. Indeed, in some types of consumer goods, imports have been almost entirely replaced by domestic production and there is even some excess capacity. That Latin America's internally geared policy of industrialization has in one sense been successful is unmistakably clear from a few figures: Average per capita income is 60 per cent higher than what it was in 1930. During the period 1950–64, Latin America's gross product (in 1960 dollars) increased from around $50 billion to $90 billion.[2] Her total output of goods and services stands today just about where the GNP of the United States stood in 1931. Production of goods and services increased during 1964–5 at a rate of 2.5 per cent. During recent years, the chemical industry has expanded its annual output on an average of 10 per cent. Over the past decade, steel production has increased from under 2 million to 7 million tons. Cement production moved from 12 million to 17 million tons during the period 1956–63, and paper and cardboard from 897,-000 to 1,890,000 tons. The output of transportation equipment, appliances, spare parts, and electrical equipment has shown an annual increase, on an average, of 15 per cent. During the first half of the sixties, production of automobiles increased 53 per cent; in 1963, around 600,000 refrigerators were manufactured, and the value of electronics production was about $170 million.

These are impressive figures. But the economic development that they reflect was accomplished under painfully harsh conditions. It is difficult for those of us who live in

[2] Economic Commission for Latin America: *Economic Survey of Latin America, 1964*, UN Document E/CN. 12/711 (March 20, 1965), Vol. 1, Eng. tr., p. 4.

advanced technological nations (where a different kind of sweat and toil is utilized) to comprehend the enormous effort of human muscle, intelligence, ingenuity, and resourcefulness which has to be expended by an underdeveloped country in order to increase a production figure by a few decimal points.

In the Latin American galaxy, Mexico is a glittering star. Her economic progress since 1940 has moved at an exhilarating pace. Though still far from being a full-fledged industrial nation, Mexico can no longer be classified as underdeveloped. Between 1939 and 1960, the annual rate of growth was around 6 per cent. Nearly half of this was absorbed by her population increase of about 2.7 per cent, with the rest going into per capita income. By 1960, Mexico's per capita annual income had risen to slightly over $300, a figure unequaled in most of Latin America, Africa, or Asia. Her output of manufactured goods, electrical energy, and petroleum has more than tripled in twenty years. The Mexican steel industry is producing about 2 million tons a year. Manufacturing makes a greater contribution to gross national product (25.6 per cent in 1960) than agriculture (20.4 per cent). Mexico is virtually self-sufficient in oil and natural gas. The Mexican people eat better than they did twenty years ago. More Mexicans work at jobs—and better jobs than they did then. It is Raymond Vernon's conclusion from his recent study of Mexican development[3] that "a very considerable proportion of the Mexican public seemed to increase its living standards by a substantial margin during the twenty-year period." Mexico's international credit is such that it is the only Latin American country that can sell its bonds in the New York money market. It was one of sixteen countries that increased its contribution to the International Monetary Fund beyond the obligatory 25 per cent. The peso is among the hard currencies of the world.

So far so good. This is one side of the profit-and-loss statement. Yet at the end of two decades of spectacular growth, the distribution of income is so lopsided as to make a conservative British or American capitalist blush. Mexico is far from being a contented or tranquil country. Tensions are higher than at any time since the era of Cárdenas.

[3] Raymond Vernon: *The Dilemma of Mexico's Development* (Harvard University Press; 1963), p. 93. In the discussion of Mexico's development, I have borrowed freely from Professor Vernon, to whom I gratefully acknowledge my indebtedness.

Most of the people still lack basic food and shelter. Over 70 per cent of Mexico's inhabitants live in one-room dwellings. Despite the fact that the budgetary appropriation for education outranks all others, in 1962, according to the Mexican Ministry of Education, only 62 per cent of the population was literate. In his annual state-of-the-nation address on September 1, 1963, President López Mateos conceded that agriculture was "unquestionably the country's fundamental problem." Fifty-five per cent of the population ekes a wretched existence from the land. Agriculture is the root of Mexico's poverty. Though the factory and office worker live in the modern world, the Indians in the backlands are scarcely aware that it exists. A large proportion of the population has yet to be integrated into an industrial culture. Many millions still speak only their ancient Indian dialects; many others, who speak Spanish, cannot read it. Industrial jobs require immense investments—about $4,000 for each job. And Mexico needs to create 400,000 jobs a year. With Mexico's appallingly high birth rate (3.1 per cent higher than that of China or India), industry alone cannot absorb the tidal wave of new mouths from the villages. Octavio Paz, the gifted Mexican writer, observes:

> With our present resources we are unable to create even the minimum amount of industrial and agricultural employment required by our excess of hands and mouths. It is clear that the problem is not only one of increased population but also of insufficient economic progress. . . . Industry is not growing with the speed which our growing population demands, and the result is underemployment. At the same time, rural unemployment is retarding industrial development, because it is not increasing the number of consumers.[4]

If, as Professor Vernon suggests, there is no solid support for "the suspicion that Mexico's growth was largely a case of the rich growing richer while the real income of the poor declined," there is, nevertheless, no sector of Mexico's political spectrum, from the *sinarquista* on the Right to the Marxist on the Left, which has not persistently, and at times raucously, asked the question: *who* has really benefited from Mexico's progress? When this question is raised so often by

[4] Paz: op. cit., pp. 178–9.

all shades of Mexican political thinkers, there would appear to be ground for some doubts about the success of Mexico's industrialization.

One of the most perceptive and sensitive observers of Mexico, the American anthropologist Oscar Lewis, offers this admonition:

> . . . the political stability of Mexico is grim testimony to the great capacity for misery and suffering of the ordinary Mexican. But even the Mexican capacity for suffering has its limits, and unless ways are found to achieve a more equitable distribution of the growing national wealth and a greater equality of sacrifice during the difficult period of industrialization, we may expect social upheavals, sooner or later.[5]

If Mexico is one of the star performers in the theater of Latin American development, Brazil was by all odds *the* star of the show until Goulart turned the lights off. Despite a ruinous inflation, a galloping rise in the cost of living, chronic balance-of-payments difficulties, fantastic losses in earnings from the export of coffee, a paralysis in government, deep social tensions arising from the very process of industrial transformation—events which would have rendered most countries impotent or turned them into a revolutionary battleground—Brazil has experienced almost continuous economic growth since the end of the war. The explanation for this phenomenon, Brazilians say, is that "Brazil makes progress at night, when the politicians are asleep." Who but the *brasileiros* could muster the supreme confidence to dismiss their staggering problems with the laughing remark: "Brazil can't go over the brink; the hole isn't big enough"? Since 1947 the over-all growth in real output has been between 5 and 6 per cent annually. The increase in industrial output has been from 8 to 10 per cent. Over the past fifteen years, Brazil has progressively increased the domestic manufacture of consumer goods that were previously imported. By 1960, consumer goods represented only 6.4 per cent of total imports. This means that for all practical purposes Brazil has completed the first phase of industrialization. Outlays for intermediate materials —steel, aluminum, heavy industrial chemicals, newsprint,

5 Oscar Lewis: *The Children of Sánchez:* Autobiography of a Mexican Family (New York: Random House; 1961), xxxi.

fertilizer, and fuel—now make up the bulk of imports. The most striking trend in Brazil's industrial development is growing self-sufficiency in the production of industrial equipment. Her own industrial system can now supply about 70 per cent of this demand. This is clearly evident in the extraordinary expansion of the capital-goods industries. During the period 1955–61, steel production increased 100 per cent; the output of the machine-building industries, 125 per cent; electrical and communications industries, 380 per cent; and transport equipment, 600 per cent. In the South—São Paulo, Rio de Janeiro, and Belo Horizonte—Brazil has created an industrial center that is rapidly approaching self-sustaining economic growth. Although the Northeast has not shared in the general growth and there remain critical imbalances in the economy—transportation, power, agriculture—Brazil has, nevertheless, made enormous strides in transforming itself from a colonial agricultural economy into a modern industrial state.

However, as in Mexico, this notable development, in which Brazilians take justifiable pride, has its critics. The criticism centers on the disproportionate social cost that has been paid for it. Let Celso Furtado, Brazil's internationally known economist, speak to the point:

> We know that this development of which we are so proud has brought about no change at all in the living conditions of three-fourths of the country's population. Its main feature has been a growing concentration of income, both socially and geographically. The large mass of people who toil in the fields and constitute the majority of the Brazilian population have reaped no benefit. Worse than that, the masses have witnessed a relative decline in their standard of living as compared to those engaged in commerce and other services. As for the industrial workers, who represent a sort of middle class in the Brazilian social framework, they have grown both in absolute and relative terms, without having improved their standard of living to any large extent. They, too, have suffered a relative worsening of their economic position as compared to higher income groups employed in urban services.
>
> It is not only in the concentration of income that economic development has produced social results of an extremely negative character. Because of the anachronistic structure of Brazilian agriculture, it has led

in many regions to a relative increase in the rent from land, thus rewarding parasitic groups. Similarly, in the absence of a conscious policy designed to further the social purposes of state action, a variety of subsidies have been improvised, which—in the name of development—have very often put a premium on investments which either were superfluous or fostered a still greater concentration of income in the hands of privileged groups. Through capital contributions, such as subsidized exchange and credit, large amounts of social wealth have been transferred to a few hands.

In political and administrative fields the distortions are still more glaring. The expansion and diversification of state functions—both as cause and effect of the development—have not been followed up by the necessary basic reforms within the state structure, and as a result waste in public administration has enormously increased. This, combined with the state's increased role in the field of investments, has created ideal conditions for the illicit acquisition of capital at the people's expense. Big contracts for public works have become the current source for amassing fortunes both within and without the government.[6]

In terms of human values, Latin America has paid a heavy price for its industrialization. Whether it has been an exorbitant price is a moot question, for to remain underdeveloped exacts its own intolerable price.

Forced-draft industrialization has, however, created artificial, hothouse industries, along with "an industrial structure virtually isolated from the outside world." [7] Latin America's industries are, in the main, sustained by their ability to exact high prices for their products. Their underpinning rests not upon technological proficiency, but upon the sanctuary of protective tariffs that are among the highest in the world. Much of Latin America's industry would collapse at the first hot breath of price and technological competition—the missing ingredient in Latin America's economic development. Indeed, behind much of the hostility to American business is the fear

[6] Celso Furtado: "Brazil: What Kind of Revolution?" *Foreign Affairs*, April 1963, pp. 526–7.

[7] Economic Commission for Latin America: *Toward a Dynamic Policy for Latin America*, UN Document E/CN. 12/680 (April 14, 1963), Eng. tr., p. 107.

of American competition. The foreigner, it is argued, has access to a superior technology, has easier credit, and a management experience which enables him to crush domestic competition. Consequently, many Latin American businessmen believe that foreign competition is "unfair."

The absence of the competitive spur is the most critical defect in Latin America's industrialization. It is the function of capitalism not only to create new enterprises and to expand the old, but also, through its managerial skill, to utilize capital resources—especially where they are limited—to the greatest extent possible. Under a protected industrial system, there is no incentive for management to utilize resources efficiently. A subsidized system automatically encourages wasteful practices and habits. Only when the sharp cutting edge of competition exists is there a necessity for technological innovation and manufacturing efficiences—elements which contribute powerfully to the reduction of costs and to the effective use of resources.

Latin America's closed industrial system has generated a vicious circle. High initial manufacturing costs created the need for protection. The coddling effects of protection eliminated the incentive to reduce the high costs. A closed market perpetuated built-in inefficiencies of production, handling of materials, and utilization of manpower. A profitable internal market surrounded by import safeguards prevented the export of industrial products. Not only has the policy of substituting domestic manufactures for imported goods failed to stimulate the export of these manufactures; it has also increased the need to import costly capital equipment, which now accounts for more than one third of the total of Latin America's imports. These purchases have greatly exceeded her capacity to make payments in cash, and as a result short- and medium-term external debt has increased. The debt service to which Latin America is now obligated can become a critical impediment to continued growth and development. As an illustration of the severity of this service, to which virtually all of Latin America is subject, consider the case of Brazil. For the period 1963–65, amortization and interest charges on an outstanding debt of some $4 billion amount to about $1.8 billion. Foreign-exchange earnings from exports for the same period produced around $4.2 billion. Just to meet the costs of her debt service would take 43 per cent of Brazil's annual foreign-exchange earnings. Plainly, this would cripple her economy and at the same time destroy any possibility of paying the debt itself. An onerous debt service coupled with insufficient earnings on exports could be the noose by which Latin America will be strangled. The political implications are frightening.

Given the conditions of the time, perhaps there was no other way to achieve rapid industrial development. Nevertheless, the policy of protected industries has reached the end of the road for much of Latin America. By the late 1950's in Mexico and Brazil, there were no more easy opportunities for investments in domestic industries manufacturing goods that were previously imported. As the 1963 ECLA report itself notes, "it was relatively simple to substitute imports of industrial items of current consumption and some durable consumer and capital goods." [8] As the industrial economy of Latin America moves into a phase that requires increased quantities of intermediate or capital goods, she will need steel instead of bedsprings, aluminum in place of frying pans, tin instead of tin cans. Not only are capital goods such as precision and heavy-duty machinery difficult to manufacture; they also require a larger initial investment, more sophisticated engineering, and an entirely different market structure.

In entering into this second phase of industrial substitution—the capital-goods stage—Latin America is confronted with serious problems. True, she can attempt to force foreign companies to produce capital goods locally—as was done with consumer goods—by prohibiting imports. But foreign companies may react unfavorably to such action. They will be loath to invest their capital and technical resources to supply such limited markets as exist within the geographical boundaries of a single country. While the Latin American Free Trade Association (of which more will be said later) will in the future open a vast market, it is still a long way from realization. The ready markets for capital goods are in Europe and the United States. Latin American industry is not attuned to reaching out beyond its own local markets; moreover, its high cost structure militates against competing in the already established markets. Although the markets of other underdeveloped regions may offer the more developed countries—Mexico and Brazil, for instance—opportunities for the sale of cars and steel products, those markets will not provide the stimulus for over-all cost reductions.

Finally, there is the formidable obstacle of the critical

[8] *Ibid.,* p. 105.

shortage or nonexistence of important raw materials and energy sources without which industry is unable to operate. Although there are fair reserves of available waterpower which can serve to accelerate short-range industrial development, they are considered to be insufficient for Latin America's long-range power needs. It is frequently assumed that the presence of mineral resources is all that an under-developed country needs to begin its climb toward indus-trialization. Latin America—notably Brazil—has enormous reserves of iron ore and manganese. Brazil's reserves alone could supply Latin America's projected steel mills for an-other generation. However, the availability of ore deposits is only the beginning. Unless they are exceptionally rich and easy to transport, a heavy capital investment is required for mining and transportation. To convert ore into finished metal involves still another level of technology and capital invest-ment. Refining requires supplementary minerals, some of which may not be available. The increased utilization by in-dustry of new alloys that require special additives, some of which were unheard of only a few decades ago, vastly com-plicates the mineral-supply requirements. Iron production, for example, requires metallurgical coal that can be converted into coke. There are no high-grade coal deposits of conse-quence in Latin America. Even the technologically advanced nations have as yet found no way to produce iron without high-grade coal. Latin America must weigh the cost of estab-lishing facilities for the beneficiation of ores against other demands for capital. Venezuela probably has sufficient pe-troleum reserves to supply the continent's fuel needs. But crude oil has to be refined, transported—and paid for.

I concede that Switzerland and Japan, for instance, though lacking in mineral resources, have succeeded in attaining a high state of technological proficiency. Even the United States is today a "have not" nation in regard to minerals. It is, however, virtually impossible for Latin America to attract private capital for the development of her minerals. The re-luctance of private capital to invest in the development of a minerals resource base for Latin America has nothing to do with the economics or the technology of the problem: it has everything to do with its politics. Foreign capital is scared out of its wits by Latin America's resort to expropriation. A blind, irrational nationalism which would rather see valuable mineral resources hoarded than developed by foreign companies may make good campaign oratory, but it makes no contribution to economic development.

The hard truth of the matter is that Latin America is largely unprepared for its second great step into industrialization. Postwar shortages, import substitutions, the liberal use of government funds, have exhausted themselves. Responsible Latin Americans in government and business know that they cannot rely, as in the past, on public spending to provide the thrust for sustained growth. The inexorable march of population in Latin America—2.7 per cent annually (it is even higher in some individual countries)—demands increasing amounts of "nonproductive expenditures" for schools, hospitals, and housing. Moreover, if Latin America expects to rely on external public financing, it has to meet the standards of fiscal orthodoxy upon which the international lending agencies insist. This necessitates holding the line on inflation and keeping the printing presses from working overtime in the production of paper currency. As every Latin American president who has tried it knows from bitter experience, fiscal orthodoxy is politically unpalatable—it has no friends.

If public spending and deficit financing have their limitations, and if "austerity" programs prescribed by the international lending agencies are political liabilities, what, then, is the answer? Plainly, it is increased private investment—domestic and foreign. This fact of life has, I believe, finally penetrated the fortresses of the bureaucracy. Belatedly, the policy-makers in Washington have come to the realization that, without a massive participation of private capital, the Alliance for Progress is like a stick of dynamite without a percussion cap. The Latin American mandarinate, too, has begun to accept the idea that private capital is necessary if Latin America's industrialization is to enjoy a sustained growth.

CHAPTER SEVEN

The Shame of the Cities

FOR MOST North Americans it is something of a shock to discover that three of the ten largest cities in the world are in Latin America. Mexico City's population is close to 5 million. Buenos Aires is rapidly approaching this figure. São Paulo has almost 4 million inhabitants. Latin America's cities are growing at the phenomenal annual rate of 5 per cent. Sometime during this decade Latin America's urban population will outnumber her rural population. This concentration of population in the cities of Argentina, Chile, Venezuela, Mexico, and Brazil parallels similar urban concentrations in West Germany, Sweden, France, and Great Britain.

For half a century or more, Latin America's cities have been magnets for a migratory horde from the countryside. Over the past fifteen years the surge to the cities has had the appearance of a flood tide. In this experience Latin America is not unique. Cities throughout the world have become swollen and shapeless by the pressure of populations which can no longer be supplied with the civilized amenities of living. Athens, birthplace of the Western city and its civilization, was for several thousand years never inhabited by more than 200,000 people. Yet, in our time, within fifty years it mushroomed into a metropolis of almost 2 million people. Lady Jackson, better known to her world-wide admirers as Barbara Ward, has warned that the contemporary failure "to adapt human settlements to dynamic change may soon outstrip even disease and starvation as the gravest risk, short of war, facing the human species."

The city slum with its fetid tenements is older than the Industrial Revolution. Latin America's industrial revolution has produced a new kind of exhibition of human degradation. In Mexico City, they are called *colonias proletarias*. In Panama City, *casas brujas*. In Caracas, *ranchos*. In Lima, *barriadas*. In Santiago, *callampas*. In Rio de Janeiro, *favelas*. In Buenos Aires, *villas miserias*. However bizarre or picturesque the name, it means the same thing: shanty town. Like hideous running sores they are to be found on the outskirts of every Latin American city. They crawl in cancerous disorder over the hills of Caracas and Rio de Janeiro. In the midst of the glitter and tinsel of urban prosperity, the shanty towns taunt Latin America for its neglect of the human condition. They are the tinder for Castro's match.

Of Rio de Janeiro's three million inhabitants one third are *favelados*, who dwell in "vertical islands of squalor." Thirty per cent of the half million inhabitants of Guayaquil, Ecuador's largest city, live in shanty towns. Of Caracas' one and a third million inhabitants, one quarter occupy makeshift *ranchos* overlooking the hills of the city. A Venezuelan government report states that almost one half of the entire population lives in shanties. A Mexican housing expert, Jaime Ceballos Osorio, reports that 76 per cent of the Mexican people live in "subhuman conditions in homes that should be condemned for human occupancy." American housing experts believe that it would take 12 to 14 million housing units to replace the substandard dwellings of Latin American cities. This would require a minimum investment of about $30 billion. A million new homes are needed each year just to keep pace with population growth. Another half million units must be rebuilt yearly to replace dwellings that have deteriorated. This would require an additional investment of $4 billion. The magnitude of Latin America's housing problem is staggering. But the effort being made to solve the problem is almost negligible.

Rural migrants are lured to the cities by the tales that percolate into the countryside telling of good jobs at high wages in the factories and the booming construction industry. The migrants come to escape the bleak poverty and the hopelessness of their lives in the backlands. Prolonged drought—or even the rumor of another dry spell—propels an exodus from the arid *sertão* of the Northeast of Brazil. The migrants are attracted to the cities for other reasons too—for the world of excitement and color and movement that contrasts so sharply with the dreariness of their drab peasant lives.

The new arrivals from the hinterland become squatters on vacant land, owned either by the government or by private individuals. At times there are "invasions" by numerous families moving into a vacant area at the same time. The invasions generally take place at night. They are well organized. At first, the shelters consist of hovels made of cast-off lumber, packing cases, corrugated-iron sheeting, odd pieces of tile and brick, and thatched palm leaves. The hovels are windowless; light enters through the doorway. Bedding consists of old rags and, for the more fortunate, hammocks which they have carried along with their few pitiful possessions. Sometimes a chair and a table may be seen; more frequently, a box serves as furniture. The floor is hard-pressed earth. There is no sanitation, drinking water, or electricity. This is the basic shelter for the great mass of Latin America's population whether they live in the country or the city.

In Lima, where the *barriadas* are mainly populated by Indians from the *altiplano,* the traditional communal system of organization is followed. First, a "residents' association" is organized, its officers chosen in a public election, in which all adults who represent a family are entitled to vote. As in the communities on the *sierra,* the elected officers mete out punishment to the refractory members of the association and act as a court of justice in the settlement of family disputes. This indigenous system of representative government is in sharp contrast with the prevailing official Peruvian system, in which municipal and provincial officials are selected by the central government—a system which President Belaúnde seeks to reverse by emulating the representative democracy of the Indian communities. After an area has been invaded, it is divided into plots of varying sizes and allotted to the individual families in accordance with their needs. Squatters' "rights" are established by the immediate erection of a shelter, using whatever materials are at hand. The association acts in behalf of the members in the protection of their rights as squatters. The help of local religious and charitable groups is sought to find jobs or to obtain medical assistance. As the migrants find employment, they pay dues to the association. An effort is made to persuade the city officials to provide the community with water, electricity, and sewage. Later in the life of the *barriada*, a clinic, a school, a church, and a community meeting place emerge. When the *barriada* no longer has any vacant land and begins to feel the pressure of crowding, a system of rentals and subtenancies is instituted by those who wish to move to other areas. As the settlement becomes a part of "suburbia," the earlier thatched roofs and improvised shacks give way to painted adobe brick houses. "Zoning" regulations are imposed by the association on the "style" of future building. The invasion which began surreptitiously one night results in a permanent residential district for the better-off members of Lima's rural proletariat.

This striking effort at adaptation to city life does not mean that the great body of the Indian population of Lima lives in Peruvian "Levittowns." Or that their daily diet of 1,200 to 1,500 calories—slightly above the level of starvation—is the Peruvian version of Nirvana. It does not require the trained eye of a health or building inspector to recognize in a casual stroll through the streets of the "City of Kings" that Lima's slum tenements are not surpassed by those in the Chinese quarter of Singapore or Bombay. *El Montón de basura*, the mountain of garbage in which thousands of shanty town families root for food, is Lima's monument to the living who have been abandoned by God and man.

The slums of Brazil became a reality for the readers of *Life* (June 16, 1961) through Gordon Parks' photographs of Rio's *favelas*. What Parks' brilliant photographic essay could not capture was their oppressive stench. Or the panorama of labyrinthine gullies winding their way over the *morros* and serving at the same time as channels for the movement of humans and their sewage. Nor could he convey the devastation of flash floods and landslides on habitations glued precariously to the hillsides. Frozen in memory is the shattering spectacle of man's inhumanity, understood only by the compassionate figure on the *Cristo* whose brooding silhouette looms over the *favelas* from its crown on the hill of Corcovado.

The typical *favela* hut with its coconut-palm fronds is African in origin.[1] There is no regular water supply for the *favelas;* the *favelados* themselves must illegally tap fire hydrants or obtain water from nearby drinking fountains. Although no electricity is furnished by the city, some dwellings have radios and TV sets. Many have a solitary electric

[1] Gilberto Freyre: *The Mansions and the Shanties* (New York: Alfred A. Knopf; 1963), p. 133.

light. Electricity is supplied by enterprising neighbors who string wires from their own homes, which adjoin the *favela*, to the shacks of the *favelados*. Mail is delivered to the *favelados* by still another group of entrepreneurs who, like the electrical subcontractors, charge a fee for their service. The *favelados* generally obtain the bare necessities of living in their own *favela* stores, which carry odds and ends of supplies purchased by the storekeeper from retail stores in the city because he has no access to wholesale merchants. Like their brethren in the backlands and the cities throughout Latin America, the *favelados* are unable to afford shoes, clothing, medicine, education, or bread for themselves and their children. They are the marginal people—spectators of Brazil's march of progress.

An insight into the mind and heart of the *favelado*, which should give pause to Brazil's politicians, has been given us by Carolina Maria de Jesus, a self-educated Negress of São Paulo. In 1960, her diary, *Quarto de Despejo*[2] (colloquially: "garbage dump"), became the literary sensation of Brazil. On a day when she was too dispirited and weary to forage in the city dump for food for her three children and herself, Carolina Maria made this ominous entry: "When I am hungry, I want to kill Jânio. I want to hang Adhemar and burn Juscelino." [3]

The shanty town is a transplanted rural village. The inhabitants follow the traditional and folk customs of the countryside. It is common for them to raise chickens and to keep pigs. The slum inhabitants carry the blight of the backlands to the city. They also acquire the ailments typical of the city: delinquency, criminal violence, job instability, alcoholism, prostitution, and mental illnesses. The rural migrant is lost without the intimate help, guidance, and protection of the *patrón*. There are very few public welfare facilities to help him adjust to city life. The labor unions show little interest in helping him. To the impersonal bureaucracies, the shantytown dweller is a despised peasant. Yet, with all of its human waste and tragedy, the shanty town provides its inhabitants with a modicum of social cohesion. In *The Culture of the*

[2] Carolina Maria de Jesus: *Child of the Dark* (New York: E. P. Dutton & Co., Inc.; 1962), trans. from the Portuguese by David St. Clair.

[3] Brazilian politicians are popularly referred to by their first names. When she wrote this, Juscelino Kubitschek was President of Brazil. Jânio Quadros and Adhemar de Barros were candidates for the presidency.

Vecindad in Mexico City, Oscar Lewis makes the point that the *vecindad* (neighborhood), owing to the similarity between its peasant culture and that of the familiar countryside, acts as a shock absorber for the rural migrant.

Lacking occupational skills, the rural migrants constitute a steady pool of cheap labor which depresses the level of wages and the standard of living. Employers have no incentive to introduce operational efficiencies in their businesses when they can readily tap this reservoir of cheap labor. Thus the unassimilated rural mass retards industrial development, and the reserve of cheap labor intensifies underemployment and unemployment.

The shanty towns bring into sharp focus the social, economic, and political combustibles which are close to the blazing point in Latin America. As Galo Plaza, former President of Ecuador, says, "most of the explosive problems of Latin America start precisely in the slums that surround the large modern city." The *bogotazo* which put the torch to Colombia's capital and the *descamisados* who gutted Buenos Aires showed what savage fury can erupt from Latin America's slums. With a mastery of modern propaganda and organizational techniques, a Latin American demagogue could plunge any of the capital cities into a long night of elemental violence.

Latin America's politicians are making no serious attempt to defuse this time bomb ticking away in the centers of squalor; they resemble the French aristocrats frolicking in the gardens of Versailles on the eve of 1789. In most Latin American countries there are programs for public and private housing. But they are primarily for the benefit of middle-income groups—white-collar employees, civil servants, and the better-paid industrial workers—those who can afford to amortize the cost of a home over fifteen to twenty years through annual payments ranging from 15 to 30 per cent of their income. Housing for the families of the lowest income brackets—the dwellers in the shacks and the tenements—who cannot afford the cost of housing under the prevailing construction and financing standards, is neglected.

It is usually taken for granted that housing for the poor cannot be built without subsidy. Under the prevailing standards of construction and financing, this is, of course, true. The question is whether these standards represent the only approach to low-cost housing. With very few exceptions, Latin American housing authorities have not even attempted to answer this question. I am not an expert in housing, but I do know from personal experience that in the Dominican Republic, it was found feasible to build concrete prefabricated houses containing simple but essential amenities for as little as $750. Dominican stevedores and sugar workers could pay for these houses without too much difficulty. Their monthly amortization payments amounted to some $8 to $10. A "down payment" of 15 to 20 per cent in lieu of cash was made possible by permitting the prospective homeowners to supply labor for clearing land and constructing roads and ditches.

Outside of Puerto Rico, very few Latin American architects have been even remotely interested in low-cost housing. Indeed, it is a serious question whether most practicing architects of this hemisphere (who seem to be preoccupied with the monumental building) are by training or temperament capable of designing low-cost housing, let alone housing practicable for rural migrants. Very few Latin American housing agencies have given serious consideration to reducing costs by utilizing self-help methods, or to furnishing at low cost a central housing core to which additional rooms could be added as the financial circumstances of the owner permitted.

The chief promoter of low-cost housing for Latin America should have been the Agency for International Development (AID). Fearful of its critics in Congress and lacking imaginative boldness, AID turned its back on the poor of the shanty towns and gave its financial support to the well-to-do among the middle-income groups.

You cannot get rid of the shanty town by moving its inhabitants to a new housing project. The peasant is clearly unwilling to live in and to maintain modern-style housing, particularly the multi-story filing cabinet known as an apartment house. Country people traditionally are suspicious of and hostile to governmental authority. They are fearful of urban living which subjects them to supervision by police or health officials. Contemporary experience shows that slum dwellers—even in the United States—are reluctant to abandon the security of their slum environment. The failure of the attempt to move the entire population of a shanty town in Barranquilla, Colombia, into a new housing project is a dramatic warning that the substitution of new houses for rural hovels will not solve the problem. Only 20 per cent of the inhabitants of the shanty town moved into the new houses

when their shacks were demolished. The remainder scattered
to other slums in the city, some because they felt alien to the
new housing, others because of distrust of the city officials.
Without adequate social and psychological conditioning, moving the inhabitants of a shanty town into modern buildings
is only treating the symptoms of the disorder. Shanty towns
are the end product of a long chain of causes: the flight from
the poverty of the countryside; the highest population growth
rate of any area in the world; resistance to birth control; concentration of industry in the big cities; haphazard development of urban centers; real estate speculation and profiteer-
ing in construction; and, finally, sheer neglect by the politicians of a marginal population which at present is politically
inert. Each is a separate problem but all are indissolubly
linked.

The ultimate solution to the continuing migration to the
cities lies in the rural areas. The city will lose its attractive-
ness when the opportunity for individual landownership and
better standards of living make their appearance in the backlands. The problem of Latin America's system of land tenure
will not be solved overnight. Nevertheless, significant interim
measures can be undertaken. As economic integration pro-
gresses, industrial decentralization can be speeded up. Tax
incentives, leasing new plants at low rentals, establishing
training centers for workers, and other familiar devices can
be employed to encourage industries to relocate or to establish themselves in smaller communities.

Southern Italy offers an instructive lesson in what can be
done to attract industry into a backward region. The Italian
Government has successfully lured northern Italian industrialists and foreign companies into the South. Prosperous
new communities have been established in an area which for
generations knew only brutal impoverishment.

We have the knowledge to design a community for the
special needs of the inhabitants of shanty towns. Private
capital is available. The difficulty is to find the politicians
who have the compassion, the imaginative boldness, and the
will to bring the two together. There are a number of political
leaders who have the sense of urgency to start pilot projects:
in Argentina, Governor Anselmo Marini of Buenos Aires
Province and Governor Francisco Gabrelli of Mendoza
Province; in Peru, President Fernando Belaúnde Terry; and
in Chile, President Eduardo Frei. Mexico presents a challenging opportunity for the establishment of a pilot project.

The need for housing is acute in all sectors, not just in the shanty towns. Because of her revolutionary tradition, Mexico's political leaders are sensitive to popular demands for housing. Among her practical revolutionary leaders, men who have demonstrated a keen interest in housing, are President Gustavo Díaz Ordaz; Don Ernesto Uruchurtu, Mayor of Mexico City; and Don Antonio J. Bermúdez, director general of the Programa Nacional Fronterizo, the national border program that has as its objective a vast social, economic, and physical transformation of the communities along the Mexican-United States frontier, stretching 1,600 miles from the Pacific coast to the Gulf of Mexico.

Probably the only architect and "master builder" in the West who has the practical experience to undertake the design and construction of "human communities" for the inhabitants of shanty towns, is Constantinos Doxiadis of Athens. Doxiadis was selected to submit the design for Islambad, the new capital of Pakistan. His ideas for handling the problems created by the flood of rural migrants have been solicited by the governments of Ghana, India, Iraq, Jordan, Lebanon, Sudan, Syria, and Greece. In 1960, Doxiadis was awarded the city-planning study for the largest urban renewal project in the United States—Eastwick, Pennsylvania. In 1963, Governor Carlos Lacerda asked him to study the relocation of Rio's *favelados*. The Society of Mexican Architects in 1963 conferred upon Doxiadis their highest award in recognition of his outstanding work in community planning and building in the emergent countries.

The pilot project should be financed in the main by private capital. The actual amount of capital required by a specific project will vary with the size of the project, the accessibility of water, electricity, and other public utilities, the cost and availability of materials, and so on. The amount of money needed is not excessive. The customary heavy cost of land acquisition can be eliminated, for land can be donated by the state or national governments. The government authorities can also contribute public services—water, electricity, streets, sewage. Working capital can be obtained from several sources—in Argentina and Brazil, for example, from the trade unions, which have substantial pension funds. I believe that a number of American, European, and Japanese companies with factories in these two countries would co-operate. Similarly, some of the American and European trade unions will be interested in helping. Some financial assistance can be provided by the local governments. With ingenuity, it should be possible to evolve a system to protect the investment of foreign private capital against inflation and currency devaluation.

The Inter-American Development Bank might undertake the role of organizing a pilot project, charging a management fee for its services.

The tools and materials are available for at least a beginning in the fulfillment of the promises of the twentieth century for Latin America's forgotten people. The major problem is the inertia of the politicians. Unless Latin America's politicians are anxious to be hung by their heels from the lampposts of their cities, they would be well-advised to give their immediate attention to their shanty towns.

CHAPTER EIGHT

Strength Through Unity

The Central American Common Market

ATTEMPTS to unify Central America into a single state began almost with the break-up of the Spanish Empire. For over a century, the five states of Guatemala, El Salvador, Honduras, Nicaragua, and Costa Rica—aggregating roughly 200,000 square miles (equal in size to Wyoming and Colorado) and containing some 8 to 9 million people—sought to unite under various forms of government. Each effort resulted in failure. As one reads the story of these doomed ventures by a small band of patriots—Manuel José Arce (a Salvadorean); José del Valle (a Guatemalan scientist-philosopher, one of the truly brilliant men of the hemisphere, the first to see the advantages of co-operation among all the states of the hemisphere); Francisco Morazán (Honduran by birth, governor in Guatemala and El Salvador, a soldier who fought and lost battles in every province and who found death in Costa Rica, he was the embodiment of the idea of Central American confederation)—one is impressed not so much by the failures as by the courage which mounted the repeated endeavors.

The Central American leaders had no experience with government comparable to that of the English colonials to the north. Fully three quarters of the signers of the American Declaration of Independence had held office under the Crown before the Revolution and under the state governments thereafter. None of the Central American provinces

of the captaincy general of Guatemala fought for its liberation—it came about almost as a matter of default. There was
absent that common struggle which, if only momentarily,
binds men together. They had no militarily strong central
government or any war debt that required amortization by
a central regime. There were no large tracts of land which
could be played off by a central government against the ter-
ritorial ambitions of the provinces. Nor was there any vast
"moving frontier" to absorb the energies of the people.
Federalism failed and the *idée fixe* of Central American
unity was destroyed by the disease that has infected all of
Latin America—"the rancors that grew from making decisions." [1] Domingo Sarmiento, out of his own not so dis-
similar experience in Argentina, saw the inherent weakness
of the Central American struggle when, with the brilliance of
a shaft of lightning, he wrote: "Central America made a
sovereign state of each village."

The urge for unity has continued into our time. Thoughtful Latin American leaders began to share the conviction
of European political leaders that the day of national sovereignty was over. Just as it has been apparent that the
European nation-state no longer makes political sense, there
was an increasing awareness in this hemisphere that Latin
America's nation-states had outgrown their usefulness. Indeed, most of Latin America's political units are more
analogous to the Greek city-state than to the modern nation-
state. As such, in the twentieth century they are political
museum pieces. European thinking on "economic integration" and the establishment of the European Coal and Steel
Community found a refrain in this hemisphere. There was
also the fear that a world organized into great power and
trading blocs would give short shrift to a Latin America
whose voice at the council tables would be only the cacoph-
ony of twenty separate entities. Experience with local manufacturing had, moreover, driven home the realization that
continued progress in industrialization was possible only if
markets extended beyond the boundaries of a single country.

The movement for a Central American Common Market
and the broader grouping of a Latin American Free Trade

[1] Thomas L. Karnes: *The Failure of Union* (Chapel Hill: University
of North Carolina Press; 1961), p. 45. I am greatly indebted to Professor Karnes for the insight he has afforded me into this historic
chapter in Central America's quest for unity.

Association were responses to this need for the sovereignty of the community.

It was not, however, until 1951 that the idea of a Central American Common Market finally took hold. In June 1951, at the yearly meeting of the United Nations Economic Commission for Latin America, and at the request of the Central American representatives, a Central American Economic Cooperation Committee was established to study the problems of economic union. Over the next six years the Committee forged two draft treaties, one dealing with the elimination of internal customs barriers and establishing common external tariffs, the other defining "integration industries"— those that would require access to the entire regional market in order to be economically feasible. The draft treaties, after some revisions, were signed by the presidents of the five Central American countries on June 10, 1958.

The first was the Multilateral Treaty for a customs union. It listed some two hundred commodities on which import and export duties were to be eliminated. The second of the treaties was the Agreement on the Regime for Central American Integration Industries, designed to promote expansion of existing industries as well as to encourage new industries in the region. A Central American Industrial Integration Commission was created for the purpose of administering this program and to designate which industries were to be "integrated." These were to receive special preferential treatment through tariff protection and tax exemptions or reductions, as well as preferences in government orders. Such "integrated industries" would be: the manufacture of tires in Guatemala, copper wire and cables in El Salvador, insecticides in Nicaragua, sulphuric acid in Honduras—all intended to serve the entire region.

In December 1960, the member nations adopted still another treaty: the General Treaty on Central American Integration. Under this, it was agreed to accelerate the creation of a free-trade area for Central America within a period of five years and to adopt common tariffs on goods from other countries. Tariffs and quotas on almost all the products of the member countries were eliminated. The General Treaty established an administrative machinery for governing the Market, with headquarters at Guatemala City. Three administrative groups were created: (1) the Central American Economic Council to direct and co-ordinate economic integration, its members to consist of the Ministers of Economy of the five countries; (2) the Executive Council, with the duty of administering the General Treaty, its members to consist of a delegate and an alternate selected by each member country; and (3) the Permanent Secretariat, to provide technical and other services for both Councils.

At the December 1960 meeting at which the General Treaty came into existence, there was also established a Central American Bank for Economic Integration with headquarters at Tegucigalpa, Honduras. The Bank's initial authorized capital was $16 million, to be subscribed by the member states. This amount was increased to $20 million when Costa Rica's decision to join the Bank was ratified by her National Congress. The Agency for International Development has made available to the Bank grants of $3 million. The Bank has received loans from AID and the Inter-American Development Bank for $27.5 million and $6 million respectively for industrial and agricultural projects. The Bank had authorized as of June 30, 1965, credits of some $38 million to finance plants for the production of such items as metal tubing, insulated wire, and processed meat. Further structural changes are contemplated to enable the Bank to participate in direct investments through the purchase of stocks in the companies that it assists, and to enable it to contribute toward setting up a Central American stock exchange.

To further integration, the following regional organizations were created:

1. A Central American Institute of Industrial Research and Technology, to advise the governments and private enterprise throughout the area. Its headquarters are in Guatemala City.

2. An Advanced School of Public Administration with headquarters at San José, Costa Rica, to provide training for officials of the governments and autonomous agencies.

3. An Institute of Nutrition of Central America and Panama, responsible for studying the problems of nutrition among the five countries, with headquarters at San José. ("Incaparina," a low-cost protein-rich vegetable mixture, was developed by the Institute to supplement protein-deficient diets. Over 3 million pounds of Incaparina were sold in Colombia and Guatemala in 1965 to make a drink with the protein value of milk at one fifth the cost, and the food will soon be marketed in Venezuela, Brazil, and the rest of Central America.)

4. A Central American Clearing House, with headquarters at Tegucigalpa, to expedite intra-Central American payments and to develop closer relations among the central banks of the region.

5. A Federation of Central American Chambers of Commerce, to operate within the private economy and furnish advisory services to the various chambers. Its headquarters are at San José.

6. A Central American Corporation of Air Navigation Services provides flight information, aeronautical communication, and radio aids to all aircraft in the Central American region. Facilities are located at the capital airports of each country. The office of the General Manager is at the airport at Tegucigalpa, Honduras.

7. A Central American Superior University Council is developing an integrated system for the national universities of the region. The rectors of the five universities constitute the Superior Council. As member universities are autonomous institutions, the Council is not a government organization.

8. An International Regional Organization for Agricultural and Livestock Sanitation conducts campaigns against plant and animal diseases, and advises the member governments on quarantine procedures. Its Executive Secretariat is in El Salvador.

9. A Central American Institute of Business Management provides management training for Central American business leaders and future executives, promotes modern management concepts, and seeks to improve business education throughout the area. Its headquarters are in El Salvador.

Other steps have been taken to accelerate the realization of a Common Market. The central banks of the region have agreed to promote a Central American check system, with a new monetary unit to be known as the *peso centroamericano*, equal to the United States dollar, for use in transactions between member countries. The separate telecommunications systems of the five countries, in all of which the respective governments hold a controlling interest, have agreed to integrate by means of a new corporation to be known as the Central American Corporation of Telecommunications. Consideration is being given to the establishment of a telecommunications network and passport- and visa-free travel within the region. The Foreign Ministers have agreed in principle to establish a Central American Court of Justice, and a Labor Council to establish common labor and social policies.

It would be quite erroneous to compare the movement toward integration of the Central American Common Market with the comparable development of the European Economic Community, despite superficial resemblances. And it would be quite unjust to measure results through such a comparison. With a highly developed industrial technology, the European Common Market, in its expansion and the elimination of internal tariffs, sought an intensification of competition, with the objective of raising productivity. It was expected that the inefficient, high-cost producer would fall by the wayside. It was never intended to supply him with crutches. Capital and resources were expected to move freely into the countries with the lowest production and distribution costs. In the pre-ECM era, French industry was notoriously opposed to competition. The story is told of the French automobile manufacturer who, at the end of the week, was given a glowing report by his general sales manager of the increased volume of sales and the excellent prospects for the future. The reaction of the head of the company was: "Excellent, Henri. Now cut back production and increase our prices." Today, the French manufacturer has ceased to be protectionist-minded and is no longer fearful of competition. Indeed, he is fully capable of creating gales of competition himself.

In the Central American integration effort, the base from which operations must start is entirely different. Here, the region's economy is dependent on four commodities—coffee, cotton, cocoa, and bananas. These commodities account for 90 per cent of the area's exports. To expect an economy in which 55 per cent of the population over the age of fourteen is illiterate, in which 53 per cent of the population has no water supplies, and 25 per cent lacks housing, in an area which is predominantly agricultural, with a low standard of living, which suffers from a critical maladjustment in its international trade, and which is only on the threshold of industrialization—to expect such an economy to embrace the classical concept of a free-trade area or a customs union would be absurd.

The architects of the Central American Common Market proceeded along Latin American lines. Industrialization is being promoted to decrease imports, to provide employment for the swollen urban population, and to attract private foreign capital. The flow of capital and resources is to be directed into "integrated industries." The removal of internal tariffs and duties is designed to swell intra-regional trade. In 1961, the five countries' trade among themselves was only 7 per cent of their total trade; trade in manufactures was only 5 per cent of the total. An increase in intra-regional trade is the key to the success of the Market. It is also the purpose of integration to increase the production of other cash crops, such as cotton in El Salvador and Guatemala. In short, the Central American Common Market has provided a number of tools to further the economic and social development of the region.

The progress toward integration has been successful beyond expectation. The Dominican Republic has applied for membership and Panama for associate membership. Intra-regional trade in 1963 was 36 per cent greater than in 1962. Total intra-regional trade for 1963 was about $66 million, an increase of 32 per cent over 1962. Intra-regional trade for 1964 was $105 million, an increase of 59 per cent over 1963. In a historic state visit to Central America early in January 1966, Mexico's President Díaz Ordaz offered his neighbors up to $30 million in credit and loans. The institutional framework for integration is proceeding at an exhilarating pace. For this generation of Central Americans there is no turning back: theirs is a commitment to the future.

The Latin American Free Trade Association

The same stirrings from across the ocean, the same inner compulsion for economic integration, working with the same ECLA technical assistance but with a different cast of countries, produced in South America the Latin American Free Trade Association (LAFTA). This free-trade area came into existence when Argentina, Bolivia,[2] Brazil, Chile, Mexico, Peru, and Uruguay initialed the Montevideo Treaty in February 1960.

Although the term "Association" corresponds to the designation employed by Europe's Outer Seven—Austria, Denmark, Norway, Portugal, the United Kingdom, Sweden, and Switzerland—the Montevideo Treaty was born of a different inspiration. Because of tactical considerations, its ob-

[2] Bolivia did not sign the treaty at its inception. In May 1961, Colombia and Ecuador announced their decision to subscribe.

jectives were deliberately restricted. The studies and negotiations that preceded the draft of the Treaty were extraordinarily cautious to avoid any suggestion that a European-style free-trade area or common market was contemplated. Indeed, Dr. Raúl Prebisch, addressing a working group in November 1956, warned against adopting "broad formulae for economic integration." He urged more limited arrangements such as "selecting a number of commodities from industries about to be established . . . which require expanded markets, and trying to establish systems of industrial reciprocity on the basis of limited schedules." [3] LAFTA was born hobbled. Prebisch knew his fellow Americans and he saw that a sweeping program—one resembling the Central American conception of integration—would have foundered on the conflicting rivalries and jealousies of Argentina, Brazil, Chile, and Mexico. It was the part of wisdom first to involve these countries in the mere act of co-operating—no mean accomplishment in itself—and then to allow the unfolding events to work their will on the member governments.

Inherent in the trade relations of members of the Association were circumstances which militated against a European conception of integration or a customs union. For instance: Colombia is more closely integrated with Venezuela than she is with Argentina; Mexico, more closely with the Central American area than with Uruguay. Indeed, northern Mexico is in many respects more integrated with the southern part of the United States than with the rest of Mexico. Similarly, Argentina is far more integrated with Uruguay, Bolivia, and southern Brazil than she is with Venezuela or Ecuador. (This gravitational pull between countries and regions has led some to question whether the organizational structure of LAFTA may not be too unwieldy and whether initially smaller—but more natural—geographical groupings might have been better.)

The European Outer Seven had existing arrangements for reciprocal trade which accounted for a large percentage of their total trade, to say nothing of the close economic ties between them. Prior to the organization of LAFTA, no such close economic ties obtained among the member countries. Pre-LAFTA trade among the nine member countries represented barely 7 per cent of their total trade. Even this small

[3] Quoted in Victor L. Urquidi: *Free Trade and Economic Integration in Latin America* (Berkeley and Los Angeles: University of California Press; 1962), pp. 52–3.

percentage was largely confined to trade among the southern countries. Argentina, Brazil, Chile, Peru, Uruguay, Bolivia, and Paraguay account for 80 to 90 per cent of all of Latin America's intercontinental trade. Argentina and Brazil together conduct more than 60 per cent of the total. Although Argentina was a focal point for trade among various countries—as among Mexico, Colombia, Peru, Brazil, Chile, or Uruguay—there was very little reciprocal trade.

There was another inherent difficulty. Such commerce as there was among the southern Latin American countries depended upon certain national currencies—Argentina's in particular. Later, trade among the southern tier of countries was dependent upon bilateral payment agreements which required the use of "money of account" and the availability of substantial reciprocal credits. In short, convertible currencies for intra-Latin American trade were not available prior to LAFTA.

The economic potential of LAFTA—even excluding Central America and Venezuela, which have not yet elected to join—is striking. Some 140 million people live within its boundaries. It accounts for 79 per cent of the territory and 72 per cent of the population of Latin America. It has a GNP of between $75 and $80 billion. The LAFTA countries are pre-eminent in manufacturing. Argentina, Brazil, Chile, and Mexico account for all of Latin America's output of motor vehicles, wood pulp, newsprint, and machinery, almost all of the primary steel products, and a high percentage of food products, textiles, consumer goods, chemical machinery, and transport equipment. It is not without interest that more than half of the total United States direct investment in Latin America is in the LAFTA countries.

Following the first round of negotiations among the member countries, significant changes in the trade patterns were discernible. Exports within the Association increased by 37 per cent, with every member participating in the growth. This increase in trade, moreover, was not the result of the exchange of traditional products, but represented the flow of new products under the negotiated tariff concessions, which now cover more than 7,000 individual items. Mexico has fared better than any of the other members and offers a meaningful illustration of the beneficial results that flow from the lowering of trade tariffs. During 1962, Mexico's manufacturing exports rose 150 per cent and her chemical exports 425 per cent. Her trade with the zone increased 90 per cent, from $12 to $23 million. By 1964, total trade with LAFTA was around $52 million, and in the first half of 1965, $28 million. Mexican businessmen roam the continent searching for markets. The government has established a credit agency to finance exports. Businessmen in the southern tier of republics complain that Mexico is reaping the lion's share of the benefits.

The LAFTA compass may be pointing toward a common market rather than a free-trade zone. An indication of this direction may be seen in the exploratory discussions between Chile and Brazil for a resolution of one of the thorniest problems inhibiting integration—the existence of an automotive industry in several of the member countries. Brazil and Argentina have fairly well developed automobile plants. Mexico is about to enter the field. A solution to the problem appears to be emerging in the arrangements between Chile and Brazil. Under this arrangement, Chile will develop its automotive industry by concentrating on diesel trucks and buses, medium-sized and small trucks, and compact cars, all of which are to be assembled in Chile from Brazilian-made parts. Companies with mixed Chilean and Brazilian capital, it is hoped, will be established in Chile for the manufacture of cars. Plainly, if this experiment is successful, it could lead to manufacturing specialization and to the interchange of parts, components, and assemblies for a wide variety of products.

At a meeting in November 1965 of Foreign Ministers of LAFTA countries at Montevideo, Uruguay, a Chilean proposal to accelerate the transition of the zone into a common market by the establishment of a High Authority similar to the European Coal and Steel Authority was rejected in favor of an advisory body. A majority of the ministers believed that it was premature to give the association supranational powers. The inarticulated reason was Latin American reluctance to accept a limitation on sovereignty. That it was the Mexican Foreign Minister who took the lead in working out the compromise indicates not only Mexican involvement in integration, but also an increasing prospect of leadership by Mexico in an area in which she has heretofore remained aloof. Ironically, the same Foreign Ministers, who were unwilling to take a concrete step in furtherance of a common market for LAFTA, showed no reluctance in approving the Act of Rio de Janeiro—also promulgated in November 1965—under which their countries were pledged to pursue the objective of a common market for the whole of Latin America.

There are, however, many who believe that LAFTA is liberalizing trade too timidly, and that greater immediate attention must be given to economic integration of the region through such measures as "the interlocking of Latin American capital markets," the creation of a regional securities exchange, the establishment of investment companies (to sell shares throughout the region, as well as in Europe and the United States), and mechanisms for bringing to the attention of private capital opportunities for the establishment of regional industries.

Regional integration offers a unique opportunity for the rationalization of many LAFTA industries. Foreign companies can assist in the reorganization and consolidation of existing enterprises whose technology is largely obsolete, whose handling of materials is costly and wasteful, and whose business efficiency leaves much to be desired. Rationalization of existing industries would provide room for North American, European, and Japanese technology, marketing, and capital to accelerate economic integration. The experience of the United States common market and the emerging European Common Market shows that the small unit cannot compete effectively. Big consumer markets require big businesses with strong engineering, manufacturing, and financial resources.

The business elite of Latin America has to make a choice: either they will remain big frogs in small ponds, not to be taken seriously in the industrial North, or they can begin to think and act like centers of industrial power, accepted as peers among peers by the industrial power centers of the North Atlantic Community and Japan.

If Latin America is to become an industrial power, her industries will have to compete in world markets. In these markets, Latin American business can compete successfully only through large industrial complexes—her own or multinational companies.

History may bypass LAFTA if it fritters away a decade on conventional tariff negotiations to the neglect of regional consolidation and the merger of industries, and if it fails to supply imaginatively conceived regional mechanisms to support economic integration.

LAFTA has demonstrated the economic advantages of lowering tariff walls. It must now hasten regional integration. Economic federation in Latin America is the inevitable first step toward political federation. Unless Latin America begins to think and act as a continental power, she has no future on the world stage. In the contemporary world of power and economic blocs, there is no room for the political anachronism of coffee, tin, banana, and sugar sovereignties. Latin America is eager to be respected. But what respect can there be for a Balkanized political structure divided by petty rivalries and bickerings, scarcely able to govern, which prefers domestic contentions to continental solutions?

What does Latin America require to become a continental power with a unified voice that will be heard with respect and could throw the weight of a continent into the scale of world politics? Only to demonstrate to herself and to the world that she has the competence, the tenacity of purpose, and the political maturity to make economic integration work.

In the Central American Common Market and the Latin American Free Trade Association, Latin America has within her grasp the repudiation of the bitter indictment of Ortega y Gasset that Latin America shares a past but no future.

CHAPTER NINE

Death of an Alliance

THE now world-famous slogan "Alliance for Progress" was first heard at Harvard University in December 1960, at a meeting of members of the United States international business community and a number of distinguished representatives of the academic community.[1] It burst over the world in President Kennedy's celebrated Inaugural Address. Although stamped in the U.S.A., the underlying philosophy of the Alliance for Progress is distinctly Latin American. The grand design for this inter-American partnership was first propounded in 1958 by Juscelino Kubitschek, former President of Brazil, in his *Operacão Pan Americana*. Kubitschek's plan was in turn influenced by the studies of the Inter-American Economic and Social Council and the United Nations Economic Commission for Latin America. Running through all of these plans and programs were certain common hopes and aspirations which had been articulated for years by Latin America's leading statesmen. In 1960, at a hemisphere conference at Bogotá, a coherent philosophy to meet Latin America's social problems was embodied in a continental doctrine through the Act of Bogotá.

"Alliance for Progress" might have remained merely a cleverly contrived catchphrase or slogan. As a United States senator, John F. Kennedy had not shown any special interest in Latin America. His knowledge of the area was prob-

---

[1] *Alliance for Progress: A Program of Inter-American Partnership.* A Statement Developed at a Conference on December 19, 1960, Faculty Club of Harvard University, Cambridge, Massachusetts.

ably as limited as that of the average citizen. Yet he sensed instinctively that Latin America—as he was later to phrase it—was "the most critical area in the world today." In the hands of the President the phrase "Alliance for Progress" became the keystone in the arch of a new United States policy for Latin America. Subsequently filled out with flesh and bone in an address to the assembled Latin American diplomats at the White House on March 13, 1961, the Alliance for Progress was to become the most significant pronouncement affecting Latin America since the Monroe Doctrine placed the New World out of bounds for European colonial powers. At Punta del Este, Uruguay, in August 1961, at a meeting of the Finance Ministers of the hemisphere, the "constitution" of the Alliance was hammered out in the form of two basic documents: the Declaration to the Peoples of America and the Charter of Punta del Este.

Let us be clear that, in its original conception (the operative words here are "original conception"), the Alliance for Progress was not designed to be another conventional foreign-aid program utilizing the conventional tools of foreign aid—money, men, and materials. What was originally proposed under the Alliance was unprecedented and without parallel in the experience of the Western world. In essence, the United States Government offered to underwrite a Latin American social revolution. The reforms were to run the whole gamut of social change: better land use and distribution, more and better housing and education, more efficient collection of taxes, the elimination of corruption in government, a reduction in the wastefully overblown armies; a greater rate of savings and economic growth, a narrowing of the gap between the rich and the poor. *They* were expected, as the late Ambassador Adlai Stevenson said, "to take the bold, brave, difficult steps" to achieve peaceably and democratically the reforms which historically had been accomplished only through a revolution of blood and violence.

For roughly a year and a half following the promulgation of the Alliance for Progress, *they* sat on their hands and *we* floundered in a swamp of bureaucratic organization. The great hopes and high expectations engendered by President Kennedy's speeches were not realized. Disillusionment, cynicism, frustration, and resentment spread over the continent like a blanket of wet fog. Indeed, the Alliance for Progress became the butt of jokes and a term of derision. The fortunes of the Alliance were in the dead season of its despair.

For a variety of reasons, the constellation of reforms embedded in the Alliance for Progress could not be put into action immediately. Some of our expectations were grounded in illusions about Latin America. Some of what we believed was politically unrealistic. Organizationally, the New Frontier simply lacked the requisite skill for managing a social revolution of the magnitude to which it had committed itself. In some situations luck deserted us.

I suspect that the root of our difficulty lay in a fundamental misconception regarding Latin America—a misconception which the principal architects of the Alliance unwittingly accepted as a result of their experience with the Marshall Plan in Europe. The misconception was that Latin America was a continental community in the way that Europe was a community of shared interests, possessed of a common heritage and a collective sense of responsibility. This community did not exist in Latin America. Moreover, there is a profound difference between the motivation for reconstruction (Europe's problem in 1947) and the motivation for reform (Latin America's problem in the sixties). The Ernest Bevins, the Paul-Henri Spaaks, the Robert Schumans, the Jean Monnets were able to furnish the necessary political drive in Western Europe. They were assisted powerfully by the Paul Hoffman-Averell Harriman axis, which insisted upon a continental response to General Marshall's offer of aid.

The same kind of leverage for reform didn't exist in the summer of 1961, following the first Punta del Este conference, at which the representatives of Latin America committed their countries to the principles of the Alliance for Progress. On the contrary, something resembling a shock effect was recorded on the hemispheric seismograph as the implications of the Charter of Punta del Este began to register on Latin America's traditional centers of power.

Although Latin American governing groups possess the capacity for survival, they do not resemble, for instance, the English Tories, who instinctively recognized that to preserve you must reform, and who in the first half of the twentieth century were able to capture the British Labor party's welfare state and make it their own. Latin America's conservative class reacted to the Alliance for Progress with psychotic fear. Having always enjoyed the friendship of American diplomacy, they felt betrayed by the reformist thrust of the Alliance, particularly its emphasis on land reform. As the shortest route to Washington is via Moscow, they cried "Communism" and passed the word to their legislative mercenaries to prepare for a rear-guard action.

Still other elements blunted the purpose of the Alliance. A formidable deterrent was—and is—anti-Americanism. Like an ocean current, it runs deep and wide through the southern part of the hemisphere. Its presence renders suspect virtually anything that emanates from the Colossus of the North.

In the intellectual circles of Latin America the Alliance was greeted with skepticism. For many, there remained the unanswered question: does the Alliance for Progress represent a commitment of the heart? For still others, the Alliance had the smell of another cold-war gambit: Washington's answer to Castro and his revolution.

As a personality, President Kennedy had not yet been able to identify himself with Latin America's people as Franklin Roosevelt had succeeded in doing through the radiance of his own personality and his Good Neighbor Policy. Then came the Bay of Pigs. As nothing fails quite like failure, in Latin American eyes the United States appeared to be adrift in a sea of indecision; cynicism toward the Alliance became universal.

But there were even more fundamental difficulties. Washington's policy-makers had assumed that the big countries—Mexico, Brazil, and Argentina—would carry the torch for the Alliance. Mexico, however, is wrapped in a mystical cocoon of nonintervention. Mexicans believed that their country, as the senior member in the hemisphere's revolutionary business, had nothing to learn from any other revolutionaries and especially from the elite of the New Frontier. It was not interested in the Alliance for Progress. As a Mexican minister once told me, the Alliance is an interesting gimmick which could help Mexico with its balance of payments. That is all. Reference to the Alliance is conspicuously absent from official pronouncements. President Díaz Ordaz in his 1965 message to the Congress departed from precedent by saying a kind word for the Alliance.

Following the flight from the presidency by Jânio Quadros, Brazil for all practical purposes was for a period of four months without a functioning government. Her own financial chaos was so great that she could not serve as a leader of the Alliance. Indeed, under former President Goulart, Brazil turned her back on the Alliance.

The military seizure of power in Argentina plunged that nation into a political and economic wasteland. Argentina was unable to provide leadership for herself, let alone for her neighbors.

In its eagerness to have the Alliance accepted, the New Frontier forgot Harold Nicolson's reminder of Talleyrand's celebrated advice to a young diplomat: *"Et surtout pas trop de zéle"* ("And above all not too much enthusiasm"). First we wooed Argentina. When poor Frondizi was hustled off to prison by his soldiers, we gave our embrace to Brazil. With indecent haste Goulart was built up into the Western Hemisphere's man of the hour. In a matter of months we had washed our hands of Goulart. Then it was Colombia's turn. At last we had found our true love. But our ardor cooled. Though still romantically attached to Venezuela, Ecuador's military junta became our favorite. I suspect that it must also be true of diplomacy that "Heaven has no rage like love to hatred turned,/Nor hell a fury like a woman scorned."

Another implied assumption by Washington was the existence of a sufficiently broad base of representative, popular democracy which could overcome the resistance to reform from the traditional, conservative centers of power. Aside from Muñoz Marín of Puerto Rico, Figueres of Costa Rica, and Betancourt of Venezuela, the democratic leaders of the political Left lacked effective political power. The parties of the democratic Left do not have a broad base of middle-class support. Acción Democrática and APRA, for instance, have been unable to attract the support of the urban groups described as "middle class" in Caracas and Lima. The parties of the Left find their strength in the rural areas, not in the cities. Salvador Allende, the leader of the Chilean Marxist coalition, FRAP, has increased his vote in the rural areas from 1958 to 1964 by 58 per cent.

This pattern repeats itself elsewhere in Latin America. Left-wing strength is diminishing among the urban middle sector but increasing among the peasants. (In the 1964 Chilean presidential elections, Allende's strength in the rural areas was not great enough to overcome a combination of circumstances—the traditional opposition from the *fundo* owners; the heavy financial support from the Chilean Right, which was willing to spearhead anti-Communism as the major issue in the campaign; Frei's promise of agrarian reform; the massive support for Frei by Chilean women, strongly influenced by Frei's Catholicism and Allende's Marxism; the superb campaign organization run by the Christian Democrats *"como una empresa"* ["like a business"]; and, finally, the reformist mood of the country which responded overwhelmingly to Frei, an extraordinarily gifted reformer and a professional politician.)

Latin America's middle groups are not hell-bent for reform. They are essentially conformist. They are emotionally identified with the institutional *status quo*. They want a bigger slice of the pie, but they do not believe that upsetting the apple cart is the way to get it.[2]

The Alliance for Progress, nevertheless, assumed that the pressure for reform would come from Latin America's middle groups and the left-of-center political parties that reflect the need for change. With the defeat of Figueres' party in Costa Rica and the repudiation of Bosch in the Dominican Republic, with the overthrow of Frondizi in Argentina and Paz Estenssoro in Bolivia, with the *colorados* of Uruguay and the *apristas* of Peru out of power, with Muñoz Marín and Betancourt no longer in office, is there a meaningful democratic Left in Latin America? Whether the parties of the democratic Left (the chosen instruments for implementing the Alliance for Progress) have the political leadership and are capable of communicating the need for social change and of formulating programs that will identify social change within the context of the originally inspired *Alianza,* is a basic problem that requires re-examination.

Nowhere is the barrenness of the appeal of the demo-

---

[2] My own skepticism regarding the existence of any great surging middle class in Latin America is fortified by the views of Dr. Claudio Véliz, Chilean scholar, currently Senior Research Fellow in Latin American studies at Chatham House. Writing in *The World Today* (January 1963), Dr. Véliz states (pp. 22–3): "The fundamental error in the U.S. approach, however, has to do with its definition of the middle class. U.S. scholars, politicians, and journalists have gleefully discovered a Latin American middle class and, without pausing to find out what kind of a middle class it really is, they have proceeded to credit it with all sorts of qualities it does not possess. In fact, the only claim which the Latin American urban middle groups have to the description 'middle class' is based on the fact that they are in the middle, between the traditional aristocracy and the peasants and workers." For a similar viewpoint regarding the so-called middle class of Chile, see Professor Fredrick B. Pike: *Chile and the United States, 1880–1962* (South Bend: University of Notre Dame Press; 1963), pp. 284–5: "Chile's urban middle sectors have traditionally demonstrated colossal indifference to the social problems and have dedicated themselves to defending the value-judgments of the upper classes . . . the readily observable traits of the middle class have led to the introduction into the Chilean vocabulary of the world *siútico. A siútico* is a middle class individual who emulates the aristocracy and its usages and hopes to be taken for one of its members. It is generally agreed

cratic Left more apparent than in the lack of response on the part of Latin America's youth. Everywhere (especially among the youth, who constitute more than 40 per cent of the population), the concept of democracy is suspect, if it is not, indeed, a dirty word. "Democracy" has been so debased by dictators that it has lost its value. These young people have little faith in democracy as a process for attaining peaceable reform: for them, social justice and revolution are synonymous. As "heroes," they prefer personages like the adventurer-opportunist Colonel Francisco Caamaño Deñó, former *jefe* of the Dominican revolutionaries, who was elected "honorary President" of the youth branch of the Christian Democratic party (Copei) of Venezuela at a recent national convention. (*Diario de las Américas,* November 2, 1965, p. 1.) The paramount political challenge in Latin America is to channel the energies and interests of the young into democratic habits within the context of the original conception of the Alliance for Progress.

If Latin America failed to respond to the call for mobilization, the United States was unable to furnish the requisite organizational structure to provide a continental framework for conducting the business of a social revolution. Here, I believe, we ourselves misunderstood our own trumpet call. President Kennedy signaled for an Alliance. This term is commonly understood to mean joint effort, joint responsibilities, mutual involvement—in short, a partnership. But the organizational response was not commensurate with Mr. Kennedy's own vision. The Alliance became just another area in a foreign-aid structure competing with aid for Asia, Africa, and the Middle East. It soon lapsed into an American assistance-granting agency, which spent almost half its capital on emergency transfusions to meet balance-of-payments crises.

One of the popular illusions of the United States is the omnipotence of its President. Yet, as everyone familiar with the workings of government knows, a bureaucracy with a stubborn will of its own can render impotent a President's will. In splendid isolation and with lonely courage, President Kennedy defended the promise of the Alliance as a "peaceable revolution" which would change the lives of our fellow Americans. The Establishment, however, gave the impression

that Chile's middle class abounds in *siúticos.*" Professor Federico G. Gil of the University of North Carolina also concurs in these views. See *The Political System of Chile* (Boston: Houghton Mifflin Company; 1966), p. 27.

of men at work on another planet. The excitement, the sense of dedication, the high drama of participation in the forging of Latin America's brave new world were missing.

During its first two years the Alliance succeeded only in lighting a spark. As it was constituted in Washington and administered by the bureaucracies of the hemisphere's capital cities, the Alliance could not envelop the people of Latin America in a "consuming fire or a flood of light." Because of its focus on governments and technicians—the mandarinate of the capital cities—the Alliance was unable to reach the broader stratum of public opinion. Tied to conventional habits of thinking about foreign aid and geared to a bureaucratic machinery (which communicates only with its counterpart in other governments), the Alliance could neither reach the people nor involve them in its goals. And without a sense of mutual involvement, without a sense of shared participation by the ordinary people, the Alliance was only a brooding presence in the sky.

Then came the American success in meeting the Soviet Union's missile thrust in Cuba. That provided the United States with its most favorable image and its highest moral authority in Latin America in a generation. American leadership had exerted itself decisively. Latin America, which loves a *caudillo* (even when named *Tío Sam*), was eager to follow—and did. For the first time since the Alliance had been enunciated there were discernible a sense of solidarity, an urge for co-operation, and a feeling for collective responsibility. A beginning, although modest, was made in land-reform legislation. Tax reforms were undertaken. Chile, for example, with the help of the Internal Revenue Service, for the first time in her history has begun to collect taxes from those who had developed evasion into a fine art. In what must be one of the classic understatements of the year, Brazil's current Director of Internal Revenue, Orlando Travancas, said: "Tax evasion is considered one of the serious national problems by this government"—as well it might be. For only 5,000 persons—the Director reported—paid individual income taxes exceeding 2 million cruzeiros (about $1,000) in 1964. For the first time in the history of the inter-American system, the hemisphere's trade-union leaders and the Ministers of Labor met as equals. It is a notable event when the government of El Salvador sponsors a week-long seminar on the Alliance for Progress. Change was in the air.

While new opportunities beckoned for American diplomacy in this new atmosphere, we failed to seize the initiative by proceeding with swift and reassuring action to revitalize the Alliance. Latin America was ready to follow decisive and determined leadership, the kind of leadership she witnessed (and followed) at the moment of the U.S.-Soviet confrontation over Cuba. Because Latin Americans are not Anglo-Americans, they were ready to subscribe with enthusiasm to a new structure for the Alliance, one which would embody both poetry and power, which dramatized their own high destiny and had the bold sweep of Bolivarian prophecy. Washington either could not make up its own mind on what it wanted or was barren of ideas.

It was left to the former Presidents Lleras Camargo and Kubitschek to recommend a structure that would provide the Alliance with continental political leverage. They recommended an Inter-American Development Committee analogous to the Organization for European Economic Cooperation (OEEC), under which Europe's recovery was achieved. Almost everyone concerned with the reorganization of the Alliance believed that some such body was needed if the Alliance was to be turned from an American check-writing agency into a hemisphere partnership. The Lleras-Kubitschek proposal was adopted by the Inter-American Economic and Social Council at São Paulo in November 1963. Significantly, Brazil at first opposed the plan but ultimately gave it her reluctant endorsement. The support of other delegations was not enthusiastic. The plan had come too late: the stride of events had overtaken it.

President Kennedy's death deprived the Alliance of political, intellectual, and spiritual leadership. For a variety of reasons there is no political leader on the Latin American scene who can fill this void. Betancourt of Venezuela is unacceptable to the military regimes because he refused to recognize their illegitimate seizures of power. Lleras Camargo of Colombia lacks the necessary physical strength—not the vision—for leadership of the continent. Figueres of Costa Rica and Muñoz Marín of Puerto Rico are Caribbean statesmen who suffer from the disadvantage of a passionate commitment to democracy in a region which prefers its leaders to pay only lip service to democratic ideals. Mexico's revolutionary tradition places her in the vanguard of those eligible to provide leadership for the continent, but she does not aspire to lead. Mexico prefers the more satisfying power relationships to be found in Europe and Asia to the parochial bickerings of the Western Hemisphere. The big countries of South America—Argentina, Brazil, and Chile—are too engrossed in their own political and economic crises to supply solutions, let alone leadership, for the whole continent. That President Johnson will fill the vacuum is a foregone conclusion. As he himself is fond of saying, "You can't expect the people to follow a vacuum." To suppose that the Johnson administration is trying to scuttle the Alliance is, I am entirely certain, malicious nonsense. What the administration has not been able to determine is the proper mixture of conventional diplomacy (essential to the conduct of the business of the state), the role of private business (to provide the underpinning for economic development), and the fervor and idealism without which the Alliance will remain unintelligible to Latin Americans. The measured cadence of the elegant dialogue is not part of the Johnson make-up. Mr. Johnson may be expected to look at Latin America through his own eyes, and to articulate its hopes through his own voice. By focusing on America's own poverty, President Johnson has effectively identified himself with the ordinary people of Latin America. By his active espousal of civil rights for the American Negro he has given the Alliance a new dimension.

The resurgence of the military makes one doubt whether the Alliance for Progress is really Latin America's alternative to authoritarianism of the Left and Right, to revolution and regression. It is this altered environment which leads me to question whether the Alliance, as it is now conceived, has any operative validity. What the chain of military coups dramatizes is that Latin America's "problem" is primarily political and only secondarily economic. The Alliance has evolved a master plan for the economic development of Latin America. What is really needed is a master plan for its political development. The chain reaction of military seizures of power began with the precipitate flight from the presidency of Brazil by Jânio Quadros. It was here that the seeds were sown for the gradual disintegration of democratic government in Latin America. The military seizures of power—in Argentina, Brazil, Peru, Ecuador, Guatemala, Bolivia, and Honduras—demonstrate that national development plans do not automatically produce strong democratic governments. To put the matter differently: of what avail is it to insist upon long-range development plans when the democratic environment necessary to accommodate the re-

CHAPTER TWELVE

Has Foreign Capital Lost Confidence in Latin America?

ONE of the less noble aspects of statistics is that they sometimes give birth to grave misunderstanding. A case in point was the "discovery" late in 1962 by some of the readers of the balance-of-payments figures published by the U.S. Department of Commerce that a disinvestment of $49 million from Latin America had taken place during that year. What this meant in plain English was that some American companies were bringing their capital back from Latin America. At that juncture, reacting with alarm, some drew the wholly erroneous conclusion that American capital had joined forces with Latin American capital in headlong flight from the area. A spate of stories appeared in the press that American capital had "lost confidence in Latin America."

Actually, from the day that the *barbudos* poured into Havana from their Sierra Maestra stronghold, American direct investments in Latin America began to taper off. That they merely slowed down instead of coming to a complete halt is in itself extraordinary. For it should be recalled that American private investment was a major casualty of the Cuban Revolution. With no more formality than a TV harangue, Dr. Castro wiped out $1 billion of American investments in Cuba.

A subsequent refinement in the balance-of-payment figures by the Department of Commerce disclosed that a more accurate estimate of returned capital was $23.8 million. At this point one might tend to assume that the flow of capital to Latin America had been arrested. But we must first consider Venezuela, which has a way of distorting the whole investment picture. For example, the year before Dr. Castro seized power, American direct investments in Latin America came to $1.163 billion. But this figure was inflated by $734 million, the extraordinary payments made to Venezuela in that year by the petroleum companies. Similarly, in 1962 the Venezuelan figures reveal a heavy outflow of funds from the oil companies in the form of earnings, depreciation allowances, and other transferable items. This was a normal movement of capital by internationally organized companies who customarily shift capital from one part of the globe to another as the needs of their operations dictate. So if we eliminate the "negative" figures for Venezuela, we find that the net capital flow into Latin America in 1962 was actually $159 million.

Far from indicating that American capital had lost confidence in Latin America, this amount of direct investment was not substantially less than that of preceding years. Thus, in 1958 the figure stood at $299 million; in 1959, $218 million; in 1960, $95 million; in 1961, $141 million; and in 1964, $156 million.

There is still another difficulty in connection with the statistics that show the movement of capital into Latin America: they fail to take into account changes in the composition of investments. Public utilities are being expropriated in various countries. Under the lash of nationalism, mining has lost its former appeal to investors. Except for defensive investments, no great surge of new oil money is pouring into Latin America. But manufacturing has captured the interest of foreign investors. In 1962, $91.4 million was invested in manufacturing. This area now accounts for 24 per cent of the total United States investment in Latin America.

When a company makes an investment in Latin America— or, for that matter, in any other part of the world—it does not always involve the use of cash from the United States. Frequently the investment consists of a contribution of equipment which has become surplus (note: the word is "surplus," not "obsolete") to the company at home as a result of model changes or improvements in the manufacturing process.

Investment also takes the form of retained earnings and depreciation and depletion allowances. Indeed, over 50 per cent of all overseas manufacturing investment is derived from these sources.

What do we find if we look at the Latin American investment picture for 1962 in the light of these facts? We find:

a capital flow *plus* equipment *plus* reinvested earnings *plus* depreciation and depletion allowances, amounting in all to about $1 billion

Clearly, this tells quite a different story about our investment in Latin America. Incidentally, this $1 billion of private investment was as much as was pumped into Latin America under the Alliance for Progress in 1962. Not only did American business meet a commitment which had been made for it by the United States authorities at Punta del Este—that $300 million would be invested in Latin America under the Alliance for Progress—but the amount was exceeded by some $700 million.

In judging whether or not American business has lost confidence in Latin America, another question must be asked: *Who* is pulling out?

Companies with long experience in Latin America are not. A United Fruit in Central America or an Anaconda Copper in Chile may wish that it could take its cash and come home. But it can't. For all practical purposes the investments of such companies are frozen. The Chase Manhattan Bank had enlarged its banking operations in Peru and Brazil. The First National City Bank of New York—a pioneer in the development of career overseas banking—is not removing itself from the scene. Sears, Roebuck and Company, whose warehouses and stores have been gutted and bombed in Venezuela and Colombia by Castro-Communist gunmen, has not taken fright. The internationally structured companies, who realize an impressive amount of their earnings from overseas, have no intention of departing. Ford is expanding its automobile production in Brazil. A group of chemical companies is proceeding with a $72 million petro-chemical complex in Argentina. Bethlehem Steel is expanding its operations in Brazil. Caterpillar is doubling the size of its São Paulo plant. Deere intends to build a completely Argentine tractor by 1966. Whirlpool showed its confidence in Venezuela by joining with other firms in the establishment of a consumer goods industrial complex.

Senator Jacob Javits and Hubert Humphrey, then also a

member of the Senate, sponsored the Atlantic Community Development Group for Latin America (ADELA)—an organization of American, Japanese, and European companies set up to provide investment funds for joint ventures. ADELA was formally organized in Paris on January 10–11, 1964. Its initial capitalization was $40 million. Subscribers to the capital stock are: Standard Oil Company (New Jersey), Ford Motor Company, IBM World Trade Corporation, the Chase Manhattan Bank, the National City Bank of New York, Istituto Mobiliare Italiano, Fiat, Swiss Banking Corporation, Sybetra, and Petrofino (Belgium). Several Japanese industrial and banking firms are participating through one of their traditional international trading companies. It is anticipated that other Japanese companies will subscribe directly. French, German, and Swedish banking and industrial firms are also expected to participate in ADELA. The International Finance Corporation—an affiliate of the World Bank—has expressed its willingness to purchase stock in ADELA, and the Inter-American Development Bank (whose charter bars the purchase of capital stock) has indicated a desire to assist through loans and credits for Latin American enterprises in which ADELA invests its funds. The directors of ADELA believe that this multi-national investment company will eventually have resources of $200 million.

Who, then, is pulling out? Mainly the newcomers to Latin America. It is worth noting that for the vast majority of American companies overseas, investment is a relatively new experience. Most American companies are still in the transition stages of passing from Export Manager to International Division to World Corporation, in which the entire globe is meshed into a unified system of production, distribution, and financial planning and the United States is only one of several world centers for production, research, and marketing. For instance, Ford Motor Company has plants in twenty foreign countries, manufacturing fourteen different lines of cars and trucks. Any Ford plant anywhere in the world can sell parts to, or buy them from, any other Ford plant. Ford of England exports diesel engines to Ford of the United States. The latter exports spindle forgings and steering assemblies to Ford of West Germany. Engineers from Ford of England designed the transmission used in the Falcon, which was built in the United States. Ford engineers from the United States and West Germany jointly designed the Taunus 12M automobile, built in West Germany for export to the European Common Market.

It should be remembered, too, that overseas investment is not without its own styles and fashions. Latin America was very popular in the late forties and early fifties, but it was replaced somewhat later by the European Economic Community. Most of the American manufacturing companies who entered the Latin American field during the recent period were new. They are the ones who have lost confidence.

There is no indication that investors from other countries have lost confidence in Latin America. Japanese businessmen swarm over the region in search of opportunities. The West German Krupp empire looks upon Latin America as the most attractive area for its investments. Swedish, Italian, French, and British firms continue to search for profitable investment opportunities.

The former British Minister of State for Foreign Affairs, Lord Dundee, expresses the British position bluntly: "It is certainly not the view of Her Majesty's Government that Latin America is the preserve and responsibility of the United States." If this means anything, it would indicate that Great Britain is preparing to exploit her nineteenth-century hold on Latin America. During this period, it will be recalled, the British consul and *chargé*, William Chatfield, was the most important foreigner in the Federal Republic of Central America, the River Plate was an estuary of the Thames, Brazil and Argentina were economic colonies, and British styles in architecture and culture were *de rigueur*.

Investments and supplier credits from the European Economic Community have reached about $400 million annually. General de Gaulle has made it plain that Latin America too falls within the orbit of his grand design. Although his state visits to Mexico, Brazil, and other countries in South America are more likely to have greater political than economic consequences, he has nevertheless made it unmistakably clear that France intends to launch a concerted drive for trade in Latin America. De Gaulle's special brand of anti-Americanism, combined with the magnetic pull of French culture on Latin Americans, could be a strong asset in a Gaullist offensive to rid the southern part of the hemisphere of United States influence.

By the end of 1964, West Germany had invested almost $379 million in Latin America. This is more than five times

Germany's investment in Africa and more than seven times what she has invested in Asia. Most of the German investment is in Brazil ($205 million) and Argentina ($72 million), the two countries that are generally regarded as the areas of greatest risk. Spain, in an attempt to restore her ancient influence, has offered $1 billion to Latin America for economic development over the next decade. This would make Spain potentially the second largest supplier of credits, after the United States.

Of Japan's total overseas investment of $1.602 billion, Latin America accounts for $420 million—in iron ore and the new fish-meal industry in Peru, fishing fleets in Guatemala and Venezuela, automotive production in Mexico, car and truck assembly in Chile, scooter assembly in Colombia, textiles, shipbuilding, banking, insurance, and cement, machinery, glass, and steel production in Brazil.

I believe that America's businessmen have been exceptionally courageous in comparison with their European and Japanese competitors. In the first place, the Europeans and Japanese are much more sympathetic to Latin America, to say nothing of their far greater experience in investing abroad. For the Milan industrialists, São Paulo and Buenos Aires are for all practical business purposes Italian "colonies." How can the Japanese businessmen become overly concerned with political instability in Latin America when his neck is scorched by the hot breath of the Red Chinese dragon? How can the mad dance of inflated pesos and cruzeiros unnerve the Japanese industrialist when he has been through a similar experience in Southeast Asia? When, before de Gaulle, has the French industrialist known political stability in France?

There is less alarm over Dr. Castro's revolutionary intentions among businessmen in Düsseldorf, Milan, Paris, Tokyo, and Stockholm than among their opposite numbers in Chicago, Cleveland, New York, Detroit, and San Francisco. This is not solely a question of nearness to Cuba. It is, I think, more accurate to say that many American businessmen are ill equipped by historical experience to grasp the significance of the revolutionary impulses running through Latin America. The non-American investor, on the other hand, generally understands better the meaning of revolution. Why shouldn't he? It's been part of his experience. Moreover, he has another signal advantage over the American investor: he has a more developed capacity to adapt to a new environment.

There is something of a paradox in the attitude of that minority of American businessmen who have lost confidence in Latin America. On the one hand, the absence of neat and tidy methods of doing business, political instability, and losses sustained through erosion of the currencies are disquieting. They act as a deterrent to many of the medium-sized companies which could contribute to Latin America's industrialization and at the same time expand their own profitable operations. On the other hand, adapting to a revolutionary environment involves nothing greatly different from what most American companies are accustomed to doing at home. It consists of nothing more than supporting education, training local people for responsible supervisory and managerial positions, sharing profits, bona fide collective bargaining, opening up stockownership to the people of the country—in short, doing those things which help to bring about a better standard of living and a better distribution of income and thus improve the market, all of which we have learned to do at home. And it is important that the company's local manager (and his wife) be selected with infinite care. A successful manager has to be something more than just competent. He has to speak the language, understand local customs, and be able to fit into the society of which he is to become a part—without losing his identity as an American. Honorary membership in the Jockey Club ought not to transform an ordinary American, with all of his democratic instincts, into a Spanish grandee. Nor does it seem necessary, in the exchange of the social amenities, for the good American to adopt the obsolete social and political philosophies of the oligarchy.

The American manager stationed in Latin America must be politically antiseptic. But it scarcely follows that he should be ignorant of—or indifferent to—what is going on. Indeed, his staying power may well depend upon how accurately he can assess the strength of the opposition parties and their leaders. For they may be the government of tomorrow.

In brief, the day has gone when all that was expected of the overseas manager was that he turn in a profit and "keep his nose clean." He must be aware of the social and political ferment beneath the surface. His political and economic intelligence has to be first-rate. If he relies exclusively for his information upon his friends at the Jockey Club, he is likely to be as dead wrong as the professional diplomat who relies upon the same source and neglects the opposition politicians, trade-union leaders, university students, writers, and artists.

One pitfall in particular against which the American businessman must be on guard is that of equating American private enterprise (which means one thing in the United States) with private enterprise in Latin America (which means something quite different). Failure to heed this admonition can lead to disastrous consequences. A classic example was a public statement made on January 29. 1963, by three prominent members of the American business community—Emilio Collado of the Standard Oil Company, Walter Wriston of the First National City Bank of New York, and David Rockefeller of the Chase Manhattan Bank.[1] Among other things they urged a greater participation in the Alliance for Progress for American private enterprise. Press accounts of the substance of this statement caused some of our best friends in Latin America to recoil with amazement and sorrow. To them, it appeared that American business was endeavoring to convert the Alliance for Progress into an instrument of private enterprise. Such prominent Latin Americans as former President Lleras Camargo of Colombia and Ambassador Gonzalo Facio, president of the Council of the Organization of American States, reacted against the symbol of a private enterprise which in Latin American eyes is still part of a nineteenth-century exploitive, unprogressive capitalism. To these old and tried friends of the United States, to involve the Alliance for Progress (which they believe to be the best hope for Latin America) with a private enterprise system (which for the great majority of Latin Americans is thoroughly suspect) was tantamount to letting a brace of rabbits into a lettuce bed.

The moral is plain: We need to be less doctrinaire about private enterprise. We need to keep in mind that Latin America—even more than the United States—has a mixed economy. Latin America intends to keep it that way. Latin Americans do not look with favor on the American businessman who seeks to impose on his operation in Latin America a brand of capitalism which has long ceased to exist in the United States except as a myth invoked at the annual trade association banquets.

[1] This statement was in the form of a memorandum sent to Mr. Peter Grace, chairman of the Department of Commerce's Committee on the Alliance for Progress. Messrs. Collado, Wriston, and Rockefeller were members of the committee, as was the author.

On March 16, 1964, in a memorable address before a special session of the Council of Organization of American States, Dr. Carlos Sanz de Santamaría, chairman of the Inter-American Committee on the Alliance for Progress, emphasized the same point that I have been endeavoring to make. A successful Colombian businessman-engineer and distinguished minister-diplomat, Don Carlos observed:

> The Alliance for Progress is not meant to supplant the free enterprise system. It fully recognizes the important role private initiative should play in the task of development. But make no mistake about it: the private enterprise system conceived of in the Charter of Punta del Este is not that of the nineteenth century.
>
> Today, a system of mixed economy, involving both government and free enterprise, governs to a greater or lesser extent in all industrialized countries. It is accepted as desirable and necessary. In trying to stimulate development in Latin America, it would be illogical for us not to apply the historical experience of Western capitalism. We cannot declare ourselves advocates of untrammeled free enterprise to suit minority groups within or without our countries.

The American businessman who contemplates investing in Latin America must answer another very important question: What form shall his investment take: a wholly owned subsidiary? a joint venture with local partners? a licensing arrangement whereby he makes patents and technology available at a fee, but without any direct investment on his part? or perhaps some combination of licensing and joint venture? Some managements—they are rapidly becoming a minority —take the position that the wholly owned subsidiary or, at least, majority control is most desirable because it eliminates any potential conflict over future managerial policies. Others have found through experience that local partners are more valuable. Still others prefer to participate only by licensing technical skills. I believe the joint enterprise (combined, where feasible, with the licensing of patents and the furnishing of technological and managerial skills for a fee) is by far the most effective.

At a time when the winds of nationalism are reaching gale proportions in some parts of Latin America, American business needs a stronger anchor than that provided by the wholly owned subsidiary. Probably no other aspect of American overseas business is more irritating to the Latin American nationalists than the wholly owned subsidiary. Nor is this irritation confined to the intellectuals and the bureaucracy; it is shared by Latin America's businessmen. Latin Americans particularly resent, and not without justification, the American manager who can make no decision without first obtaining the approval of his home office. From any point of view, he is seen as a boy sent to do a man's job. To the Latin American, this smacks of economic colonialism.

Hostility toward the wholly owned subsidiary is not peculiar to Latin Americans. The Canadians have their version of *"Yanqui* go home"—in their sensitivity to Canadian subsidiaries of American firms and their fear that the Canadian economy is becoming largely a branch office of American industry. Among the European Common Market countries, the French, for instance, take exception to the wholly owned American company. Both the French Government and the French business community believe that basic economic decisions laid down, say, in New York or Detroit may hinder the achievement of national investment objectives which could be attained through joint government-industry planning. A recurrent Latin American nightmare is the fear of becoming, as was pre-Castro Cuba, an outpost of American business.

There is probably no more knotty or delicate problem than this question of *when* there is too much concentration of American investment. It presents business and government with a dilemma. On the one hand, it is repugnant to American foreign-policy makers to dictate to American business in this area. On the other hand, corporate managements are in no position to act collectively.

The mixed enterprise goes far toward removing the Latin American fear of American business. It has other signal advantages. First, the joint enterprise contains one of the prime ingredients for conducting a successful business operation in Latin America: the enterprise *is* Latin American. Anti-American hostility cannot be effectively directed against a local company. Second, local partners will be as eager as their American partners to have the venture succeed. It's their money that is invested, too. They help prevent political discrimination. I have yet to see an instance in which local partners were not infinitely more effective than their North American colleagues in negotiating with the authorities. Finally, the mixed venture is most likely to attract the return of local capital that has fled the country.

CHAPTER THIRTEEN

A Challenge to America's Business Leaders

THE EMBRYONIC Central American Common Market offers an unparalleled opportunity for American business to make a spectacular contribution to the region's economic progress. Success can be achieved by organizing quickly a mixed private and public venture to supply consumer and capital goods for this potentially viable regional economy. An undertaking of this magnitude should not be exclusively North American, but should make use of Western European, Japanese, and Central American capital (both private and public) as well. Neighboring Puerto Rico and Mexico could supply technicians and managers and some capital.

This international consortium could make a significant contribution by proposing a "Charter of the Rights, Duties, and Obligations of the Investors and the Respective Governments." It could be made abundantly clear that these international investors did not intend to preserve their investments over an indefinite future, and that their stake could be bought out by either local private capital or government bodies. The Charter could declare that, although the sovereign power of expropriation is inviolable, its exercise would carry with it the duty of compensation, enforceable, if necessary, by the International Court of Justice. The Charter could also delineate those areas of the economy that would be reserved for state investment and operation and those areas to be reserved for development by the private sector. It could specify the bargaining rights of labor. It could affirm the obligation of the consortium to facilitate through training programs the early and rapid assumption of managerial and supervisory responsibilities by nationals of the region as well as its intention to encourage the widest possible distribution of stock among the people of the area.

The voluntary initiation of such a Charter by American business leadership would have an electrifying effect. It would automatically remove the lingering fear in the minds of many of Latin America's intellectuals and businessmen that foreign capital never lets go once it takes hold. It would take account of Latin America's nationalist sensitivity and pride. It would supply the missing ingredient in Latin America's economic structure—technological and price competition. It would not attempt to impose American-style capitalism, to which the Latin American is, in the main, inhospitable. It would be a genuine offer of partnership and would operate strictly within the framework of the profit system.

This is how "confidence" is born. Confidence does not come about on its own, and it can't be legislated or established by decree. It must be built up gradually from small beginnings. Out of the give-and-take of negotiation, enthusiasm can be kindled, until finally the desire to realize a particular idea becomes compelling.

I have long believed—as have many of my friends and colleagues in the international business community—that the consortium of multi-national private companies, in conjunction, if need be, with government authorities or special corporations, constitutes one of the most effective devices for the attraction of foreign capital to the poorer countries.

That this concept is eminently practical is evidenced by its use by the World Bank in the long-term development loan program for Colombia, and the recent organization by a number of international private companies of the Atlantic Community Development Group for Latin America (ADELA). The question arises: if the idea is feasible, why is it not being utilized more extensively? There are several answers. Our government does not regard overseas business as an extension of our foreign policy. On the other hand, many of the great trading nations of the non-Communist world do regard overseas private businesses as instruments of foreign economic policy. Western European, British, and Japanese diplomacy functions easily and comfortably with its business community. American diplomacy and American business by and large do not have the same relationship. The British Foreign Office and its embassies have always kept a sharp eye on British commercial interests. It was an event when Secretary of State Rusk sent a circular letter to the American embassies urging our ambassadors to direct their personal attention toward assisting American business. It is a rare United States ambassador who publicly warns the government to which he is accredited, as Lincoln Gordon, professor-turned-diplomat, at Rio de Janeiro, did, that a Brazilian tax law aimed at remittances of profits would be nothing short of *hara-kiri* (Brazilian style). It is the rare United States ambassador who publicly defends American business against accusations by xenophobic nationalists that American companies drain off more capital than they bring in—as was done by Fulton Freeman, our former ambassador at Bogotá.

There is no established machinery by which government and business can function together—as equals—in joint planning or in accomplishing mutually-agreed-upon objectives. Business is suspicious of government. And government suspects the motives of business. There are semantic difficulties in communication. We talk on different wave lengths. The bureaucracy scorns the business mind as capable only of intellectual clichés. Business is contemptuous of the doctrinaire mentality of the bureaucracy. Except during the high drama of war, American business and its government live, think, and operate in different worlds.

In the Washington establishment there is a good deal of skepticism regarding the private economy as an instrument for attacking the problems of social and economic development in the poor lands. I believe that this skepticism derives in large measure from a failure to comprehend the disparate roles of government and the private company with respect to the developing countries. Government can spend the public investment funds solely on the basis of strategic—or political —considerations. The private company can invest only on the basis of anticipated profits. Private capital, therefore, tends to move into an already established industrial complex, such as exists at São Paulo, for example, rather than into the Northeast of Brazil, where the infrastructure and the markets are still primitive. Unwittingly, private capital exacerbates social tensions in an underdeveloped land by concentrating its investments in the few, isolated oases of prosperity and otherwise detouring around the vast desert of poverty. Because its obligations to its stockholders and profit

motivation leave it no other choice, the private company un-
fortunately acquires the reputation of being insensitive to the
aspirations of the people of the hungry lands. This is not to
suggest that the international mining and oil companies, or an
occasional pioneer from the ranks of light industry, or the ad-
venturous automotive and pharmaceutical companies, will not
continue to look for investment opportunities outside the
promising industrial complexes. But most of the manufacturing industries, with their dependence on advanced technology, engineering, and sophisticated consumer markets, will
continue to avoid the world's high-risk areas.

It should be apparent, therefore, that no common ground
exists between the considerations that move private companies and the strategic considerations of the government.

Does it follow that the private economy can do little or
nothing to assist in the economic and social development of
the poor lands? In my view, we have not as yet properly as-
sessed the unique managerial, technical, and financial resources of the private economy as a *collective* instrumentality for attacking the problem.

As I have suggested, consortia made up of companies
from many nations offer the promise of a successful attack
on the problems of the poor lands. By associating numerous
companies under a central management it would be possible
to undertake a balanced and integrated development of vast
areas of an underdeveloped country—from infrastructure to
the ultimate distribution of consumer goods—through pro-
grammed phases which might extend as long as twenty years
or more.

How would the idea work in practice?

First: The United States Government would have to determine the areas and programs of strategic priority in which
the private economy would be asked to invest its resources.

Second: Where no economic, engineering, and financial
studies have been made to determine the actual requirements
of a country or region (but many are in the government files),
they would have to be underwritten by the government. Such
studies should not be academic exercises, but rather the work
of companies most likely to be concerned with the project
during the latter operational phase. Most emphatically, I am
not suggesting more "surveys": Latin America has been sur-
veyed to death. These studies would be *plans for action*.

Third: One company would be selected to serve as manager for an entire program. The managing company would

select the other companies whose skills and experience would be needed in the various phases of operations and would obtain the necessary capital from either private or government sources, or both.

We should start in Brazil. Brazil occupies almost half of the continent and has common borders with all the other countries except Chile and Ecuador. Brazil is like a gigantic suction pump in the heart of Latin America. She can pull the rest of the continent into her vortex. And in Brazil, I would begin in the Northeast, which Gilberto Freyre calls "the country's number one problem region." This is the great bulge which stretches eastward into the Atlantic and is closer to Africa than to the United States. It includes nine states in an area of 600,000 square miles. For four centuries this region has been Brazil's "geography of hunger." It is the India of the Western Hemisphere, where more than 20 million landless, illiterate, restless people—one quarter of Brazil's population—scratch a wretched existence out of a miserable soil. For generations the chief export of the Northeast has been its people. In broken-down trucks, trudging on foot, their few belongings bundled over their backs, they swarm over the dusty roads into the nearby coastal cities and even to distant Rio de Janeiro and São Paulo. There they join the other denizens of squalor in the *favelas* of Brazil's festering slums. The Peking Chinese see in Brazil's Northeast the ideal laboratory for their own brand of revolution. Portuguese translations of Mao Tse-tung's writings have flooded the region. The Cuban brand of subversion is on the scene, too; thousands of copies of Major Ché Guevara's book *Guerrilla Warfare* have been distributed, along with 16-mm. films on how to make a Molotov cocktail. If the Northeast explodes, Cuba will seem like a firecracker. Gilberto Freyre, himself a *nordestino*, a man of the Northeast, urges "direct American and European aid of a financial and technical nature toward the industrial development of the region—direct, that is, to regional public and private organizations and not through the slow federal bureaucracy of Brasília and Rio." With the intimate knowledge of a lifetime in the region, Freyre concludes with a warning:

Because so little is being done at present, some industrialists in the Northeast who are in financial difficulties are being approached subtly by Soviet representatives offering the possibility of financial help directly to them and through them to the region as a whole. These representatives are using methods that should have been followed long ago by citizens of the United States. By dealing almost exclusively with the bureaucrats of Brasília and Rio, the United States now seems to some observers to be repeating in Brazil the same mistakes it made in pre-Communist China.[1]

Using the Northeast as a pilot project, the member companies could undertake to build a power plant, dams for an irrigation system, roads to connect newly opened lands or new farms with markets, and a chemical plant to supply fertilizers, fungicides, herbicides, and pesticides. A credit system could be established to enable small farmers to purchase fertilizer and modern agricultural equipment and to build homes; marketing co-operatives could be organized; a food-processing plant could be built for meat and agricultural products; a canning and packing facility could be erected to provide fish for the people in the interior; a successful Midwest farmer could manage and supervise the development of new grain crops and hog and dairy herds; a pharmaceutical company could be organized to provide basic drugs; an agricultural-equipment company, to develop a simple tractor that could be used by barefoot *caboclos;* and an export company, to promote the overseas sale of local products.

What happens if a participating company sustains operating losses because a cash market does not exist and it will take too long to bring one into being? Up to 75 per cent of such losses can be covered by the United States Government acting through the President under authority granted by the Foreign Assistance Act of 1963. Because it would be less cumbersome, a more desirable method is private insurance under which a participating company could purchase a policy to cover its losses. Premium rates could be established on an ascending scale in accordance with the degree of protection desired. The assets of the protected investor would be subrogated to his insurers until such time as the operation became profitable, when repayment of advances to cover temporary losses would be made to the insurers. This method of writing insurance for losses sustained by participating companies would involve only an extension of the mechanism now in effect for covering export commercial insurance by

[1] *Foreign Affairs*, April 1962, p. 462.

the Foreign Credit Insurance Association, a group of private American insurance companies. The point is this: high risks and inadequate markets should not be permitted to prevent the fulfillment of the strategic objective of providing development assistance to a country that needs it—and wants it—and is prepared to participate with its own capital, whether government or private or both.

Through this kind of collective action on the part of a number of business organizations both large and small, by bringing to bear a multitude of technological, engineering, and managerial resources over large areas of a country or over whole regions, it is possible to achieve a balanced and integrated development with proper emphasis upon economic growth, but without neglecting the immediate social needs of the people.

The cardinal advantage of this kind of arrangement is that it provides machinery whereby the resources of the private economy can undertake collectively what no single company could accomplish by itself. It avoids overconcentration of investment in existing pockets of prosperity and intensifying a disequilibrium that already exists in the economy. It makes available in concentrated form the unique features of the private economy—its self-imposed disciplines; its experimental methods; its capacity for avoiding emotional judgments; its trained technical and managerial manpower accustomed to work under organizational restraints. And it affords the free play of individual initiative and ingenuity. Through the financial participation of government—many governments, not just the United States Government—the element of risk (so frequently the decisive barrier to investment by the private company) is minimized.

This flexible approach allows for joint public and private planning, operation, and financing. It can separate the private and public phases of activity or it can consolidate them. The criterion is: what combination of facilities, organizations, and finanical support can best do the job required in the particular country or region?

Two other objectives of supreme importance would be accomplished by this method. First, it would provide the public (foreign aid) sector with the supplementary economic stimulus to ensure economic growth. Each sector would feed the other—with markets, suppliers, and new investment opportunities. Together, the public and private sectors would ensure what each, functioning separately, fails to do—provide the dynamic elements for sustained economic growth. Second, the proposed arrangement would create an environment of confidence which would attract into these investment pools the substantial local capital that is now in exile or, when invested locally, finds its way into the building of luxury apartments or the acquisition of additional idle landholdings rather than into industrial enterprises.

The idea of an association of companies to undertake large-scale projects is not new: it is being used in Africa for the development of an aluminum industry, in Argentina for the development of a petrochemical industry, in Iran for the construction of dams and irrigation systems, in Greece for laying the foundations for a steel-oil-chemical complex. In the United States we have for years utilized, in our military procurement, a system analogous to the proposed association of companies: a prime contractor who has, working under his direction, a satellite system of subcontractors sometimes numbering into the hundreds.

What is required in order to begin an experiment of this type?

Financial tools to provide the underpinning. A number of these tools are already available through the Foreign Assistance Act. They have, however, been used haltingly and some are already rusty from lack of employment. Others might have to be added. But the single most important ingredient now missing is the will to utilize the resources of the private economy as an instrument of high policy.

There is a "right" way and a "wrong" way to go about the accomplishment of this objective. The wrong way consists of bureaucratic oratory which periodically attempts to assure the business community of its dedication to private enterprise. This is not necessary. A moratorium should be called on the appointment of Committees of Businessmen to give advice. This represents a misuse of talent, knowledge, and energy. Businessmen are at their best when they are engaged in doing, not talking. Setting up offices in the departments to "assist" the business community in geographically locating the underdeveloped countries is nonsensical. Obviously, none of these conventional approaches gets to the heart of the problem—the mobilization of the *collective* resources of the private economy in undertaking a sustained program of development. Which leads us to the right way to come to grips with the problem. In the American system, all roads eventually lead to 1600 Pennsylvania Avenue—the White House. In my opinion, only the President of the United States can launch such a great experiment. He will succeed where lesser lights will fail, for a simple reason: irrespective of his political views, no responsible American business leader will refuse a Presidential request to assume direction of a strategically selected project. For, as Thomas Jefferson said: "There is a debt of service due from every man to his country proportioned to the bounties which Nature and Fortune have measured to him." Moreover, I am persuaded that, if any one of our prominent business leaders could be assured of direct access to the President in his role as manager of the project, the undertaking would be launched successfully. By the same token, the experiment will not succeed if it becomes an appendage of the bureaucracy.

I believe there are boards of directors and managements in this country who would participate in international consortia such as I have suggested—not only because of a presidential request, but also because of an awareness that in a revolutionary epoch in which the entire world is undergoing a transformation, neither government-as-usual nor business-as-usual will be able to survive the dynamic, ruthless, and effective competition of an adversary who makes no bones of his intention to "bury" us.

These directorates and managements are also fully aware that to meet the challenge of the revolution of rising demands in Latin America—and elsewhere in the emergent lands—the conventional and orthodox methods of investment, whether public or private, are inadequate. There is ample awareness among these sectors of the business community that when great numbers of people are without hope, when whole societies are mired in economic stagnation, when the educated and intellectual elite seethe with political and social tensions, there can be no real security for the United States. Among this select company of men there is the gnawing anxiety—perhaps it would be more accurate to call it an atavistic fear—that unless the private economy is willing to work as hard and as eagerly for the kind of world we want as the Communists work for the kind of world they want, there is probably little chance of our survival.

Epilogue

LATIN AMERICA'S nemesis is her galloping rate of population growth and inability to supply a burgeoning population with food. Uncontrolled population and unproductive agriculture will not only wipe out Latin America's hard-won industrial gains but inexorably turn her into one of the most miserable and devastated regions of the world in which human life will scarcely be distinguishable from animal existence.

In little more than three decades at the end of this century, Latin America's share of world population will be exceeded only by Asia. She is expected to add over a half billion more people to her current population of just over 200 million. It took 50 years—from 1900 to 1950—for the *entire* world to add 1 billion more people to the total global population. Latin America will have the dubious distinction of contributing half this amount in 35 years.

Former President of Colombia Alberto Lleras Camargo, in anguished despair, says: "If the population increase were not proceeding at such an inordinate rate, the problem would be manageable. *But at the current rate, it is beyond manageable proportions, and certainly beyond the capacities of the Latin Americans to cope with it.* Latin America is breeding misery, revolutionary pressures, famine, and many other potentially disastrous problems in proportions that exceed our imagination even in the age of thermonuclear war."[1]

---

[1] Testimony before the U.S. Senate Subcommittee on Government Operations in connection with Senate Bill 1676 (to co-ordinate the dissemination of birth control information among the governmental departments), sponsored by Senator Ernest Gruening, *Congressional Record*, July 9, 1965, p. 15630.

Like most of the world's heavily populated regions, Latin America has a high proportion of young people. More than 80 million—between 40 and 50 per cent of the population —are under fifteen years of age. (In the industrialized countries the proportion of children under the age of fifteen ranges from about 25 to 30 per cent.) This age profile has an adverse economic effect. A larger proportion of national income must be invested in feeding, clothing, housing, and schooling the young than is required in the highly industrialized countries, in which population increases more slowly. A country with a fast-growing population must spend such a large percentage of national income on rudimentary education to attain a bare minimum of literacy that little or nothing is left over for the education of engineers or agronomists. Indeed, the probability of a child, one of eight in the family of an illiterate peasant farmer who must support his family with the produce of 2 acres of land, ever becoming an engineer or agronomist is remote. Almost a million new homes are needed each year just to keep pace with population growth—an impossible requirement for Latin America to fulfill.

Eventually, dependents under the age of fifteen seek work. It is frequently overlooked that mere additions to the labor force do not increase a country's total production. In developing countries, the ratio of labor to capital is high. Consequently more entrants to the working force actually increase unemployment and underemployment. Modern technology is designed to produce more with less labor. When Mexico or Chile or Brazil, for example, invests capital for a new cement factory or steel mill it wants the latest technology; it cannot afford to invest scarce capital in an obsolete facility. Hence the very process of modernization exacerbates unemployment and underemployment. Moreover, even semi-automated plants can employ only a bare minimum of illiterate and unskilled workers.

Religious reasons are generally adduced for the failure to arrest Latin America's "Malthusian swamp of humanity." Part of the problem is the Roman Catholic dogma which opposes any form of birth control except the rhythm method. As a method of family regulation, it is far too sophisticated for Latin America's illiterate masses. Another factor is *machismo,* the *latino* masculine vanity that extols sexual prowess and large families—in or out of wedlock. Among the peasantry—and even among city-dwellers—the man who has fathered only five or six children is apt to be regarded as a laggard, if not impotent.[2]

Lest it be thought that the United States is immune from opposition to birth control to forestall a population rise that demographers warn can be ominous, it is well to recall the controversy between Catholic "literalists" (who oppose all forms of family-planning services under the auspices of the federal government of the United States) and Catholic liberals (who regardless of personal religious convictions are profoundly concerned with the need for family planning, particularly among the poverty-stricken who are unable to provide adequate food, guidance, and education for their children).

Dr. J. Mayone Stycos, Director of the International Population Program at Cornell University, has put his finger on another inhibiting factor: the unrealistic attitudes of many Latin American political leaders. Population growth is regarded as an immutable fact of life but the staggering demographic statistics are utilized to justify larger budgets and increased foreign aid. A second school of thought endeavors to turn a liability into an asset by a mystical view of population growth as the expression of the "dynamism" of the country. There are the complacent optimists who deplore rampaging population growth but believe that "education" and "economic development" will slow it down "as has inevitably occurred in Western European countries."

These three attitudes emulate the ostrich that buries its head in the sand. There are profound differences between the inordinately high rate of population growth in Latin America and the circumstances under which the industrialized countries underwent their demographic transition. In the latter part of the nineteenth century, an exodus began to North America, Australia, South Africa, and South America that totaled an estimated 27 million people by 1932.

---

[2] *Machismo* is also a North American addiction—at least in some circles. On a tour of Latin America, Senator Robert Kennedy was reported as having received loud cheers when he challenged a crowd of Cuzco Indians to outdo him in the production of children; he has nine. (*The Washington Post* November 13, 1965, p. A-11.) Mr. Kennedy's flippant remark did not serve President Belaúnde's national objective of encouraging the Indian population to reduce the size of their families, or the policy of the United States Government in fostering family planning at home and abroad.

Many prominent *porteños* in Buenos Aires and *paulistas* in São Paulo are descended from European emigrants. Northern Europeans recognized the need for limiting the size of families if they were to provide education for their children and enjoy the amenities of growing affluent societies. The surge in population brought about by the decline in mortality (through public health measures introduced around 1920) is occurring in Latin America at an earlier stage than the comparable development in Western Europe. In Great Britain, for example, "the peak of human multiplication came when the country was already highly industrialized and urbanized, with only one-fifth of its working males in agriculture." [3] The rate of natural increase (births minus deaths) was around 1.5 per cent in nineteenth-century Europe. Compare this percentage with the 3.8 per cent of tropical South America today. Few Latin American countries show evidence of a decline in fertility. Indeed, the only countries showing relatively low birth rates are Argentina and Uruguay. In these countries, European populations predominate and consensual marriages are uncommon.

It is wishful thinking to expect industrialization alone to bring down birth rates in Latin America within the next few decades. As the Brazilian economist Glycon de Paiva puts it tersely: "Without population control, any real economic development is impossible."

In his address commemorating the twentieth anniversary of the founding of the United Nations, President Johnson dramatized the problem by juxtaposition of two figures. He said: "Let us act on the fact that less than five dollars invested in population control is worth a hundred dollars invested in economic growth." We shall not be exaggerating in paraphrasing President Johnson's conclusion by saying that, unless we invest less than five dollars in birth control, a hundred dollars invested in economic development will be lost.

Increasingly, the suspicion grows that the attitudes of many Latin American political leaders regarding birth control do not reflect popular attitudes. Dr. Stycos reports that studies of Catholic attitudes in Puerto Rico, Peru, Chile, and Mexico show women of the lower classes to be over-

[3] Kingsley Davis: "Population," *Scientific American*, September, 1963, p. 69.

whelmingly in favor of smaller families. Still other statistical data disclose an overwhelming proportion of mothers favoring a limitation on additional children—for example: in Brazil, 79 per cent; in Mexico, 66 per cent; in Colombia, 61 per cent; in Costa Rica, 59 per cent; and in Panama, 57 per cent.[4]

That induced abortion has reached epidemic proportions in Latin America attests to the desperate plea for a method of family planning and contraception. In some hospitals, complicated aftereffects of abortions accounted for occupancy of as much as 70 per cent of the beds. For every birth in Uruguay, there are three abortions. In Brazil, some 2 million women have abortions each year. According to Dr. Walter Rodrigues, a leading Brazilian obstetrician, for every 2 hospital births there was an abortion requiring medical attention. In Argentina, 6,000 registered midwives specialize in illegal abortions.

In Chile, Dr. Jack Lippes, inventor of the celebrated contraceptive device known as the "Loop," reports that for every 100 live births occurring in hospitals, there were 31 hospitalizations from induced abortions. Out of every 100 liters of blood for transfusion, 27 liters were used on abortive cases. Induced abortions occurred in 35 to 40 per cent of all pregnancies in Chile. In one year alone, Dr. Lippes reports, there were 54,000 hospital admissions for complications resulting from secondary to criminal abortion.

Though the Church opposes the use of contraceptives many *padres* have braved the wrath of their bishops by quiet participation in government family planning information programs and—as in Brazil—in dispensing birth control devices. Chile's President Eduardo Frei has launched a birth control campaign in Santiago's shanty towns, and Peru's President Fernando Belaúnde Terry has established a Center for the Study of Population and Development. In Brazil, a private foundation plans to organize 600 birth control information centers across the country. For the first time in its history, the Brazilian Society of Gynecology and Obstetrics has publicly debated birth control and family planning. A sign of the times was the birth control conference

4 Testimony of Dr. Bernard Berelson, vice-president of The Population Council, before U.S. Senate Subcommittee on Government Operations in connection with Senate Bill 1676, sponsored by Senator Ernest Gruening, September 22, 1965.

held in Cali, Colombia, in August 1965, attended by educators, sociologists, physicians, welfare workers, demographers, and Catholic priests from 20 countries. Even the Agency for International Development has jumped on the birth control bandwagon by appropriating $1.4 million for 30 cooperative population studies throughout the hemisphere.

At this late date, Latin America's relentless multiplication will not be arrested by studies, conferences, plans, and public discussions. Talk is a traditional Latin American substitute for action and the refuge of her bureaucracies. Knowledge exists. What is lacking is the will to apply this knowledge by a massive campaign of education and distribution of a simple and inexpensive contraceptive device. Other world regions are far ahead of Latin America in implementing national programs that utilize the "Loop" method of intrauterine contraception—the cheapest and most effective device for mass distribution. Such programs have been adopted by the governments of Korea, the Republic of China, Pakistan, Tunisia, Turkey, and India.

Will Latin America's flood of humanity, as Pope Paul VI wistfully asked in his address before the United Nations, find "enough bread at the banquet of life"? Not unless a miracle occurs. According to the somber 1965 report of the Food and Agriculture Organization (FAO) of the United Nations, Latin America has lost the capacity to feed itself. For millions of already hungry Latin Americans, starvation is just around the corner. The projected per capita food production for 1965–66 will be 11 per cent less than the prewar average.

Chronic malnutrition is endemic; 2 out of 3 Latin Americans suffer from hidden hunger. As B. R. Sen, Director-General of FAO, reminds us: "To avoid the worst evils of underfeeding, an average diet of 2,400 calories per person per day, including 70 grams of protein" is needed. To reach this minimum standard, Latin America requires a fourfold increase in the supply of food. Dietary deficiencies and malnutrition exact a frightful toll, frequently irreparable, on the children. Malnutrition and infection interact on child mortality rates that are 20 to 40 times higher than in the United States and Western Europe.[5] Malnutrition is not merely a

[5] Nevin S. Scrimshaw, Professor of Nutrition and Head of the Department of Nutrition and Food Science at the Massachusetts Institute of Technology: "The Urgency of World Food Problems," an address before the annual meeting of the American Freedom From Hunger Foundation, Washington, D.C., October 8, 1965.

food problem; it is also an important health problem.

No other world region dramatizes so graphically the impact of unbridled population growth upon food supply as Latin America's shift from a grain-surplus region to a grain-deficit region. During the late 1930's, Latin America dominated the world grain market. She exported more grain than North America and Oceania combined. Latin America was an important supplier of wheat, and her corn exports accounted for almost three fourths of the world supply. By early 1960, Latin America had become a net deficit region.[6] Agricultural exports to Latin America from the United States alone increased from $472 million in 1961–62 to $536 million during 1963–64.

To be sure, the United States can be expected to use its agricultural surpluses, though they are rapidly dwindling, to alleviate hunger and famine—as in the case of India. But the transfer of food provides only peripheral relief: It is not a solution. Indeed, it may delay coming to grips with a country's unproductive agriculture. United States food policy is being altered by requiring increased emphasis on agricultural productivity as a condition to receiving food relief.

The strategy of economic development pursued by Latin America has emphasized industrialization to the neglect of agriculture. Industry has not grown fast enough to absorb the excess of hands and mouths. The heavy concentration of scarce resources and trained manpower on industrial development has intensified the disparities between development and underdevelopment and widened what Walt W. Rostow calls "the gap between the rich and poor parts of the developing nations themselves." Though development is an organic process and a complex of interrelated growth, as Gunnar Myrdal, the celebrated Swedish economist, says, "No drive for industrialization has much chance to be successful if not preceded and accompanied by a rather decisive rise in productivity in agriculture."

Improvement in agricultural productivity is not a single problem but a collection of complex problems. Each is a

6 Mexico's success in increasing her agricultural production to permit the export of wheat and corn has led the United States Government to cancel Food for Peace shipments of these foods. Mexico plans to continue food distribution programs itself. Venezuela has boosted her food output 63 per cent since 1953, but her population will have doubled by 1971.

separate problem but all are indissolubly linked. To be successful, all must be attacked simultaneously; a piecemeal approach dooms the effort to failure. An unfortunate example of the "piecemeal" approach is the recently concluded agreement between the Inter-American Development Bank and the United Nations' FAO for a heterogeneous series of agricultural technical assistance programs. By aiming their sights too low—on technical assistance to individual countries rather than a continental plan—this joint effort will be largely wasted.

Agricultural development depends on numerous physical variables: soil and plant characteristics, topography, climate, and rainfall. It depends on a nexus of services: roads, crop storage, irrigation, cheap credit (honestly and efficiently administered by agricultural banks), extension services (to instruct both big and little farmers in the latest advances in agricultural technology), training centers (to teach the essentials of agronomy), and marketing facilities (to provide the incentive for production beyond a subsistence level).

In Latin America, one of the most important keys to agricultural productivity is the use of chemical fertilizer. As Lester R. Brown of the U.S. Department of Agriculture says: "The use of more fertilizer in combination with other improved technology will undoubtedly be the single most important means of expanding output." With fertilizer and other modern farming practices, Latin America could double or triple her food production. Yet Latin America ranks next to Africa as one of the lowest consumers of chemical fertilizers—about 1 million metric tons annually compared to nearly 10 million tons in Western Europe and 12 million tons in the United States. Japan, whose postwar agricultural production has virtually eliminated hunger (and whose rate of population growth, 1.1 per cent, is lower than that of the United States and several European countries) uses more fertilizer than Latin America, Africa, China, or India.

Because of the shortage of good arable land, Latin America must make the transition from the area-expanding method of increasing food output to the yield-raising method followed by the technologically advanced countries. This is really shorthand for saying that intensive farming produces more per acre through use of mechanized equipment, better seeds and plant varieties, pesticides, fertilizer, irrigation, drainage, and availability of bank and supplier credit and managerial skills. Though Japan has the heaviest population per acre of cultivated land of any country on earth, her intensive agriculture provides a lesson in how much can be obtained from very limited land. Crop diversification is imperative for the single-commodity countries that are heavily dependent on the export of coffee or bananas. With a master plan for increasing the supply of food, a more concentrated effort of crop diversification can be undertaken (instead of exclusive reliance on bananas, adding beef, pineapples, and vegetables), or cushioning the transition from an oversupply of coffee to a more balanced program of poultry-raising, cattle-grazing, growing corn and other food crops—as in Brazil, Colombia, and Mexico.

Tillers of the soil in the biblical tradition, peasants whose farm implements consist frequently of stone-tipped sticks or the hoe and machete, who still clear the land by the primitive slash-and-burn method so that the soil is quickly leached, eroded by rain, and its working life-span limited—these agriculturalists (more than half the total population of Latin America, and in individual countries, as much as 70 per cent or more of the population) contribute little or nothing to the food supply. Subsistence farmers, with little or no cash incomes, cannot become consumers of the products of ·industry. They constitute the tidal wave of migrants to the shanty towns of already swollen and disfigured cities that are incapable of providing the civilized amenities of living. (It may comfort our friends to the South to know that the North American megalopolis is no prize. Urban dwellers in a motorized society are being slowly asphyxiated by lead poisoning and polluted air. Los Angeles' smog makes her unimaginable sprawl at times virtually uninhabitable. New York has rationed water, and her traffic is a nightmare out of Kafka. The Great Blackout early in November 1965 left 30 million inhabitants of the Northeast, the world's greatest megalopolis, in a state of underdevelopment for 24 hours.) Rural migrants fan the political combustibles that are close to the flash point in every Latin American capital city; in some North American cities the explosion has already occurred in the outbreak of racial violence by Negroes, who in large part are migrants from the rural South.

Of the many complex facets to Latin America's agricultural problem, by far the most difficult is the conversion of a rural peasantry into literate farmers capable of grasping and utilizing the knowledge of modern agricultural science and technology. Despite widespread belief to the contrary, we know too little about the formidable problem of transferring scientific and technological knowledge to subsistence agriculture. The universe of the peasant farmer is at the opposite pole from that of the representative of the Ministry of Agriculture from the capital city and light years away from the visiting agricultural specialist from the United States. The peasant has a profound distrust of his own countryman from the national bureaucracy—and with good reason. The foreign technician is apt to be regarded as a curiosity.

The value of much of the technical assistance by agricultural specialists sent to Latin America is questionable. Without painstaking adaptation to the particular needs and ecology of the country, the effort of foreign specialists is largely wasted. American agricultural technicians who are content to sit in the capital cities as "senior advisers" to the Ministers of Agriculture are useless appendages. More could be accomplished by using Israeli and Japanese agricultural specialists than our own. They are closer to, and more familiar with, small-scale operations, understand how to adapt modern agricultural technology to hostile environments, and know how to work with people.

The conventional economic developers give insufficient attention to rural education. Latin America can do without its annual crop of literary "doctors." Education for its own sake is a luxury that Latin America can forgo. Emphasis needs to be placed on education for agricultural development, with the rural community as the pivot in the process. High school graduates can be taught the rudiments of agronomy in short intensive courses. Working under the supervision of professional agronomists, they can enlarge the area of instruction to peasant farmers. This may not be an extension service as we understand it in the United States, but it is a beginning and better than nothing. American fertilizer and pesticide companies could be enlisted to establish demonstration centers for both big and small farmers. We have not even begun to tap the potential of the private economy for the organization and management of a wide range of agricultural and industrial services. By mobilizing the resources of the private economy, it would be possible to undertake economic development on a vast scale.[7] By greater utilization of the financial, managerial, technical, and administrative skills of private industry, Latin America could direct more of its energies into agricultural productivity without abandoning industrial development. Indeed, only by reshifting its development gears to prepare for the hard climb to agricultural productivity will Latin America assure itself of a lasting industrial development.

It serves no useful or honest purpose to exude false and complacent optimism that Latin Americans will be able to avert a Malthusian catastrophe. Organizational ability is missing. Technical skills are in short supply. The quantity of money called for is not at hand—though it can be obtained from the industrialized nations. Agriculture will not receive the attention that it deserves because industry has more prestige and glamour. Political leaders are in the main indifferent to birth control for the underlying population. With few, courageous exceptions, the Church evades the issue. Among the ruling and governing groups, the heroic effort will not be made because the will and the courage of desperation is absent.

Though the report of the White House Conference (November 28, 1965) on population lamented "that this may be the last generation which has the opportunity to cope with the problem on the basis of free choice," its recommendations were timid and woefully inadequate to meet the magnitude of the population problem which it thoughtfully recognized. It is equally true that no adequate plan exists in the Western world to prevent starvation in Latin America—or throughout the poor lands of the world. The refrain of the experts has been heard for years that, as President Kennedy told the World Food Congress in June 1963, "We do know how to produce enough food now to feed every man, woman, and child in the world, enough to eliminate all hunger completely." But in moving from high-sounding resolutions to action, we are treading water.

It is one of life's perversities that man can organize his resources for his own destruction in historic episodes of

[7] The Greek Government intends to hire Litton Industries, Inc., a leading American manufacturer of diversified products, to develop the agricultural and industrial potential of the island of Crete and the western part of the Peloponnesus. Litton Industries will prepare surveys and obtain foreign capital for, and supervise construction of, agricultural and industrial projects. See *The New York Times*, March 20, 1966, p. 5.

mass bloodletting, or a Manhattan Project for the successful production of an atom bomb, or a National Aeronautical and Space Administration to place a man on the moon, but he is not sufficiently motivated to organize a comparable effort for a massive attack on the world's most important problem of survival—too many people and too little food.

Appendix

The Dominican Revolution
and Its Aftermath

Arthur Schlesinger, in his book *A Thousand Days: John F. Kennedy in the White House,* implies that President Kennedy was disappointed but not surprised at the failure of Juan Bosch's political leadership. "In spite of the invasion of the island by swarms of Washington economists and engineers, of foundation experts and private consultants, in spite of grants and loans and blueprints," Schlesinger writes, "the Bosch government was not able in 1963 to reduce unemployment or prepare a national development program." Kennedy's fabled Olympian detachment is belied by the violent reaction of his administration to the collapse of Bosch's regime. By cutting off financial assistance and peremptorily withdrawing the American diplomatic corps, AID, and military missions, the rug was pulled from under the Dominican people, as the former Assistant Secretary of State for Inter-American Affairs Jack Vaughn correctly and courageously pointed out to the Committee on Foreign Relations of the United States Senate during the hearing on his nomination as Director of the Peace Corps. Actually, Bosch's political failure was a blow to the *amour propre* of the Kennedy administration. Kennedy's Charles River advisers had measured Bosch as a Caribbean Nehru, whereas in reality he was, in the retrospective judgment of historian Schlesinger, "essentially a literary figure, better as short story writer than statesman." By insisting on a presidential election in 1962 against the better judgment of thoughtful Dominicans (who believed the vast majority of the people were unprepared to exercise an act of citizenship after three decades of dictatorship) and then abandoning them out of pique, the Kennedy administration helped create the whirlwind that was to strike the island with shattering impact in April 1965.

On October 2, 1963, Juan Bosch sailed into another exile aboard the Dominican frigate *Mella*. Not renowned for his intestinal fortitude, Bosch demanded that General Antonio Imbert (who two years later would lead the loyalist Dominican armed forces against the revolution made in Bosch's name) accompany him as a hostage for his safety. Bosch's departure did not create a murmur of protest—students did not riot; slum dwellers did not man the barricades; *campesinos* did not march on Santo Domingo. Unlike the overthrow of the left-leaning Goulart in Brazil, neither parades nor celebrations marked Bosch's departure. For most Dominicans there was only one desire—to forget the nightmare of his ill-fated regime.

In *The True Believer* Eric Hoffer observes that though "men of words"—Bosch is the classic example—do much to prepare a revolution, they cannot face the turmoil of the revolution itself. Once the savagery of Santo Domingo had been unleashed, Bosch preferred the appearance of power to power itself. Bosch chose to remain in Puerto Rico, where he could hold press conferences, denounce his former friends, condemn United States intervention, and play the role of elder statesman of lost causes. Five months after the upheaval on September 25, 1965, Juan Bosch returned to Santo Domingo, an embittered, confused man who had lost his charismatic hold not only over his own party, but also over many who fought a sanguinary civil war under his banner.

The April Revolution had left Bosch behind; it produced its own heroes, mystique, legends, songs, slogans, glamour, and prestige. The real revolutionaries, who used Bosch to make *their* revolution, no longer needed him; they had won a victory without him.

Professor Bosch's homecoming speech was a heady Dominican cocktail, consisting of one part Caribbean romanticism and two parts anti-*yanqui* demagoguery. He told his audience —estimated by UPI at about 6,000—that the United States should be required to pay an indemnity of $1 billion for intervening in the April Revolution. More charitable toward Latin countries which sent troops to the Dominican capital, he assessed Brazil $20 million; Paraguay, a "poor country," was let off with a mere $1-million payment. Costa Rica, which sent twenty-one police officers, and Honduras, a company of troops, were exempt from indemnification. The Dominican people were exhorted to use any means to drive the foreign, i.e., American, military forces out. Consistency is not one of Bosch's virtues. One month later he called for the Inter-American Peace Force "to protect the people against the [Dominican] armed forces."

It takes as many kinds of men and women to make a revolution as to make a world. But all revolutions share one thing in common: they are hatched in conspiracy. Available evidence militates against acceptance of the view that inept political amateurs in Juan Bosch's party twisted the diverse strands of the conspiratorial rope, melded the heterogeneous elements involved in the plot, co-ordinated the peculiar organizational plan of this insurrection, and acted with the swiftness and professional skill that was evident on April 24–25.

It is also difficult to accept as mere coincidence the presence at this particular time of a cadre of specialists, trained in revolutionary techniques in Cuba, Eastern Europe, the Soviet Union, and China; or to believe that these technicians were only passive observers, ready to devour the revolution once it had been made.

A pertinent question that needs to be asked is: why did Bosch, a charter member of the Latin American democratic Left and professed believer in the democratic processes, participate in a conspiracy for the violent overthrow of a government that had scheduled presidential elections for September 1, 1965—less than four months from the bloody insurrection?

Reasonable men have concluded that a "democratic revolution" triggered by a conventional Latin American military *coup d'état* got out of hand and was taken over by Communists "in a flash almost as rapid and blinding as nuclear fusion." [1] But the instincts of common sense, let alone historic experience with the Communist strategy of deceit, caution against acceptance of this popular explanation. In his book *The White House Years: Waging Peace, 1956–1960,* President Eisenhower has a sentence pregnant with meaning for the Dominican situation. He writes: "It is easy now to look back and read Communism into Castro's actions. *But*

[1] John Bartlow Martin: "Inside the Drama and Chaos of the Dominican Upheaval," *Life,* May 28, 1965, p. 70-C.

at the time, conclusive evidence was lacking" [author's italics]. This is like saying your house has to burn down before you are willing to admit there is a fire. President Johnson's memoirs may require a gloss on his statement of May 2, 1965 that the insurrection in Santo Domingo was a "popular, democratic revolution"; but he will not lack conclusive evidence to justify his response to the dangers of that insurrection. For the Communists themselves have made it abundantly clear that they were the architects of the grand design for the armed revolt in Santo Domingo. In an article —the second of two on the Dominican uprising—entitled "Revolutionary Struggle in the Dominican Republic and its Lessons" by J. I. Quello and N. Isa Conde, members of the Central Committee of the Dominican Communist party, published in the January 1966 issue of the *World Marxist Review*, the authoritative international journal of the Moscow Communists, the authors leave no doubt that Havana was the inspiration for the revolutionaries in Santo Domingo. They write:

> . . . the Dominican revolution is another contribution to the arsenal of revolutionary experience on the continent; it may differ from the Cuban revolution in the "letter" but is fully in accord with it in "spirit, meaning and lessons."

According to Héctor Aristy, the gnomelike adventurer who served as mouthpiece for Colonel Francisco Caamaño Deñó, former "Provisional President" of the motley crowd of insurrectionaries, the conspiracy began more than a year before the day of the uprising.[2] The code name for the conspiratorial plan was Operación Enriquillo (after the legendary Indian *cacique* who organized the first New World insurrection against the Spaniards).

Aristy's admission points the compass in the direction of Havana. *Pravda* reported in January 1965 that at a secret conference in Havana in November 1964 the Soviets had re-established their control over Latin America's Communist parties. Since that meeting, all the Latin American

---

[2] Television interview with John Casserly, American Broadcasting Company, July 6, 1965. Señor Aristy was understood to have said that Dan Kurzman (Latin American correspondent for *The Washington Post*) was aware of the plot for over a year before the upheaval. "He was here in the beginning," Señor Aristy said, "and I told him what was going to happen."

Communist parties have publicly proclaimed the Caribbean region as an area for decisive revolutionary action. Santo Domingo was marked as a primary target of opportunity.

An insurrection sparked by guerrilla warfare—the technique used in Guatemala, Colombia, Venezuela, Peru, and Bolivia—was apparently deemed unnecessary under the conditions prevailing in the Dominican Republic. The Castro-oriented 14th of June Movement had been unsuccessful in mounting a guerrilla campaign because it lacked the indispensable prerequisite for Maoist-style guerrilla warfare—a strong base among the conservative Dominican peasants. Though the Moscow-aligned Dominican authors of the critique in the *World Marxist Review* are charitable toward the failure of their Havana-leaning colleagues, they were not inhibited in tagging them as a prime mover in planning the April insurrection. They write (December 1965, p. 74): *"Even before the [April 1965] uprising which was being prepared by the June 14 Movement, they tried to form their own guerrilla unit. But these guerrillas were soon taken prisoner in the Cevicos Mountains"* [author's italics]. The ascendancy of the Moscow thinking influenced a more conventional strategy for a quick seizure of power.

It was common knowledge during the first quarter of 1965 that the sixteen-month-old Reid Cabral regime was in trouble and lacked popular support. Technicians of insurrection, the managers of the plot understood how to exploit Reid's weakness. They were helped by a Dominican trait—the habit of betrayal. In the Dominican Republic, treachery is a way of life. Ironically, Reid's own sense of decency played into the hands of his adversaries. In the barbaric Dominican societal relations, tolerance and fair play were his Achilles' heel.

The problem Reid faced (which also is the problem of other poor lands) was a burning popular desire for the standard of living of the rich lands but an absence of the technical tools, social attitudes, and collective discipline that makes affluent societies possible.

With all the problems of underdevelopment, Dominicans also have peculiarly Dominican problems. They are like children who have lost the way. Psychologically disoriented by Trujillo's mutilation of their body and spirit, Dominicans do not really know what they want, cannot agree on what to do, and are unwilling to make common sacrifices to attain what is possible.

The old-line politicians—Dr. Viriato Fiallo is a notable exception—represent only their own ambitions. The Left is irresponsible, complacent toward Communism, and believes slogans are substitutes for governing. Though the Dominican Right denounces the Communists, it has consistently pampered them and has not been averse to making alliances with them. Indeed, some years ago an archconservative of the Right, General Antonio Imbert Barrera, helped finance the 14th of June Movement and furnished it with arms.

Unstable societies invariably find intellectuals pitted against the existing order. As talkers and writers, Dominican intellectuals helped set the stage for the ruthless fanatics who planned the Dominican uprising. Some in government sabotaged reform; others were informers who revealed vital information to the managers of the conspiracy. In January 1965, United States Ambassador W. Tapley Bennett transmitted to President Reid a list of well-known Dominican and foreign Communists who had managed to slip into the country undetected. This list was removed from a drawer in Reid's desk within a few hours of its delivery by a member of the President's official family, one of the country's most distinguished intellectuals. That the managers of the conspiracy were alerted is a forgone conclusion, for the cadre promptly vanished, surfacing again on April 24. When the revolution exploded, many Dominican intellectuals were to be found in the revolutionary stronghold, behind sandbags, with automatic rifles and machine guns. The "treason of the intellectuals," in Julian Benda's phrase, undermined and discredited social reform by peaceful methods.

Forty-two-year-old, five-foot-seven Donald Joseph Reid Cabral is a nervous bundle of energy who bears no resemblance to the stereotype Latin American "strongman." Reid represents a progressive, enlightened company of Latin American businessmen who are pro-United States, recognize the compelling need for social reform, and are committed to the goals of peaceful revolution under the Alliance for Progress. Reid is not a professional politician. He agonized over accepting the presidency vacated by the resignation of Don Emilio de los Santos. The presidency was his on-the-job training in the art of governing. From a councilor who was with him from the day of his oath-taking comes the observation that he was as baffling as a Hamlet and as secretive as a Richelieu in the conduct of the affairs of state. Veering and weaving between the Scylla of the old-guard politicians (who were plotting to unseat him) and the Charybdis of the Dominican military (whose support could not be taken for granted), Reid drained his energies in the business of staying alive politically.

In a sea of troubles perhaps Reid's greatest trouble was —as in every underdeveloped government—the almost total absence in his administration of men with managerial experience. Except for a scattering of businessmen and functionaries, virtually an entire generation under fifty years of age reached manhood without any opportunity to acquire skill and experience in decision-making. *El Benefactor* made the decisions for the Dominican Republic, which for all practical purposes was the private fiefdom of the Trujillo family.

In the accepted meaning of the term, Reid had no government. Delegation of authority was largely meaningless as there were few to whom responsibility could be entrusted. (Mario Mathiss Ricart, former Secretary of State for Agriculture, and Reid's colleague and close friend on the governing Executive, Ramón Cáceres Troncoso, would be rich assets in any advanced country.) Problems, trivial and significant, flowed like a river to the Palace. As the President himself had to decide both the big and little, the order of executive priorities was extinguished by the demand on Reid's time and energy from subordinates.

When Reid assumed the presidency at the end of 1963, the Dominican Republic was in critical straits. Liberation from Trujillo was heady wine. Wages, depressed for a generation, skyrocketed. Successive regimes padded the payroll of the government-owned sugar company with thousands of superfluous workers. Government departments were dumping grounds for job seekers. With pesos jingling in their pockets, Dominicans were eating more and better. Consumer goods, which only the rich had known in the era of Trujillo, filled the shops and warehouses. Superficially, the country looked prosperous; but it was like the rosy color on the cheek of the consumptive. The economy was not really productive— at least not productive enough to afford living high on the hog.

At the beginning of 1963, the trade deficit had grown to $22.8 million. Bosch sought the help of the International Monetary Fund. Lacking confidence in Bosch, the Fund declined to participate in a bailing-out operation. Reid's predecessor, Don Emilio de los Santos, did not possess the economic training to enable him to grapple with the problems of debt consolidation and budgetary controls. His colleagues, Manuel Enrique Tavares Espaillat and Ramón Tapia Espinal, were even less qualified. So trade deficits mounted while income shrank.

Reid inherited a nearly bankrupt treasury, a trade deficit of around $30 million, a tangled skein of government finances, and a catastrophic drop in the world price of sugar, which accounts for more than 50 per cent of the country's foreign earnings.

Reid inaugurated a major reform in a prevalent Latin American technique of government investment. Previously, the "autonomous agencies"—the electric power company, the state-owned sugar company, the water and sewerage institute, the agricultural bank, and others—borrowed and spent money as they saw fit. Reid insisted that their financial activities be channeled through a central body over which he himself presided. Though this procedure guaranteed future fiscal responsibility, re-examination of prior commitments before authorization of new ones, and tightened loose management practices that enabled corruption to flourish, it also brought forth bitter protests from the panjandrums of the once-independent agencies.

Ironically, Donald Reid Cabral, the capitalist, distributed in one day, January 24, 1965, more land to landless *campesinos*—1,500 certificates of title—than Juan Bosch, the professional revolutionary, managed to distribute over seven months—only 300 parcels of land.

Because Dominicans attach a mystical importance to maintaining their peso on a parity with the dollar (a tradition inherited from Trujillo), Reid, with encouragement from the United States and support by the International Monetary Fund, elected to embark on austerity rather than devaluation. Like other Latin American presidents who have tried it, Reid soon discovered that austerity has no political mileage. Tight credit, stiff import taxes, and restrictions on the amount of money that could be used for purchases abroad alienated merchants and traders; holding the line on wage increases and cancelling employee bonuses produced wildcat strikes and labor unrest; contracting the swollen government bureaucracy increased popular ferment.

Only demagogues make omelets without eggs. Reid refused to buy synthetic popularity with cheap promises on which he could not make delivery. Hence he was impaled on the horns of a cruel dilemma. On the one side, bringing order to the country's snarled finances and restoring international confidence in the country's credit meant postponement of major social reforms. On the other side, the people were thirsting for reforms and welfare measures, which Bosch had promised but which he was incapable of fulfilling.

The Gordian knot could be cut only by the United States. Tapley Bennett, on his first ambassadorial assignment but with long Latin American experience and a former deputy chief of the American mission at Athens, was committed to Reid's success. For Reid's success would be the measure of his own. Unlike some American ambassadors, who become so deeply identified with the countries to which they are accredited that they are special pleaders, Bennett never lost sight of his primary responsibility—the interests of the United States. He understood that, even in the Dominican Republic, the American ambassador is not a proconsul. Though Bennett could suggest, which he did frequently, Reid alone could decide. Even suggestions to an inexperienced government are fraught with danger. To act on the right suggestion at the wrong time can be fatal.

To be sure, economic and financial specialists on Bennett's staff supplied the technical expertise that enabled Reid's regime to keep afloat in the deep waters of fiscal and monetary controls. Reid, however, needed more than a financial life preserver to survive. Bennett appreciated this political fact of life, but he was frustrated by his own bureaucracy. It is a popular misconception that an ambassador is sovereign in his embassy. In reality, he is more often than not a presiding officer over potentates from other government agencies—CIA, Pentagon, Treasury, Labor, AID, the Peace Corps, for example—who have their own private channels of communication to Washington, their own ideas on what should be done, and sometimes their own operating budget.

Wedded to the theology of economic development, in Washington the AID bureaucracy was unable to comprehend that development cannot take root in a political vacuum, that AID programs, if they are realistic, also must provide some political benefits. Immobilized by its own red tape and conventional attitudes on the nature of economic development, AID was incapable of helping Reid to offset the effects of a siege economy.

A civil war, a near-Communist take-over, and a shattered economy brought an end to AID-as-usual. What was not done for Donald Reid Cabral was done for Héctor García Godoy, who had a nine months' lease on the office of Provisional President. Ironically, a "pot" of $2 million was allocated for public works "in areas where it will do the most good politically." [3] Now that the horse has been stolen, *The New York Times* reported (December 2, 1965, p. 17) that a $50-million aid "package" was being readied for delivery before Christmas, with the hope that it "will enhance the domestic and international prestige of the García Godoy regime."

The United States has not been niggardly with financial aid to the Dominican Republic—an island country 18,703 square miles in size, about as large as Vermont and New Hampshire, containing largely a Negro and mulatto population of about 3.5 million, the vast majority of whom is engaged in subsistence agriculture. Over a period of three years, from January 1962 (when the Council of State took office) to April 1965 (when the Reid Cabral regime was overthrown), the United States supplied about $144 million in loans, grants, and other types of financial assistance. The Kennedy administration in seven months furnished the Bosch regime with over $30 million (of which $22.75 million was a gift). The *triunvirato,* which succeeded Bosch, received over $60 million in loans—there were no grants—and the use of Public Law 480 currency owned by the United States. An impartial commission would find little evidence that this investment had produced any significant economic development. From April 25 to August 31, 1965, the OAS—acting for the United States—disbursed $48,500,000, mainly for medicine and food for the inhabitants of the rebel zone and for salaries of government workers—on both sides of the conflict. From the start of the revolution to the election on June 1, 1966, the Dominican Republic received about $131 million. Except for Brazil, the Dominican Republic received more U.S. aid than any other Latin American country in the current fiscal year. And the end is not in sight.

The Inter-American Development Bank, which is regarded as a Latin American community to foster economic development, also has nothing to show for its efforts in the Dominican Republic. According to the Bank's 1964 Annual Report, it has maintained since 1962 four advisers to the Banco Agrícola (the Dominican Agricultural Bank) to carry

[3] *U.S. News & World Report,* September 27, 1965, p. 56.

out the bank's programs. On p. 64 of this report, these programs are described as "administrative and accounting reorganization, to establish norms and policies in agricultural credit, crop diversification programs, and to train appraisers and supervised credit personnel."

Rafael Jorge Abinader, general administrator of the Banco Agrícola during the Bosch regime, retained the internationally known accounting firm of Ernst & Ernst to make an audit. The final audit was completed during the Reid Cabral administration. On March 16, 1965, Ernst & Ernst submitted the audit to Mario Mathiss Ricart who, a few days earlier, had been designated by Reid to succeed Luis Rodríguez—a Reid appointee—as the bank's general administrator.

The audit shows that about two thirds of what the bank claimed as assets were not assets at all. Of the bank's claimed $118 million in assets, the auditors approved only $43 million. In referring to the $75-million discrepancy, the Ernst & Ernst audit (p. 4), in one of the most restrained financial understatements of the year, observed: "As a result of our examination, the financial statements previously prepared by the bank, as of May 31, 1964, have been revised substantially." That is, revised $75 million downward. On the same page, the audit goes on to say: "Contracts were inspected for the respective loan ledger cards and we were unable to locate approximately 3,900." Continuing, the audit reveals that "We also inspected the mortgages and were unable to locate approximately 900 mortgages."

On p. 7 of the audit, there is the disquieting news that "titles could not be located for certain properties carried at approximately $1,300,000." On p. 8, the audit points to the crowning folly of this "bank"—it forgot to list one of its most important assets, its own bank building. Among the "assets" of the agricultural bank were loans made to borrowers who had skipped out of the country, including several Dominican diplomats. According to a Dominican official, a considerable number of these loans were made to members of Bosch's political party.

Nor has the World Bank fared better. It has twice attempted to inaugurate a miniature TVA that would bring water and other benefits to the Dominican countryside only to see its efforts frustrated by the country's endemic political instability.

Such is the record of "economic development" in the Dominican Republic. American policy-makers continue to ignore the real problem in the Dominican Republic—the illiteracy of the mass of the population and the primitive stage of political development that make a mockery of pretensions to a democratic government. American policy in the Dominican Republic has confused the relationship between economic and political development. We have employed technical assistance and economic aid to fill a political vacuum left by Trujillo. We have fallaciously assumed that economic development automatically produces democratic political development. The problem of political development eludes American policy-makers because it requires not only deep knowledge of the psychology of the Dominican people but also the conviction that the influence of the United States can legitimately be exercised in assisting the Dominicans to acquire the habit and practice of governing themselves. The political failures in the Dominican Republic since the demise of Trujillo are primarily the result of political inexperience in the art of governing. Exiles who return as strangers to their own country and political dilettantes cannot be expected to govern successfully.

Pumping money into a backward, hate-ridden country will not produce a political structure, respect for law, for property, for individual and political rights, for constitutional processes. These values can be developed—in time and by means other than economic development. Lost opportunities are rarely retrievable. It is by no means clear that we have either the time, the political program, or the influence to control the situation.

In Latin America, no civilian chief of state can survive without the support of the military. From their conspiratorial centers within the Dominican armed forces, the plotters against Reid knew that the military establishment was not united behind him.

Smuggling is a venerable institutional practice in the Dominican Republic—as in other Latin countries. During Bosch's regime as earlier under the Council of State, a number of senior officers were engaged in smuggling as a profitable sideline. Military aircraft and naval vessels were used to transport contraband merchandise from Miami and San Juan, Puerto Rico. Military post exchanges became centers of traffic in smuggled goods. These officers were encouraged by the example of, perhaps in connivance with, a member of Bosch's cabinet whose business activities also embraced smuggling. Though Bosch was informed of his ministerial colleague's illicit traffic, he did not take disciplinary action against him—or the offending military officers.

Because the United States was footing a large part of the Dominican government payroll, Ambassador Bennett, steadily but diplomatically, nudged Reid to purge the military establishment of its corrupt practices. Reid retired 76 officers, removed 10 others from key commands, closed the post exchanges, ended the misuse of naval vessels and military aircraft, and cut the military budget (which siphoned off about 19 per cent of the national budget). Reid also began a reduction in the size of the armed forces, which stood at 26,000 officers and enlisted men. The notoriously corrupt General Belisario Peguero, Chief of the National Police, was fired. Upon his dismissal, Peguero was presented with $10,000 severance pay. One of the island's wealthiest men— his home near the Embajador Hotel is a showplace—General Peguero knew how this money could be invested profitably: He turned over $8,000 to Bosch's political party.

For the first time in Dominican history, her military were brought under civilian control. Reid himself temporarily assumed the portfolio of Secretary of State for the Armed Forces. But Reid paid a heavy price for his courage. He unhinged the command structure and created a train of bitter enemies who were ripe for a conspiracy to topple him. The plotters exploited their advantage among leftist officers and the unsavory types that had been purged.

It seemed, as the year 1965 was ushered in, that luck had deserted Reid. A United States shipping strike in January and February drastically reduced government receipts of custom duties (the principal source of budgetary income). Forest fires ravaged the countryside. (About a week before the April 24 uprising, the entire central *cordillera* was on fire. Many Dominicans believe this fire was the work of saboteurs.) Strains and tensions produced by the straitened economic situation were intensified by the natural proclivity of Dominicans to intrigue against each other. Broadcasts over the radio grew more inflammatory. A series of strikes by taxicab drivers and sugar workers exacerbated raw nerves. *El Caribe* and *Listín Diario*—the big daily Santo Domingo papers—eroded waning confidence in the Reid administration by carping and, at times, irresponsible criticism. The atmosphere was heavy with rumors of coups. On April 4, Ambassador Bennett cabled Washington that the situation was rapidly deteriorating, that, as he put it, "Little foxes some of them red are chewing at the grapes"; and "we could have a very bitter wine here."

Cold, hard-eyed men trained in Eastern Europe, the Soviet Union, China, and Cuba, professional revolutionaries surveying the Dominican scene during the early months of 1965, might well have concluded that the climate was propitious for a lightning assault on the fragile regime of Donald Reid Cabral.

Professor Bosch was an ideal choice as "front man" for a Communist-dominated conspiracy. He was not allergic to the color "red." His party—or what remained of it—was honeycombed with Reds. Though the Dominican Communist parties officially boycotted Bosch's campaign for the presidency, in reality they supported him.[4] During his term of office, he had shown a peculiar affinity for the 14th of June Movement—the Castro-oriented Communists. He thirsted for revenge against those whom he regarded as the usurpers of his rightful claim to the presidency. As a political refugee in Puerto Rico, he abused the hospitality of the Commonwealth by maintaining an incessant barrage of incendiary speeches against the Reid regime and used his asylum as a base for intrigue and conspiratorial action.

He was the darling of doctrinaire American liberals. The triumvirs of the democratic Left of the Caribbean—Muñoz Marín, Betancourt, and Figueres—were his political allies. To Latin American intellectuals he was an indigenous popular leader. A popular front with Bosch as its respected leader would be a magnet to attract well-meaning but gullible Dominicans into the conspiracy and, later, into the streets.

Revolutions need the underpinning of myth. With a shrewd sense of its propaganda value, the Communists used Bosch's unique free election as a foundation upon which to erect the great myth of the April Revolution—"constitutional government."

Addressing a May Day rally in Havana, Dr. Castro, with exquisite irony, lauded the Dominican Communists in Santo Domingo for their role in defending the Constitution. He associated himself with Juan Bosch and João Goulart

[4] In the 1966 presidential election the pattern was reversed: Bosch officially boycotted the Communist parties but they openly supported him.

(deposed left-leaning President of Brazil who brought his country to the brink of chaos) as the kind of reformist leaders whom he thought the United States also should have supported (*The New York Times*, November 1, 1965, p. 1).

After the uprising and the installation of Colonel Caamaño as "Provisional President" of the revolutionary government, Juan Bautista Mejía Gómez, a leader of the 14th of June Movement, urged Havana to softpedal its radio broadcasts on the active role of the 14th of June Movement in the planning and execution of the insurrection because the Dominican loyalists, he said, were using these broadcasts to prove Communist involvement in the revolution. Mejía asked that Havana cease referring to "mountain hideouts" and "guerrilla warfare" and emphasize instead that the members of the 14th of June Movement were "Constitutionalists."

The Agrupación Política Catorce de Junio (APCJ), the 14th of June Movement, with an estimated strength (before the uprising) of more than 4,000 members, was the link which joined the military conspirators, the other Communist parties—the Partido Socialista Popular (PSP), the Moscow-oriented wing of the party, with an estimated strength of about 1,000 members; and the Movimiento Popular Dominicano (MPD), the Peking disciples, with some 500 members —and the Partido Revolucionario Dominicano (Bosch's PRD) with each other—and Havana.

(The three Dominican Communist parties and Colonel Caamaño's "Constitutionalists" were represented at the Tricontinental Solidarity Conference at Havana in January 1966. Cayetano Rodríguez del Prado, member of the delegation from Movimiento Popular Dominicano [MPD], told the conferees that "Our country took Cuba as an example for our revolution," and the Communists would make the Dominican Republic "the Viet Nam of Latin America.")

The 14th of June Movement sent many of its members to Cuba for training in guerrilla-warfare schools. It arranged forged identity papers for the technicians who were slipped across the Windward Passage and was the repository for large amounts of money brought into the Dominican Republic by couriers from Havana. It received arms from Cuba, landed clandestinely on the northern Dominican coast.

Throughout 1964, the 14th of June Movement maintained close liaison with Bosch and his party. At a convention of the PRD in San Juan, Puerto Rico, in October 1964, Bosch himself urged absorption by PRD of the 14th of June Movement because his own party lacked the youthful dynamism and revolutionary zeal of the 14th of June Movement.

In January 1965, Bosch and Antonio Rosario, leader of the Christian Social Revolutionary party (PRSC), entered into an alliance, which they termed the "Río Piedras Agreement," for the overthrow of the Reid regime. In an interview on February 1, 1965 with *El Mundo*, a Spanish-language daily of San Juan, Bosch and Rosario were quoted as saying that "Conditions in the Dominican Republic do not permit talk of elections."

The true facts were the opposite. There never was any question that elections would be held. During the interval when the Kennedy administration withdrew diplomatic recognition after the collapse of the Bosch regime, Reid's predecessors on the governing Executive, on November 27, 1963, approved a system of staggered elections, beginning in November 1964 with the *alcaldes pedános* (village mayors) in the villages, municipal elections in January, congressional elections in June, and presidential elections in July, 1965. This arrangement was endorsed by six political parties and the military establishment. Neither Bosch nor Rosario signed the agreement of understanding. The power-hungry politicians—again Viriato Fiallo was the exception—soon repudiated their commitment and demanded earlier elections than those which had been scheduled, but confined to a run-off for the presidency. In September 1964 Reid's government formally announced that national elections would take place on September 1, 1965. All the Dominican politicians were aware of this announcement. It was not lost on the Communists. The Central Committee of the Partido Socialista Popular (the Moscow wing) as late as March 16, 1965, "warned" its members and supporters that a national election in September "could definitively validate the clerical-military coup of September 25, 1963."

Reid had concluded after lengthy deliberation to stand as a presidential candidate. He intended to announce his candidacy at the end of April or early May. Don Marino Cáceres (whose father, President Ramón Cáceres, gave the Dominican Republic one of the few decent and honest administrations—1906–11—in its history) had agreed to serve as Reid's campaign manager. Reid's young friends were planning an "American-style" political campaign, with stickers, buttons, sound trucks, and other typical American political trappings.

For tactical reasons, the 14th of June Movement was not a signatory to the Río Piedras pact though its leadership was attuned to the understanding reached by Bosch and Rosario. In a stop-over at Caracas on June 1, while returning from Chile as a special emissary of Colonel Caamaño, Caonabo Javier Castillo, a member of the Christian Social Revolutionary party, held a press conference at the headquarters of Copei, the Venezuelan Christian Democratic party. Unwittingly, he revealed the true state of affairs when he referred to the 14th of June Movement as one of the signatories of the "Río Piedras Agreement."

On February 20, 1965, the Peking-oriented MPD, in a flyer entitled "The Fight Against the Coup [i.e., the Reid regime] is a Fight Against Yankee Imperialism," publicly endorsed the "Río Piedras Agreement." It asserted: "Any group or political party that does not fight for public liberty and for the Constitution of 1963, although it be through the PRD-PRSC agreement, serves imperialism and is a traitor to the struggle of the people."

On March 9, the Moscow-oriented PSP came to life with its own flyer. Though it hailed the "Río Piedras Agreement" as a significant development, the party was careful to point out that the pact was too limited in scope. Needed, it said, was a "united front" to battle for the Constitution of 1963.

On March 16, five weeks before the uprising, the Central Committee of PSP released a manifesto which cynically declared: "*It is necessary to use the slogan of the return of President Bosch as head of the constitutional government of the Republic*" [author's italics]. But "The return of Professor Bosch to the presidency of the Republic," the Central Committee pointed out, "does not signify the solution of the national problems." Freedom of the working class can be obtained only, according to the manifesto, by "eliminating the economic domination of North American imperialism." Bosch's return, therefore, was to be considered as a transitional stage in the ultimate emancipation of the Dominican people. Dominicans were exhorted to "fight in the streets, in the squares, in the factories, in the fields, for the return of President Bosch as head of the constitutional government."

In March, Victoriano Félix and Rafael Taveras of the 14th of June Movement visited Bosch in Puerto Rico to obtain taped speeches. These were broadcast throughout the Dominican Republic from a radio station owned by a member of Bosch's party.

On the night of April 9 an interview with Bosch by Victoriano Félix was broadcast over Radio Cristal (owned by the Finance Secretary of Bosch's party, José A. Brea Peña) on a program called "Aquí Santo Domingo," directed by another member of the 14th of June Movement. Bosch's message was anti-American, rabble-rousing, and pro-Communist. That Bosch's party conspired with dissident officers of the Dominican armed forces is confirmed by the Dominican Communist leaders. The *World Marxist Review* (December 1965, p. 76) states: "Although Bosch himself undoubtedly linked a military conspiracy with the struggle of the masses, the DRP [PRD] leaders in Santo Domingo did not understand this and for months engaged solely in preparing a military conspiracy, doing nothing to rally the people."

Colonel Rafael Tomás Fernández Domínguez, an intimate friend of "Ramfis" Trujillo, was one of Bosch's principal contacts with the military. He became "Minister of Interior" in the revolutionary government headed by Colonel Caamaño. Domínguez was killed on May 19 during a night attack on the National Palace.

Another important connection which Bosch had with the military was Lieutenant Colonel Miguel Ángel Hernando Ramírez (considered by knowledgeable Dominicans as the brains of the military side of the conspiracy). In his political outlook, Ramírez was regarded by many fellow officers as leftist. It was widely known that Ramírez and members of his family were ardent admirers of Bosch. For these reasons General Viñas Román, former Secretary of State for the Armed Forces, would not permit Ramírez to have command over troops.

Ramírez was involved in a curious incident on the night of June 10, 1964—the significance of which became apparent a year later. A fire broke out at the ammunition depot of the 27th of February camp, about 3 miles from the capital, on the other side of the Ozama River. Though a large quantity of munitions was destroyed by the fire, an equally large quantity of weapons mysteriously disappeared. Colonel Ramírez was the officer in charge of the security of the depot.

On Sunday, April 25, 1965—when arms were handed over

to civilians by rebel officers and Communist leaders—a loyalist officer, who had served under Colonel Ramírez at the depot, recognized familiar equipment among the weapons that were distributed. He counted over 100 German-manufactured rifles and a large number of machine guns that were allegedly destroyed in the depot fire.

Other officers involved in the conspiracy were known for their left-wing political beliefs. A responsible Dominican source estimates that the majority of the 60 officers who participated in the insurrection were members of the 14th of June Movement. Lieutenant Commander Manuel Ramón Montes Arache, who commanded the navy frogmen, deserted with 40 of his company of 70 men. Montes Arache prepared Trujillo's abortive plot for the assassination of former President Betancourt. In Montes' desk at navy headquarters, Commodoro Francisco J. Caminero, former Secretary of State of the Armed Forces, found a list of the names of the foreign and Dominican Communists, who were the directorate of the conspiracy. Ironically, virtually all the officers involved in the insurrection received training at the United States' School of the Americas in Panama. Colonel Caamaño was trained at the Marine Corps base at Quantico.

The modern technique for overthrowing a government by a small disciplined band of insurrectionaries was first developed and used by Leon Trotsky in the 1917 Bolshevik Revolution. Thereafter it was successfully utilized in Eastern Europe, Italy, and Germany, and is now standard operating procedure for revolutionaries of the Left and Right.

Like all good plans Trotsky's is simple. Its success depends upon three factors: (1) surprise; (2) manipulation of contrived disorder (more important, Trotsky believed, than a general strike) and exploitation of the ensuing chaos to (3) effect a quick paralysis of a country's nervous system through seizure of communication facilities, power plants, water systems, banks, warehouses, railroad terminals and docks.[5]

"To overthrow a modern state," Trotsky wrote in his own *History of the Russian Revolution*, "you need a storming party, technical experts and groups of armed men led by engineers." Trotsky's technique of the *coup d'état* was carried out to the letter in Santo Domingo by the leadership of the 14th of June Movement and the Moscow branch of the Communist party.

[5] See Curzio Malaparte: *Coup d'État: The Technique of Revolution* (New York: E. P. Dutton & Co.; 1932), *passim*.

In the twentieth century the masses do not make revolutions. The masses are like bit players in a movie spectacular. They are called out when needed for the pageantry of the mob scenes. Small, ruthless, fanatical groups make revolutions of the Left or Right. In the politics of revolution the directing group must be small to maintain the high pitch of fanaticism, to provide speed, flexibility, and the capacity for immediate decisions—factors of incalculable importance in the planning and execution of the Dominican upheaval.

During the first months of 1965 rumors of coups were a peso a dozen. The dramatis personae of the coups—real or fancied—ranged over the political and military spectrum. Neither Reid nor Ramón Cáceres Troncoso (the other member of the governing Executive) was aware of the depth of the conspiracy. By April 8, they knew of rumblings and mutterings at two army garrisons. On April 19, Reid asked Lieutenant Colonel Miguel Ángel Álvarez Holguín, deputy commander of the 16th of August garrison, Lieutenant Colonel Hernando Ramírez, commanding officer of the 27th of February garrison, and Brigadier General Marcos Rivera Cuesta, chief of the army general staff, to meet with him. Holguín and Ramírez protested Reid's suspicions; both assured him of their unswerving loyalty; and the Chief of Staff vouched for them.

Later in the week, on April 21, because of his continued uneasiness, Reid, his military aide, Colonel Calderón, and General Rivera Cuesta, spent three hours at the 16th of August camp.

"I thought," Reid said, "if they were going to make a coup, it would be better for the country to take me prisoner and avoid bloodshed."

Nothing untoward happened; Reid was not taken prisoner; Lieutenant Colonel Holguín and his commanding officer, Colonel Giovanni Gutiérrez, played out the charade as loyal officers.

At 2 a.m. on Saturday, April 24, General Wessin y Wessin was awakened at his home by an army corporal who informed him of a meeting which had taken place in the residence of Captain Mario Peña Taveras, a G-1 staff officer attached to the headquarters of the army general staff. The corporal's information was that Captain Peña Taveras and a group of officers were planning to arrest General Marcos Rivera Cuesta, chief of the general staff, on Saturday morning. General Wessin telephoned Rivera Cuesta, who dismissed the warning as a fabrication; it could not be true, he told Wessin, because he was a *compadre* (godfather) to one of Captain Peña Taveras' children. Wessin proceeded at once to his own base at San Isidro and issued an order recalling all officers and enlisted men who were in the city on week-end passes.

About 7:30 General Rivera Cuesta went to Reid's home. He told Reid that the two garrison commanders and the principal members of their staffs were definitely involved in a plot to overthrow the government. (Informed Dominicans believe that Rivera Cuesta was himself involved in—or at least cognizant of—the plot, and upon realization that it was more than another Palace *Putsch,* lost his nerve. He consistently "vouched" for officers suspected of complicity. On Friday, April 23, he was at the Officers' Club, accompanied by several officers and cashiered officers who subsequently were in active command in the rebel zone.) Reid directed him to relieve Colonel Gutiérrez and Lieutenant Colonels Holguín and Ramírez of their commands and place them under arrest. Rivera Cuesta telephoned Holguín (who was at La Vega, a provincial city in the interior) and the two garrison commanders to report to the headquarters of the general staff. By mid-morning Gutiérrez and Holguín voluntarily submitted to custody. Ramírez ignored the summons and remained at his camp. The hapless and naïve Rivera Cuesta had underestimated Captain Mario Peña Taveras, who was the key liaison between the 14th of June Movement and the headquarters of the army general staff. Around noon on Saturday, with a group of armed officers and sergeants, Captain Peña Taveras took General Rivera Cuesta prisoner and, as if he were boning a fish, removed the vertebrae—such as it was—of the Dominican army.

By coincidence, the principal senior members of the American Embassy were not in Santo Domingo on Saturday morning, April 24. Ambassador Bennett, en route to Washington, was in Georgia visiting his parents. (Bennett had previously informed the Department of State that this might be the only time left for consultation at Washington.) Of the thirteen-member U.S. Military Advisory Assistance Group, eleven were in Panama for a briefing session. The newly appointed naval attaché was in the interior shooting wild doves with General Antonio Imbert Barrera, who would shortly become a stellar actor in the bloody Dominican drama. The Chief of the U.S. AID Mission was in Washington for the annual country budget and program review.

Also absent from Santo Domingo on that fateful Saturday morning were Reid's closest and most influential advisors: Don José Antonio Bonilla-Atiles (then Dominican ambassador to Washington, who divided his time between his ambassadorial duties and counselling Reid, his former university student) was in St. Augustine, Florida, attending a Pan American celebration; and Francisco (Pancho) Aguirre (who was en route from Costa Rica to Panama).

The absence from Santo Domingo of so many key persons could not have been lost on the directorate of the conspiracy. One can only speculate what effect their absence had on Reid's own fortunes.

The date for the uprising was not April 24 but April 26 (as Juan Bosch himself has confirmed in a personal letter to Theodore Draper, cited in *Commentary*, December 1965, p. 37). As the fat was already in the fire and the operational plan ready, the management of the conspiracy concluded there was nothing to gain by further delay.

Reid and Cáceres spent Saturday morning on routine business in their offices at the National Palace. About 1:30 they departed for their respective homes.

A few minutes after 2:30 Ramón Cáceres telephoned Reid that Radio Santo Domingo, the government-owned station, had been seized by a group of civilians who were broadcasting that the government had been overthrown. Cáceres came at once to Reid's residence; together they returned to the Palace. It was not long before they learned that the headquarters of the general staff and the 16th of August and 27th of February garrisons were in revolt.

On radio and TV, though they may not have grasped its significance at the time, Dominicans were witnessing a demonstration of "manipulated disorder." Led by the Cuban Communist Luis Acosta Tejeda, a parade of actors armed to the teeth, some dressed as sailors, others in army uniform; characters with *barbudos,* wearing the familiar olive-green fatigues and berets of Castro's militia; girl *milicianas,* with ammunition bandoliers and rifles, flitted across the TV screens, shouting: "We demand a return to constitutional government; we want Juan Bosch as President." Prisoners, among them criminals, released by some units of the National Police were rushed before the TV cameras to broadcast that the police had joined in the demand for the return of Juan Bosch. An announcer shouted that the armed forces had revolted. Dominicans were exhorted to "pour into the streets and celebrate the victory of the people over the downfall of Reid Cabral." This announcement sent crowds boiling into the streets, where agitators whipped them into a frenzy. Mobs invaded the central fire station, stole the engines, and drove them, sirens howling, through the streets.

Paul D. Bethel, a former State Department foreign service officer and now executive secretary of the Citizens Committee for a Free Cuba, wrote from Santo Domingo:

> Control of the radio and television by the Communists nearly delivered the country into their hands. The confusion created in the ranks of the loyalists was enormous. Skillful radio and television propaganda made it appear that the country was in the hands of the rebels.

Confronted with an insurrection of which as yet only the peak of the iceberg had appeared, Reid needed the kind of absolute power that, as Mao Tse-tung once observed, flows from the end of a gun barrel. That power did not exist at the Palace. It was to be found only on the other side of the Ozama River at San Isidro, where General Elías Wessin y Wessin had his tanks and General Juan de los Santos Céspedes his air squadrons. Reid was unable to bring that power to his support.

At the Palace, the afternoon wore on as precious hours were lost in indecision and a cascade of talk. Commodoro Caminero urged Reid to abandon the Palace and to transfer the seat of Government to the flagship *Mella*. Reid said such a move might provide him with safety but at the price of provoking bloodshed. He refused to leave the Palace. About four o'clock, Lieutenant Carlos Rocha led a detachment of loyalist troops to recapture Radio Santo Domingo. By nightfall, Wessin sent an infantry company with four tanks to occupy the eastern end of the Duarte Bridge to protect this avenue of access to his camp. Throughout the afternoon Reid endeavored to reach General de los Santos Céspedes, who had made himself inaccessible. Actually, his sympathies were with the rebels. He ignored a plea by Commodoro Caminero to strafe the rebel garrisons. He had asked General Wessin to surrender. Wessin refused. He reminded de los Santos Céspedes that they were in the middle of a "Dominican *carupano*" (the abortive Venezuelan uprising instigated by Castro-Communists and joined by marines and junior officers), and they were witnessing a Communist uprising. "I told him," Wessin said, "I preferred to fight until the end." It was not until 7 p.m. that Reid was able to reach the Chief of the Air Staff at Boca Chica, a nearby fashionable beach resort. General de los Santos Céspedes observed that darkness prevented retaliatory action against the rebellious garrisons, but promised an air strike at 5:30 a.m. Sunday. (De los Santos Céspedes owed his appointment as commanding general of the air force to Reid. Of some Dominican generals it has been said their loyalty cannot be bought, only rented.) Throughout Saturday night 40 or 50 truckloads of weapons taken from the barracks of the 6th Battalion and soldiers from the 27th of February camp were brought into the city. The soldiers were placed at strategic points in the city. Arms were distributed to old army legionnaires, officers whom Reid had cashiered, and civilians. Communist leaders had lists of names prepared and distributed arms by roll call. Arms were stored in schools and other buildings near Independence Park and in private homes.

Around nine o'clock, drawn and tense, Reid spoke over radio and TV. The country, he said, was tranquil and the greater part of the armed forces were loyal to the government. To the rebellious army units, Reid delivered an ultimatum: Surrender by 5 a.m. Sunday or face bombardment.

Reid was whistling in the dark, for his fate had already been sealed—the army stationed in the city, most of the navy, national police, and air force were committed to the rebels. Santo Domingo went to bed on a lighted fuse.

Sunday, April 25, was Santo Domingo's day of horror.

At 5 a.m. Reid telephoned General de los Santos Céspedes. After sleeping on the matter, the general informed Reid, he had concluded not to order a bombardment of the rebellious garrisons, that he could not attack fellow officers and Dominican enlisted men.

"I thought," Reid answered, "it was the duty of a general to take orders, not to decide whether to follow them."

"I knew at that moment I was finished," Reid later said ruefully.

Parenthetically, to set the record straight, Reid did not on Sunday morning request intervention by the United States.[6] In a conversation at the Palace around nine o'clock with William B. Connett Jr., *chargé d'affaires* of the American Embassy, Reid expressed his willingness to resign if it would

[6] A charge made by Senator Fulbright in a speech before the Senate on September 15, 1965.

prevent bloodshed. By Sunday, there was nothing the United States could have done. The time for saving Reid had passed.

During the afternoon loyalist officers attempted to negotiate with rebel officers led by Colonel Ramírez. Rebel officers insisted on the return of Juan Bosch to the presidency, which was not acceptable to the loyalist side, who proposed a military junta, with elections in three months. At this officers' meeting, Colonel Ramírez was réported to have made two revealing admissions: He said, first, he had been involved in the planning of the conspiracy for over a year; and, second, that he could not make any decisions unless he consulted with Captain Mario Peña Taveras, who was the army's liaison with the 14th of June Movement.

On Sunday, after a call was broadcast over the radio to members of the three Communist parties and Bosch's PRD, there was a wholesale distribution of weapons by rebel officers led by Captain Peña Taveras and Communist leaders from the 14th of June Movement and the Moscow wing of the party.[7] Between 10,000 and 15,000 weapons—rifles, pistols, grenades, semiautomatic guns, bazookas, mortars, and machine guns—were distributed to hoodlums, criminals, adolescents, soldiers from the rebel garrisons, followers of Bosch, and Communist cadres; indeed, to anybody at the scene. Thousands of Molotov cocktails, *prepared before the uprising,* were handed out. Peace Corps volunteers reported that leaflets had been passed around by Communist organizers several weeks before the revolt, with instructions on how to make Molotov cocktails out of Coca-Cola bottles and gasoline. Bottles and gasoline obtained from tank trucks were distributed to civilians for making additional Molotov cocktails. This appeared to be the principal assignment of the Peking Communists, who were more bystanders than active participants in the first hours of the insurrection. Radio Havana, in programs beamed at Hispaniola, interspersed repeated instructions: "Use your bottles!" "Use your bottles!"

The police, as the last vestige of authority and order, were the special target of the Communists. Jay Mallin, a *Time* correspondent, recounts a statement by a university student attached to the 14th of June Movement: "We joined this

---

[7] For the names of Communist leaders who participated in the distribution of arms, see Wessin: op. cit., Appendix I, p. 209. General Wessin's official log of the events of April 24 makes the interesting observation that civilians received automatic weapons, the soldiers only the hand-operated Mauser rifles.

thing in the beginning just so we could kill those bastards. And, *hombre,* we wipe them out very good." So good in fact that hundreds of police officers were murdered.

Turbas—hired thugs and musclemen used by Trujillo to terrorize the people—were deployed to loot, burn, sack, intimidate, and kill. Denizens of the shanty towns joined the orgy of plunder and pillage. To the cries *"!Al paredón!" "!Al paredón!"* ("To the wall!" "To the wall!") men were herded to their execution. Paul Bethel tells of his companion, a Scottish news photographer, who counted 90 bodies in a single block, and was sickened at the wanton murder. Foreign embassies were violated. With racial overtones, black mobs surged through white residential areas screaming: "Kill the *tutumpotes!*" (a favorite Bosch expression for the rich and wellborn). Significantly, the first building to be gutted by the mob was the headquarters of the Confederación Nacional de Trabajadores Libres (CONATRAL), the Dominican free trade union. The pride of the Hispanic world, the New World's oldest cathedral, was looted and desecrated.

Downtown Santo Domingo looked more like a war zone than the quaint capital of the hemisphere's oldest city as a pall of smoke from gutted buildings curled over the city, and as rifles cracked, machine guns stuttered and flaming Molotov cocktails spread a holocaust.

This was only the beginning of Professor Bosch's "democratic revolution," designed and stage-managed for him by the Communist directorate. Before the madness ended—if it really has—probably 3,000 (nobody knows the exact figure) lay dead, and perhaps five times that number were wounded.

Maneuvering behind the screen of organized anarchy, Communist technicians efficiently went about their business —seizure of the telephone and cable exchanges, newspaper plants, the waterworks, the post office, the power plant, banks, warehouses, and docks. Santo Domingo was a paralyzed city without electricity, water, telephones, newspapers, and food.[8]

In approximately three hours, under the leadership of the 14th of June Movement and Partido Socialista Popular Dominicano (PSPD), platoons and squads with machine guns, bazookas, and recoilless rifles were stationed at prearranged street intersections and key traffic centers. Snipers with machine guns and rifles were in position on apartment roofs.

[8] Organization of American States: *Combined Reports on Communist Subversion,* U.S. Government Printing Office, 89th Cong., 1st sess. (1965), p. 108.

Strongholds were established at strategically located buildings. Block by block, the city was systematically converted into armed command posts.

A Western diplomat, who had fought in the Second World War, said many of the street fighters showed evidence of the most sophisticated urban guerrilla-warfare training. Directing the paramilitary units was Manuel González González, a veteran of the Spanish Civil War, a member of the Central Committee of the Moscow Communist wing, and, later, Caamaño's principal military adviser. Between 1,000 and 1,200 regular officers and enlisted men were under arms in the rebel zone Sunday afternoon, but civilians with weapons outnumbered the soldiers.

Now the managers of the revolution were ready to deal with Reid and Cáceres. Out of the wings—more precisely out of the embassy of El Salvador where he had taken asylum—stepped Colonel Francisco Caamaño Deñó. A typical product of Trujillo decadence (his father, General Fausto Caamaño, was one of Trujillo's most accomplished killers), Caamaño, thirty-two, stocky, brown-skinned, never harbored an enlightened political or social idea during his checkered career as naval cadet, marine, aide-de-camp to Trujillo, and policeman. During the entire period of the uprising, his wife and children remained in the Argentine Embassy. Caamaño himself skipped in and out of asylum during the first days of the revolution.

In 1959, Caamaño participated in the extermination of the June 14th invasion by Castro-trained Dominicans, for which he was decorated by Trujillo. In November 1962, the Council of State sent an army detachment under General Rodríguez Reyes and a police unit commanded by Colonel Caamaño to investigate a religious sect at Palma Sola, near the Haitian border. General Reyes was killed in an encounter with the sect and his body mutilated. Colonel Caamaño as senior officer ordered the liquidation of the inhabitants of Palma Sola. In his book *The Unfinished Experiment: Democracy in the Dominican Republic* (p. 106), Bosch characterized the incident as "the bloody Palma Sola episode." Nonetheless, during his presidency Bosch permitted Caamaño to command the Cascos Blancos, an elite police riot unit. The records do not disclose that Caamaño, the "Constitutionalist," protested the abrogation of the 1963 Bosch Constitution or raised his voice in support of Bosch.

A compulsive plotter, Caamaño plotted to oust his police chief, General Belisario Peguero. At the request of the High Command of the armed forces, President Reid removed Caamaño from the National Police. To get him out of the country, Reid appointed Caamaño consul general at Kingston, Jamaica. Caamaño pleaded to be restored to the armed forces. The navy and army refused to have him. The air force agreed to take him. Promptly, he began to plot against Reid.

Caamaño could claim he was not a Communist though he had no difficulty in using the clenched-fist salute of the international Marxist brotherhood on his swearing in as "Provisional President." Under the 1963 Constitution, Caamaño, as a military officer, was disqualified from the presidency. But in the upside-down Dominican universe, Bosch hailed him as the man "who was able to restore a constitutional government without the fraud and sham of elections." Ambitious, pliable, Caamaño like Bosch was a useful "front" for the Communists.[9]

On Sunday morning around ten o'clock, with about 50 armed men, Caamaño appeared at the rear of the Palace. "He distinguished himself," says the *World Marxist Review* (December 1965, p. 76), "by persuading the palace guard not to offer resistance and arresting their officers with their assistance." Reid and Cáceres were placed in custody. But Caamaño's heart apparently was not in his work; he skipped back to the safety of the embassy of El Salvador, emerging on the following day.

With singular irony, at four o'clock, four P-51 Mustangs (denied Reid for a pre-dawn strike on the rebellious garrisons) circled over the capital for a strafing run on the Palace, where Reid and Cáceres were prisoners.[10] Later, a frenzied howling mob supplied with clubs and rifles, led by armed Communists, forced the iron gates at the entrance to the Palace; like hot lava from a volcano in eruption they flowed across the grounds, seized, and sacked the building. From the third floor of the Palace, Reid said the scene re-

[9] See *Testimony of Juan Isidro Tapia Adames*, Hearing before the Subcommittee of the Committee on the Judiciary, United States Senate, 89th Cong., 1st sess. (October 18, 1965), pp. 22, 42.

[10] According to the testimony of General Wessin y Wessin, Lieutenant Colonel Beauchamp Javier at gunpoint ordered General de los Santos Céspedes to give the order to strafe the National Palace and other positions held by the rebels. Op. cit., p. 161.

sembled something out of Dante's Inferno. "It was," he said, "primeval savagery."

During the early evening, Reid and Cáceres were informed their safety could no longer be guaranteed. An ambulance was waiting in the courtyard; they must flee for their lives, they were told. They found refuge at the home of a friend.

The Communist directorate had successfully accomplished the operational phase of its mission: the economic arteries of the country were severed, and the state as a political entity no longer existed.

Sunday, April 25, also witnessed the creation of the revolutionary government, with José Rafael Molina Ureña, Speaker of the Chamber of Deputies during Bosch's regime, installed as "Provisional Constitutional President." It was also the beginning of the disenchantment of the sincere, idealistic supporters of the revolution. Many soldiers, having sniffed the direction of the wind, deserted the rebel cause and eventually found their way back to their regiments. In every revolution the honeymoon of moderates and extremists is short. Lacking the fanatical discipline and organization of the extremists, the moderates are quickly pushed aside. In the famous phrase of the French revolutionary moderate Vergniaud, "the revolution, like Saturn, devours its children." The flowering of hard-core foreign and native Communists from the Moscow and Peking wings of the party, and Castroites from the 14th of June Movement rapidly persuaded moderate *boschistas* that their revolution had been betrayed. Antonio Francisco Martínez—like Donald Reid an automobile distributor and a successful businessman—Secretary General of Bosch's Dominican Revolutionary party, appealed over radio to party members to lay down their arms.

The testimony of John Bartlow Martin, United States Ambassador at Santo Domingo during the Bosch regime, a liberal and a friend and admirer of Juan Bosch, is significant. Martin wrote in an article for *Life* that he undertook his assignment to Santo Domingo in May 1965 as special emissary for President Johnson with "grave misgivings," fearing "we were in danger of getting on the wrong side, against the people."[11] In less than forty-eight hours after his arrival, he was able to corroborate the earlier assessment made by Ambassador Bennett—the revolution was Communist-controlled.

11 Martin: op. cit., p. 29.

By Sunday the Chiefs of Staff clearly understood the significance of the pattern of events. Though the military chiefs had been unwilling to use their power in support of Reid on Saturday, they mobilized on Sunday to prevent Bosch's return as a Dominican Fidel Castro. From the armed forces radio at San Isidro a warning was broadcast to civilians to stay clear of the vicinity of Duarte Bridge. De los Santos Céspedes' aircraft made repeated strafing runs on the western approaches to the strategic Duarte Bridge—the route into the city from San Isidro—to soften up rebel positions—taken Saturday night—in preparation for an assault by Wessin's tanks, supported by infantry. From the harbor, Commodoro Francisco Rivera Caminero's naval vessels opened a bombardment on the rebel-held Palace. From the San Cristóbal army garrison to the west of the capital, the elite "Mountain Battalion," consisting of 500 troops under the command of General Salvador Montás Guerrero, was approaching the city. (Montás was a member of the San Cristóbal clique of corrupt and *golpista* officers. Both Caminero and Wessin were distrustful of Montás's intentions. They suspected him of moving his troops into the city in order to take advantage of the confusion, that he would attempt to hoist himself into supreme power.)

To force Wessin's troops to hold their fire, Communists took wives and families of soldiers to the bridge. Before TV cameras they provided a ruthless demonstration of psychological warfare. A woman and two children were presented as Wessin's "wife and family." They "pleaded" with the general to desist from attacking the bridge. Soon afterward, a second woman appeared before the cameras, posing as the "mother" of Wessin. She repeated the pleas. The same technique was employed with characters depicting other officers' relatives. This was not entirely play-acting; bona fide wives and children of air force pilots were dragged before TV cameras. The announcer warned: "We are going to hold them at the bridge. If you strafe there, you kill them."

On Tuesday at 9 a.m. Wessin's tanks and infantry launched their attack. Wessin's infantry and tanks encountered strong resistance from the Communist paramilitary forces. They were not an armed rabble but highly skilled guerrilla fighters who counterattacked with a withering enfilade. Losses on both sides were heavy. By 11 a.m. Wessin's troops had secured the bridgehead and a small perimeter within the city. Why Wessin did not secure the city has baffled observers

of the Dominican Revolution. General Wessin offers this explanation. His effectives consisted of two infantry battalions,
totaling 1,000 men, and a company of 60 tanks. He attacked
with about 600 troops. This number of troops was insufficient
"to effect the capture of the city." The remainder of his soldiers was trapped in Santo Domingo. Many succeeded after
several days in making their way back to their camp. "We
began to reorganize and to assemble more troops to begin
the final operation against the city."[12] During this period the
Papal Nuncio, Monsignor Clarizio, had arranged the first
cease-fire. By nightfall on Wednesday, April 28, Wessin's
troops holding the bridge were relieved by American units.[13]

If the Dominican loyalist forces had no coherent view of
the tactical situation, the revolutionary provisional government was equally blanketed by the fog of combat; it was
out of touch with its own fighting units. Actually, it never
exercised any control over them.

On Tuesday, the hierarchy of the revolutionary government apparently believed the revolutionary cause was hopeless, and that Wessin's troops would enter the city by nightfall. Colonel Hernando Ramírez—the most prominent rebel military leader—had taken asylum in the Argentine Embassy during the morning (though it may well be, as he
claimed, that he was in urgent need of medical attention). "Foreign Minister" Jottin Cury was in an embassy.
By late afternoon, Molina Ureña and other leaders of the
revolutionary government were at the American Embassy, be-
seeching Ambassador Bennett to arrange for a cease-fire and
to dissuade Wessin from entering the city and de los
Santos Céspedes from continuing his air attacks. "President" Molina Ureña took refuge in the Colombian Embassy.
In the words of the *World Marxist Review* (December
1965, p. 76), "almost the entire leadership of the DRP [PRD]
found asylum in the embassies of Latin American countries."
The revolutionary government had vanished.

On the evening of Wednesday, April 28, elements of the
3d Battalion, 6th Marine Regiment, in helicopters from the U.
S.S. *Boxer*, were landed on "Ramfis" Trujillo's former polo

[12] Wessin: op. cit., pp. 158–9.

[13] Former Under Secretary of State Thomas C. Mann has advanced a
version of the sequence of events at variance with the account given by
General Wessin y Wessin. See Address before the Annual Meeting of
the Inter-American Press Association at San Diego, October 12, 1965, p. 8.

field adjoining the Embajador Hotel. This was the first wave of an armed American force which eventually exceeded 20,000 troops.

Critics of the Dominican intervention contend that evacuation of American citizens and foreign nationals was used as a cloak to conceal the real purpose of the intervention—to prevent the victory of a revolutionary force, judged to be Communist-controlled.[14] The Department of State hotly denies the charge.[15] And former Ambassador John Bartlow Martin argues that the cease-fire actually helped the rebels by leaving them in control of the center of the city.

The debate is silly. Of course the United States intervened (1) to evacuate American citizens whose lives were endangered, and (2) to prevent a Communist seizure of power. Civilized governments have a responsibility for the protection of their nationals. The United States also acted to protect its strategic interests in the Caribbean.

All great powers indulge in a certain amount of hypocrisy in their conduct of foreign affairs. Soothing semantics are invariably used to obfuscate what is obvious. The Caribbean Sea—perish the unthinkable thought—has been an American sphere of influence since the days of the Monroe Doctrine.

[14] Senator J. W. Fulbright, *Congressional Record,* September 15, 1965, p. 22998 *et seq.* The "background information" on which Senator Fulbright relied in making his charge against the Johnson administration is available as a Committee document of the Senate Committee on Foreign Relations. See *Background Information Relative to the Dominican Republic,* U.S. Government Printing Office 89th Cong., 1st sess. (1965). Other members of the Congress have criticized Chairman Fulbright's reliance on selected newspapers, principally *The New York Times, The Washington Post* and the New York *Herald Tribune.* See Senator Thomas J. Dodd, *Congressional Record,* September 16, 1965, p. 23294 *et seq.,* and Representative Armistead Selden, Chairman of the Inter-American Affairs Subcommittee, *Congressional Record,* September 23, 1965, p. 24073 *et seq.* Actually, Senator Fulbright and other members of the Senate Committee on Foreign Relations had access to the same factual information with which the Department of State was working. As Senator Fulbright has pointed out, his evaluation of that information led to a different conclusion from that of the Johnson administration and other members of his committee.

[15] Former Under-Secretary Thomas Mann in a speech to the Inter-American Press Association on October 12, 1965 (reported in *The Washington Post,* October 13, 1965, p. 1, and *The New York Times,* October 13, 1965, p. 10) said the decision that there was a "clear and present danger of the forcible seizure of power by the Communists" was not made until a day after the first Marines had arrived to assist in the evacuation of Americans and foreign nationals.

As long as there is a Canal, the Caribbean Sea will be an American *mare nostrum*. The Good Neighbor Policy did not abolish the classic concept of the great power sphere of influence: it merely civilized the "blatant assertions of the hegemonic rights of the United States" to intervene in hemisphere affairs under the obsolete Platt Amendment and the Roosevelt Corollary to the Monroe Doctrine, promulgated in an age of crude imperialism. Countries on the Caribbean littoral are within the defense perimeter of the United States. It is a fact of life of international politics that no other great rival power may enter this area with its military forces, or establish puppet regimes that can be used for the spread of "wars of national liberation."

General Eisenhower gambled on Castro and lost. No President of the United States will again risk a repetition in the Caribbean of the pattern followed by Castro in Cuba. The Cuban missile crisis, which brought us to the brink of nuclear war, made it abundantly clear that the United States will not allow its security to be threatened in the Caribbean.

The Caribbean offers Communism ample targets of opportunity—the Dominican Republic, Haiti, the Guianas, Panama, and, on the northern rim of South America, Venezuela and Colombia. Honduras—wretchedly poor, sparsely populated, ineptly ruled by a military man on horseback, with a political opposition that is incompetent to govern—offers Communism a choice target. In 1954, the United States helped overthrow a Communist-oriented government in Guatemala; this country is again a primary Communist objective. Hispaniola is an island of prime strategic importance to the United States. A Communist regime on either part of the island would threaten the vital interests of the United States. The United States will not sit on its hands while Communists attempt to fill the Haitian void on the demise of Duvalier. A Havana-dominated regime will never be permitted in Panama.

We would do well to remember Lin Piao's dictum in the Peking revolutionary offensive of encircling "the cities of the world" by "the rural areas of the world": American influence is to be attacked by use of the tactic of the united front, with the help of local nationalism but with Communists in actual control. The woods abound in power-hungry demagogues who will lend themselves to Communist popular fronts. They have yet to learn that "he must have a long spoon that must eat with the devil." The role of Juan Bosch in Santo Domingo mirrors the threat in the Caribbean—and the rest of Latin America.

A great power does not expect small countries to be sympathetic to its security interests, least of all Latin American city-states that are neurotically obsessed with hallucinations of the Colossus of the North. When a Communist country— in this instance, Cuba—trains, finances, and organizes indigenous Communists to seize control of another Caribbean country—in this instance, the Dominican Republic—the President of the United States will not defer action until the OAS, an organization that is not renowned for the speed with which it makes decisions, is able to function. In the veiled language of diplomacy, Secretary of State Rusk intimated at the November 1965 meeting of Foreign Ministers at Rio de Janeiro that in the protection of its security the United States will not hesitate to intervene unilaterally— in the absence of prompt collective action—when other Santo Domingos arise. In the Inter-American system all states are equal but the United States is more equal than others.

The hot breath of American domestic politics invariably scorches the neck of American foreign policy. Though Saigon is at the other end of the world from Santo Domingo, both are within the context of domestic United States politics. In deep trouble over Vietnam, and with Kennedy's Bay of Pigs fiasco seared in memory, it is difficult to imagine that Lyndon Johnson through inaction or indecision would jeopardize his political fortunes and those of his party by handing the loyal opposition a made-to-order campaign issue: who lost the Dominican Republic?

Such are the realities of the world of power.

The critics of Dominican intervention are, however, missing the point in an area where there is room for legitimate criticism: what happened in Santo Domingo *after* the Marines went ashore?

In Santo Domingo a domino principle was at work; the first big mistake engendered all the others, and error compounded error. Whatever the reasons—uncertainty as to the reaction of public opinion, humanitarian considerations, reluctance to risk a heavy loss of American lives in house-to-house combat, a belief that containment of the revolutionary force would allow time for an eventual diplomatic settlement, the syndrome of the hawks and the doves, with its resultant ambivalence toward Bosch and the insurrection made in his name—*an immediate military solution was not imposed*.

In the Bay of Pigs, President Kennedy refused to commit American armed forces. In Santo Domingo, President Johnson did commit them—decisively and massively. The point is this: having engaged our military power, we recoiled from the implications of its effectual use. We applied a poultice, but did not excise the malignant growth. Now the entire Dominican body politic is infected. Because the United States is a prisoner of its own misjudgment, there can be no effectual political solution to the Dominican crisis. What was manageable on April 28, 1965—when troops went ashore—is now insoluble.

In December 1944, Winston Churchill was confronted in Greece by a situation somewhat analogous to that in Santo Domingo. The Communist-controlled Greek EAM (National Liberation Front) and ELAS (People's National Army of Liberation) had violated solemn promises made to the British Government not to take the law into their own hands. Having murdered the bulk of the police officers of Athens, ELAS troops were preparing to seize the city. Churchill recounts ordering General Scobie, the British Commander, to intervene and fire upon the treacherous aggressors. "It is no use," Churchill wrote, "doing things like this by halves."[16] General Scobie's directive from the Prime Minister was explicit: *"We have to hold and dominate Athens. It would be a great thing for you to succeed in this without bloodshed if possible, but also with bloodshed if necessary."*[17]

In words that have overtones for Santo Domingo, Churchill wrote of his decision to destroy the Greek Communists:

Now that the free world has learnt so much more than was then understood about the Communist movement in Greece and elsewhere, many readers will be astonished at the vehement attacks to which His Majesty's Government, and I in particular at its head, were subjected. The vast majority of the American press violently condemned our action, which they declared falsified the cause for which they had gone to war. If the editors of all these well-meaning organs will look back at what

16 Winston S. Churchill: *Triumph and Tragedy* (Boston: Houghton Mifflin Company; 1953), Vol. VI, p. 288.

17 Ibid., p. 289, author's italics.

they wrote then and compare it with what they think now they will, I am sure, be surprised. The State Department, in charge of Mr. Stettinius, issued a markedly critical pronouncement which they in turn were to regret, or at least reverse, in after years.[18]

The cease-fire in Santo Domingo provided a breathing spell for the Communist forces to strengthen their positions. Behind the ring of encirclement of the 82d Airborne Division, snipers with impunity killed 25 American soldiers and wounded more than 100 officers and enlisted men.

Treating "President" Caamaño as if he were the chief of a sovereign state gave the extremists international status and wide support abroad. Outside of police and military circles, Caamaño was a nonentity. After his build-up by the OAS and UN, he became a revolutionary hero to Latin American youth. At a national youth conference of the Venezuelan Christian Democratic party (Copei) held in Caracas on November 1, 1965, Caamaño was elected "honorary President." Whether he meant it or not, General de Gaulle made noises that sounded like recognition.

McGeorge Bundy, former Special Assistant to the President on National Security Affairs, failed to attend a much publicized nationwide TV teach-in on Vietnam. Later, it was learned that he had gone to Santo Domingo to negotiate with Caamaño and Imbert for a "government of consensus" under the presidency of Señor Antonio Guzmán, an intimate friend of Bosch and Secretary of Agriculture during his administration. The revolutionaries applauded Bundy's efforts—they were regarded as a political indemnification of the revolution that had been strangled by the landing of American troops. Intelligent, moderate conservatives were appalled by an American policy that aimed at restoring *boschismo sin Bosch*. Mr. Bundy's mission failed.

[18] *Ibid.*, p. 292. On the comparable role of influential American newspapers in condemning intervention in the Dominican Republic and a criticism of their evaluation of the events at Santo Domingo, see Representative Armistead Selden, *loc. cit.* Presidential Press Secretary Bill D. Moyers, in a radio interview, said the President believed reporters covering the Dominican Revolution were "too often advocates of a particular viewpoint." The President, said Moyers, was concerned that some of the reporters were "advocates first and reporters second." Although Mr. Moyers did not specifically identify these reporters by name, the President was known to be angry at the coverage by correspondents from *The New York Times*, the New York *Herald Tribune*, and *The Washington Post*. See *The Washington Post*, November 2, 1965, p. A-2.

Before memory fades, it should be recalled that some ambassadors to the OAS regarded Colonel Caamaño's regime
as a true expression of the revolutionary impulses of the
Dominican people. In reality, the insurrection was confined
to the capital. The rest of the country was not involved and
did not support the rebellion. It was only after the ambiguous
diplomacy that allowed the insurrectionaries to consolidate
their position and slip their weapons into the provinces
that a countrywide crisis was created.

The revolutionaries of Ciudad Nueva, Santo Domingo's
downtown section, adroitly played the UN against the OAS
when it suited their purposes, and both bodies catered to
the insurrectionists. The United States, acting through the
OAS, fed the inhabitants of Ciudad Nueva, gave them medical assistance, and paid the salaries of government employees
who joined the revolution as well as those who remained
with the loyalists.

The political successes of the Communists have been spectacular. What they could not win by revolution they attained by appeasement.

"Those who cannot remember the past are condemned to
repeat it," wrote George Santayana. This admonition has
been poignantly ignored in the Dominican Republic by the
Organization of American States. This body has foisted a
political "solution" on the Dominicans which carries that
wretched island-country full circle to the start of a course
that has been covered before with disastrous consequences.

The OAS Mediation Committee, led by the American diplomat Ellsworth Bunker, created a "Dominican Act of Reconciliation": a Dominican zoo in which lions, lambs, foxes,
wolves, and jackals were expected to lie down side by side,
lick each other's wounds, and bury their hatreds and passions—if they had not devoured each other beforehand. At
the end of nine months of tropical euphoria, it was assumed by the OAS Mediation Committee that Dominicans
would have mastered the practice of democracy and be ready
for a presidential election.

To preside over this cuckoo menagerie, "President" Imbert
of the Government of National Reconstruction (inside the
international security zone) and "President" Caamaño (on
the other side of the zone) "agreed" on a Provisional President in the person of forty-four-year-old Héctor García
Godoy, a professional job holder who had served Trujillo as a
diplomat, with Bosch as Foreign Minister, and under Reid

Cabral in a sinecure in the state-owned tobacco company. García Godoy had no discernible qualifications or experience for the job except his blandness and family ties in Santiago de los Caballeros, where the OAS Mediation Committee is reported to have discovered among the local oligarchs a center of progressive-minded, non-political businessmen—a hitherto carefully concealed Dominican secret.

García Godoy's most newsworthy accomplishment during his first month in office was to sign his name to a request to the Peace Force Command to expel General Wessin y Wessin, a dedicated anti-Communist and a loyal and honest professional soldier, but utterly lacking political sophistication. For propaganda purposes, the Communists blamed Wessin for the air attacks on the city during the first days of the revolution, when in fact it was General de los Santos Céspedes who ordered them. (As commander of El Centro de Enseñanzas, Wessin had no operational control over the air force.) Wessin's deportation under the most shabby circumstances was the price the Communists exacted for their adherence to the compact for demobilization of Ciudad Nueva.[19]

In sophisticated countries, officers and enlisted men who betrayed their military oaths by participating in an insurrection would be court-martialed, sentenced to heavy labor, or shot. In the Dominican Republic, under the plan prepared by the OAS Mediation Committee, they were given amnesty and are to be taken back into their regiments. This is tantamount to introducing a fifth column into the armed forces. (Caamaño had the temerity to propose that all his own troops be incorporated into the Dominican military, whether or not they were in uniform before the revolution.)

That battle-blooded Castroites and followers of the Moscow and Peking wings of the Communist parties would behave like little Lord Fauntleroys and turn in their arms was a preposterous idea. In their critique of the April insurrection in the *World Marxist Review* (December 1965, p. 80); J. I. Quello and N. Isa Conde make this illuminating observation:

> At the final phase of negotiations, when the so-called Dominican Act of Reconciliation was deliberated, an at-

[19] See Wessin: op. cit., p. 169 *et seq.*

tempt was made . . . to empower . . . the "Inter-American Peace Force" to confiscate all weapons in the hands
of civilians. *This move was foiled by the threat of a
breakdown in the negotiations. The solution of this
delicate problem was finally entrusted to constitutionalist
officers, which made it possible to effect an organized
retreat* (author's italics).

This is Aesopian (Communist) use of language to conceal the
true meaning of words. In plain English, the meaning is: the
Communist leadership successfully blocked the collection of
arms; by prolonging the negotiations, it gained time to conceal them.

Jeremiah O'Leary, the respected Latin American correspondent for *The Evening Star* of Washington, reported
(September 25, 1965, p. B-10) that some 300 weapons were
turned in, mainly inoperable guns of World War II vintage
and a cannon that was more a park ornament than a weapon.
Modern weapons that could be used for another try at insurrection were cached in the countryside, behind newly
plastered walls and under floors in downtown Santo
Domingo. Large quantities of weapons were moved into
provincial towns in the interior through checkpoints controlled by the Inter-American Peace Force. They were concealed in gasoline tank trucks, trucks, ambulances, and automobiles.[20] Under the protection of the Peace Force, small
inspection parties consisting of law students and graduates
began what *The New York Times* called "a gingerly search
for weapons" among householders who, when asked whether
"they were illegally holding weapons," invariably replied in
the negative. The whole drive was soon abandoned.

The hard-core Communist directorate of the revolution disappeared; it had served its purpose. At three guerrilla-warfare
schools, under the very noses of the Inter-American Peace
Force, several thousand young commandos received training
in the techniques of street fighting, sabotage, explosives, and
guerrilla warfare.[21] These cadres established clandestine
schools in small towns and cities in the interior for the instruction of other young Dominicans. Some 20 Dominican
Communists have been sent to mainland China via Prague

[20] See Tapia Adames: op. cit., pp. 24–5. This witness testified that
about 10,000 weapons were transported into the interior. See Committee exhibit of Dominican Republic map on p. 25 for locations of
weapon caches.
[21] See ibid., pp. 27–8, for the location of the guerrilla schools.

and Karachi for paramilitary indoctrination training. Five returned to Santo Domingo as recently as the end of May 1966.

The Communists work in the open and identify themselves with their party emblems—the red banner (with Lenin's portrait) of the Moscow branch, the black and red colors of the Peking Communists, and the black and green of the 14th of June Movement, inspired by Havana. The 14th of June Movement was given legal status so that it could campaign in the June 1966 elections. They issue "advisory opinions" to the Dominican people. The Partido Socialista Popular (now known as the Dominican Communist party) announced that armed insurrection is "the correct policy" in the Dominican Republic in the months ahead. The prescription of the disciples of Peking and Havana calls for prolonged guerrilla warfare. The *World Marxist Review* (December 1965, p. 81) informs us that "the Right wing of the DRP [PRD] steers clear of any joint statements with the Communists, although it in practice [accepts] cooperation and united action with them."

In the June 1966 presidential election campaign, the Moscow-aligned Dominican Communist party announced its support of Bosch (*The Washington Post,* April 10, p. A 23). Bosch also was the nominee of the pro-Red Social Christian Revolutionary party and the Havana-dominated 14th of June Movement. Bosch rejected the nomination by the 14th of June Movement not because its Marxist-Leninist ideology was repugnant, but for reasons of political expediency. Bosch declined the nomination, he was quoted as saying, because it was "inconvenient," "made without prior consultation," and had "set conditions" (*The Washington Post,* April 20, 1966, p. A 22). That political expediency was the chief deterrent in accepting Castroite support is evident from a taped radio speech—Bosch was terrified that he was marked for an assassin's bullet and never left his house during the campaign, which led Dominican wags to dub him "Juan the cave man"—in which he was reported as saying that the 25,000 votes of the June 14th Movement would cost him more than 125,000 other votes (*Diario Las Americas,* April 21, 1966, p. 1). Whether or not he wanted their support, Bosch was nonetheless the chosen instrument of the Dominican Communist parties. At a celebration of the first anniversary of the April 1965 uprising, the Havana-style 14th of June Movement urged its partisans to vote for Bosch (*The New*

York Times, April 25, 1966, p. 4). The Movement petitioned the Electoral College to be allowed to transfer votes cast on its ballot to Bosch and his running mate. Antonio Guzmán (*Diario Las Americas,* May 12, 1966, p. 1). And in a Dominican version of an end-of-the-campaign rally, all three Communist factions—Havana, Moscow and Peking—joined forces in support of Bosch (*The Evening Star* of Washington, May 30, 1966, p. A 5).

Since the insurrection of April 24, when the Communist directorate fused the military radicals of the Left and Right with Bosch and his party and the Communist groups, and since the selection of Héctor García Godoy as provisional President, the Communists have gained control—or partial control—of key government institutions: the state-owned sugar corporation (the country's largest employer of labor), the Federation of Government Employees, the Ministry of Public Works (whose strategic transport section controls all urban transportation), the national university, all student organizations, and most of the trade unions. The Communists use these organizations and their members to stage anti-American demonstrations and to foment political strikes that are used as weapons of terror—as was done during an entire week in mid-February 1966, when the whole country was paralyzed. They demand withdrawal of the Inter-American Peace Force. They organize gangs of young rowdies to harass Peace Force troops and to provoke them into firing on the mobs. They burn American flags. The chant of these well-organized *agents provocateurs* indicates the origin of their leaders—"Quisqueya and Viet Nam, together we will win." (Quisqueya is an Indian name for Hispaniola.) To the familiar chant "Yankee, go home!" they add the derisive cry "Governor, get out!" against García Godoy (as an official of a United States "colonial" regime). Héctor García Godoy appointed Alfredo Conde Pausas as Chief Justice of the Supreme Court. Conde named his brother, a member of the Central Committee of the Dominican Communist party, as a judge of the court in Santiago de los Cabelleros. Meticulous in his dispensation of equal justice, the Chief Justice designated a member of the rival Peking faction to be an appellate judge in Santo Domingo.

"History repeats itself," Marx wrote, "once as tragedy, once as farce." Juan Bosch took office with the power of a popular mandate. He was incapable of using that power constructively. Though Héctor García Godoy is a creature of American intervention and has no political base in his own right, many *latino* politicians would envy his power base— the armed force of the United States and an unlimited expense account. García Godoy like Bosch is incapable of using power. The Dominican Right detests him; the Left holds him in contempt. His erstwhile friends, Bosch and Caamaño, withdrew their support. Bosch castigated him as "spineless"—an example of the pot calling the kettle black. The High Command of the regular armed forces, in an *opéra bouffe* spectacle, defied his order dismissing them from their commands and ordering them into "exile."[22] The *reductio ad absurdum* of the pretenses surrounding García Godoy was demonstrated in mid-February 1966 when his own "Government" went on strike against itself.

For all practical purposes, there is no Dominican govern-

[22] Capture of the command structure of the Dominican armed forces is the grand prize in the revolutionary struggle for the conquest of the Dominican Republic. Control of the armed forces can deliver the country to the Right or Left. The power vacuum left by Trujillo's demise has not been filled by strong leadership within the Dominican armed forces. The military establishment is still in a stage of transition from an *ejército de monteneros* to a professional body. There are many patriotic officers who are deeply committed to the modernization of the country and the military establishment. They do not, however, believe these objectives can be achieved at the price of violent revolution, or that the Dominican social revolution should emulate the Cuban way. In the recent past, some senior officers have been more *condottieri* than professional soldiers. Others like Colonel Caamaño are psychologically unsuited for service in a modern military establishment—they are attracted to conspiracies like a moth to a flame. There is no tradition of obedience to the civil authority. A weak and divisive political leadership since Trujillo's assassination has not been conducive to the development of obedience to the civil authority. The expulsion of General Wessin y Wessin, carried out by American diplomatic and military authorities, was a shattering blow to the morale of the armed services. The abortive effort in January 1966 by García Godoy to purge the High Command, albeit "balanced" by the temporary "exile" into lush diplomatic posts of Caamaño and other rebel officers, would have carried the *conquistadores* from Moscow, Peking, and Havana and the leftist revolutionary parties such as Juan Bosch's PRD a long step forward in the fulfillment of a cardinal objective—progressive demoralization and disintegration of the Dominican armed forces. It is to the credit of the Brazilian Government that it would not sanction the participation of Lieutenant General Panasco Alvim, former commander of the Inter-American Peace Force, in an illusory diplomatic attempt to stabilize the *status quo* at the expense of the dismemberment of the Dominican military hierarchy. President García Godoy had so far retreated from his earlier position as to have told the Dominican people over radio and television that the "armed forces may be at present the best factor for order that the country has," and a "destroyed armed forces would be no use to us" (*The New York Times,* March 11, 1966, p. 15).

ment. With their highly developed olfactory sense, Dominicans know where the real power resides—with Ambassador Ellsworth Bunker.

Until the June 1, 1966 election, which repudiated Juan Bosch, the management of the April Revolution had every reason to congratulate itself on having attained a psychological and political conquest of the Dominican Republic. Only the victims of illusion can believe the Dominican people will not undergo boundless grief in their anguished struggle to attain political maturity.

INDEX

Abinader, Rafael Jorge, 268
Acción Democrática, 36, 208
Acosta Tejeda, Luis, 279
Act of Bogotá, 204
ADELA (Atlantic Community Development Group for Latin America), 229, 238
Agency for International Development (AID), 28, 74, 128, 195, 251, 266, 267, 278; housing, 188
agrarian reform, *see* land reform
Aguilar de León, Juan de Dios, 111–3
Aguirre, Francisco (Pancho), 279
AID, *see* Agency for International Development
Alegría, Ciro, 101
Alejos, Roberto, 110
Alende, Oscar, 88, 90
Alexander, Robert J., 95n
Alianza Popular Revolucionaria Americana (APRA), 93, 95–102, 166; *see also* Peru
Allende, Salvadore, 61, 208
Alliance for Progress, 53, 54, 66, 81, 97, 109, 116, 122, 152, 161, 165, 181, 204–14, 221, 222, 223, 228, 233; President Kennedy's role in, 122, 204–5; origin of term, 204; "constitution" of, 205; original conception of, 205; misconceptions of, 31, 205; goals of, 205; influence of Marshall Plan on, 206; re-

sistance to, 206–7; difficulties encountered by, 207–13; and Cuba, 211; recommendations of Lleras Camargo and Kubitschek for reorganization of, 212; attitude of President Johnson toward, 213; effect of military on, 213; political shortcomings of, 213–14; self-determination and, 214
Alliance for Progress: A Program of Inter-American Partnership, 204n
Alvin, General Hugh Panasco, 32, 299n
Amazon River, vii
American Freedom From Hunger Foundation, 251n
Amiama Tío, Luis, 120, 121, 125, 133
Anaconda Copper Company, 222, 228
Andalusia, 44
Anderson, Robert, 171
Andes Mountains, vii, 102, 143
antioqueños, ix
APRA, *see* Alianza Popular Revolucionaria Americana
aprismo, 96
Arabs, *see* Moors
Arab Socialism, 103; *see also* Nasserism
Aragão, Candido da Costa, 72, 77
Aramburu, Pedro, 88, 90
Arbenz Guzmán, Jacobo, 104, 105–7
Arce, José Manuel, 192

301

Liga Militar, 66–7; *see also* Ecuador
Lilienthal, David, 26
limeños, viii
Lin Piao, 35, 290
Lincoln, Abraham, 48; Emancipation Proclamation of, 45
Lippes, Dr. Jack, 250
Lippmann, Walter, 29
Listín Diario, 271
Litton Industries, Inc., 256*n*
Liz, Ángel, 129
Lleras Camargo, Alberto, 40, 52, 61, 212, 233, 246
Lleras Restepo, Carlos, 62
Lozano, Julio, 55
López Contreras, Eleazar, 64
López Mateos, Adolfo, 174
L'Ouverture, Toussaint, 20
Luna-Pérez, Miguel Atila, 132
Luque, Crisanto Cardinal, 61

MacArthur, Douglas, 134, 155
Macauley, Thomas Babington, 17
Machiavelli, Niccolò, 31, 92, 163
machismo (cult of virility), 49, 87, 248
McLellan, Daniel B., 38
McNamara, Robert S., 134–5
Madariaga, Salvador de, 41
Magalhães, Juracy, 32
Mahan, Alfred Thayer, 20
Malinche, 214*n*
malinchismo, 214
Malthus, T. R., 150
Mamede, General Jurandir de Bizarria, 83
Man and Land in Peru (Ford), 94*n*
Mandate for Change: 1953–1956 (Eisenhower), 106–7
Manhattan Project, 257
Mann, Thomas, 32, 288*n*, 289*n*
Mansions and the Shanties, The (Freyre), 185*n*
Mao Tse-tung, 35, 78, 147, 241, 280
Marañón (shanty town, Panama City), 28
Mariátegui, José Carlos, 94

Marini, Anselmo, 189
Marshall, George C., 150, 171
Marshall Plan, 168, 206
Martin, John Bartlow, 260, 286, 289
Martínez, Antonio Francisco, 286
Martínez Durán, Carlos, 114
Marx, Karl, 103, 215, 225, 298
Marxism, 36; in land reform, 144
Masters and the Slaves, The (Freyre), 146*n*
Mathiss Ricart, Mario, 264, 267
Maya: civilization, 43; Indians in Guatemala, 104
Mazzilli, Paschoal Ranieri, 78
Medellín, ix
Medina Angarita, Isaias, 56
Meija Palacio, Jorge, 161
Meir, Golda, 22
Mejía Gómez, Juan Bautista, 272
Mella, 279
Méndez Montenegro, Julio César, 111–4
Méndez Montenegro, Mario, 112
Mendoza, Antonio de, 42
Mendoza, Eugenio, 219
mestizo (child of European father and Indian mother), 41, 49, 50
Mexico, 18, 37, 59–61, 145, 190; elimination of military from politics, 59; merger of military and civilian groups into official party, 59–61; military revolts, 60; myth of the revolution, 60; military budget, 63; industrialization, 173; land reform, 144, 153, 155; housing, 183, 190; LAFTA, 198–201; Alliance for Progress, 207, 212
middle class: in Argentina, 85, 91; in Peru, 102; housing for, 187
military, 38–9, 55–140, 213; praetorian attitudes of, 38–9, 57–8, 65–6; political involvement of, 55–8, 59–67, 103–4,

Other MENTOR and SIGNET Books
on Civilizations of Today

THE NEW ASIA: Readings in the History of Mankind
Guy Metraux and Francois Crouzet, editors
Essays originally published in UNESCO's *The Journal* of World History, on the development of Asian countries in the 20th century. (#MQ652—95¢)

THE CHANGING SOCIETY OF CHINA
by Ch'u and Winberg Chai
The nature of Chinese civilization as revealed in its social institutions, philosophy and religion, art and literature, and the impending threat of Communist totalitarianism. (#MT365—75¢)

ASIA IN THE MODERN WORLD
edited by Helen G. Matthew
Prominent authorities study the people, culture, and political history of Asia and provide the background for understanding its current role in world events. Illustrated with maps. (#MT542—75¢)

THE ISLAND CIVILIZATIONS OF POLYNESIA
by Robert C. Suggs
An anthropologist reveals the origin and culture of the primitive people of the South Seas. (#MT653—75¢)

THE ANGUISH OF INDIA *by Ronald Segal*
A highly controversial view of India and the fate toward which she is moving. "An event in the literature about modern India"—*The Observer*. Maps and tables. (#T2947—75¢)

FIVE FAMILIES *by Oscar Lewis*
An intimate and objective study of a typical day in the lives of five Mexican families. A great anthropological study by an expert in the field of Mexican studies. (#MQ658—95¢)

RUSSIA (revised) *by Bernard Pares*
An authoritative study of the background of the most controversial country in the world today. (#MP398—60¢)

RUSSIA AND AMERICA: Dangers and Prospects
by Henry L. Roberts
A penetrating analysis of our relations with Russia, in view of the sinister global tensions created by atomic discoveries. Foreword by John J. McCloy. (#MT589—75¢)

MENTOR Books on History

THE ORIGINS OF ORIENTAL CIVILIZATION
by Walter A. Fairservis, Jr.
An archaeological and anthropological study of the beginnings of culture in China, Korea, Japan, Mongolia, and Manchuria. Illustrated with drawings and photographs. (#MP445—60¢)

HISTORY OF THE WORLD IN 240 PAGES *by Rene Sedillot*
World history from prehistoric times to the present, in one volume. Ideal for rapid reference. Translated from the French by Gerard Hopkins. (#MP411—60¢)

IMPERIAL SPAIN, 1469-1716 *by J. H. Elliott*
The portrayal of one of the most remarkable epochs in history during which an impoverished, disunited land rose to the fore as a world power for a brief and glorious period. (#MQ664—95¢)

A SHORT HISTORY OF JAPAN *by Malcolm D. Kennedy*
The cultural and political development of Japan from the time of its first emperor through the Second World War—to its present position as a member of the Western alliance. (#MT559—75¢)

A SHORT HISTORY OF IRELAND *by Roger Chauvire*
The history of Ireland and her people from pre-Christian to modern times, written by a renowned French scholar who called his book a "work of Love." 16 pages of illustrations. (#MT602—75¢)

A SHORT HISTORY OF INDIA AND PAKISTAN
by T. Walter Wallbank
The political, economic, and social forces and events which have shaped modern India and Pakistan. A revised, abridged, up-dated edition of *India in the New Era*. (#MQ615—95¢)

A SHORT HISTORY OF AUSTRALIA *by Manning Clark*
An account of Australia's development from its first scattered settlements of aborigines to its emergence as a prosperous and dynamic power. (#MT522—75¢)